BILLY McNEILL

IN PRAISE OF CAESAR

ALEX GORDON

BLACK & WHITE PUBLISHING

First published 2018
This edition first published 2019
by Black & White Publishing Ltd
Nautical House, 104 Commercial Street,
Edinburgh, EH6 6NF

1 3 5 7 9 10 8 6 4 2   19 20 21

ISBN: 978 1 78530 250 3

A CIP catalogue record for this book is available
from the British Library.

Typeset by Iolaire, Newtonmore
Printed and bound by CPI Group (UK) Ltd, Croydon, CR0 4YY

This is for Billy McNeill: above all else, a good human being.

Also for his wife Liz and children Susan, Libby, Carol, Paula and Martyn.

Billy McNeill passed away on the evening of Monday 22 April 2019 at the age of seventy-nine.

'They never die who live in the hearts of those they leave behind.'

Publisher's Note

We first published *Billy McNeill: In Praise of Caesar* in 2018 and are proud to publish this paperback edition in 2019. We have retained the original text for its authentic perspectives upon Billy's life at the time of writing.

Contents

Acknowledgements

Roy Aitken, Steve Archibald, Bertie Auld, Pat Bonner, Craig Brown, Chic Charnley, John Clark, John Collins, Jim Craig, Pat Crerand, Sir Kenny Dalglish, John Fallon, Sir Alex Ferguson, Eddie Gray, Davie Hay, Robert Harvey, Harry Hood, John Hughes, Mike Jackson, Peter Latchford, Denis Law, Peter Lawwell, Bobby Lennox, Jimmy Lumsden, Murdo MacLeod, Frank McAvennie, Jim McCalliog, Frank McGarvey, Danny McGrain, Alex McLeish, Paul McStay, Sandro Mazzola, Joe Miller, Charlie Nicholas, Davie Provan, Brendan Rodgers, Billy Stark, Gordon Strachan, Andy Walker and Willie Wallace.

The valued contributions of Paul Brennan, Sandy Devers, Liam Donnelly, Eddy Grady, Kevin McKenna, Greg Maclachlan and Peter Marshall.

The sterling assistance of Mary Gemmell, Olive Wallace, Kevin Hughes, John Keeman, Gordon 'Syd' Sydney and Arthur Grant.

Campbell Brown, MD at Black & White Publishing, is also due a round of applause for his complete and professional support throughout and, of course, editor Graham Lironi, assistant editor Rosie Pierce and the production team.

John Paterson, my good friend and constant companion at Celtic Park in the sixties.

Last, and certainly not least, my wonderful and understanding wife Gerda, who, as usual, was my wee rock throughout the entire project. She played a blinder. And fed and watered me at regular intervals.

If I have overlooked anyone, please accept my profuse apologies.

Author's Note

It would have been impossible to write an exhaustive book such as this without the kind assistance, co-operation and collaboration of so many others.

To those who so willingly, enthusiastically and freely gave their time for interviews and to offer well-appreciated guidance, I can only say thank you.

It became a humbling experience to write this book. The engaging warmth and extraordinary affection Billy McNeill so obviously holds in so many hearts did not surprise me. However, I admit the emotive and endearing fondness generated from all the meetings and conversations with an array of individuals – two Knights of the Realm among them – did verge on the overwhelming.

It was an absolute joy to hear of the wonderful and often moving reminiscences of the man's friends, teammates and opponents: those who shared a dressing room, those who faced him on the field of combat, those in rival dugouts who pitted their wits against him and those who simply came in contact with Billy McNeill.

The treasured memories away from the field of play simply exemplified the stature of a fine and caring human being and a devoted family man.

It was a privilege to be involved in this work and it was also an honour to spend time in the company of individuals who played a significant role in the life of a person whom I, too, was fortunate enough to call a friend.

And one thing is assured: once you have made a friend in Billy McNeill, you have an ally for life.

Once again, I owe a debt of immense gratitude to each and every one of those who assisted in putting this tribute together for a rather special human being. Thank you.

Perhaps the following sentiment best sums up the man behind the legend.

'If ever a person was made for a specific club, it was Billy McNeill and Glasgow Celtic. He was never really manager here or at Aston Villa. His heart was always at Parkhead.'

The words belong to former Manchester City chairman Peter Swales.

Foreword

Peter Lawwell, Chief Executive
Celtic Football Club

Billy McNeill was born to lead Celtic.

Wonderfully inspirational on the field of play in those famous green and white hoops and equally as impressive in the dugout, Billy McNeill is the absolute epitome of this football club. He will always be a man of genuine stature; someone who has given so much of his life to Celtic and, at all times, with such grace, humility and dignity. He is, of course, respected by all in football and will always be loved dearly by all Celtic supporters. Recently, he has had personal challenges to face, a situation he has met with true bravery and unflinching fortitude, qualities synonymous with Billy McNeill.

Throughout his journey, both in the early years and now in more difficult times, Billy has been supported so strongly by his wonderful wife Liz and loving and caring children, who rightly will always be so proud of all he has achieved and all that he is. On a personal note, it has been an absolute pleasure and privilege to have known this gentleman over such a lengthy and memorable period. To me, he will always be an inspirational figure.

I can reminisce about the days when I was at Celtic Park, along with friends and relatives, to support the team. There was always an aura about Billy McNeill as he led the players out of the tunnel for another ninety minutes of frantic action. He always looked immaculate as he made his appearance, followed by excellent teammates who respected him so highly, and welcomed by the customary din from the Celtic fans, eager to urge their team to victory.

Billy McNeill more than played his part in making this club such a monumental success at home and abroad during the remarkable Jock Stein era. No one could have looked more noble or resplendent than Billy McNeill when he held aloft the European Cup following the historic 2–1 triumph over Inter Milan on 25 May 1967 at the Estádio Nacional in Lisbon. The glorious sunshine that early evening in the Portuguese capital perfectly highlighted the Celtic captain; dignified, chest puffed out in pride, as he accepted the trophy on a truly unforgettable occasion for our football club.

As a manager, we can never forget how he skilfully directed the team to their League Championship and Scottish Cup double in the club's centenary year in 1988.

He deserved every bit of success that came his way, but Billy McNeill remained a humble man, despite the adulation. Integrity was always his watchword. And he never wavered in his devotion to Celtic.

A few years ago, we were delighted to welcome Billy as our ambassador and to honour all he did for this club when we unveiled his statue at Celtic Park in December 2015 – a fitting and enduring tribute to Celtic's greatest-ever captain.

He was imposing and proud as a Celtic player and with this magnificent sculpture he will be overlooking the Celtic Way forever. And that is how it should be for Billy McNeill, a very special member of the Celtic family.

A Personal Thought

Brendan Rodgers

It was Christmas Day and I was in Paradise. I stood in the centre circle at Celtic Park and looked up at the stand. I gazed at the words 'Celtic Football Club 1888' and, for a moment, I thought, 'My God, I'm manager of this club.'

It was a magical little passage of time.

I was at the ground with the players on 25 December 2017 as we prepared for the Premiership game against Dundee at Dens Park on Boxing Day. The boys had gone through their paces, I was alone and was simply walking towards the middle of the pitch. And somehow I found myself staring skywards. And that mystical name of my boyhood idols looked back at me. Once again, I acknowledged I was in a privileged position. I was living the dream. I was the manager of the club I had adored as a kid growing up in Ireland. After my pleasant reverie, the following day we travelled to Tayside and won 2–0 with first-half goals from James Forrest and Leigh Griffiths.

You can't help but think of the famous names associated with

Celtic, all the remarkable characters and unforgettable individuals, the club's folklore is packed with glittering personalities and special games. I grew up watching the fabulous team that won the Centenary League and Cup double. The family would gather round the television when BBC Scotland was on and showing the highlights of a Celtic match. I could reel off the line-ups starting with the great Packie Bonner in goal. What a fabulous side that was in such an illustrious season, the 1987/88 campaign when the club celebrated its one hundredth birthday.

The manager was Billy McNeill. It is with the greatest regret I never saw him play. I was two years old when Billy retired as a player following Celtic's 3–1 Scottish Cup Final victory over Airdrie in 1975. Typical of the man to go out in style. But, living in the village of Carnlough, in County Antrim, I soon got to know the name of the legendary Billy McNeill. My mother's side of the family was Celtic daft. At a very early age, I was brought up on a diet of some possibly imaginative tales about Big Billy and the Lisbon Lions.

As I informed the TV reporter after the Scottish Cup Final win over Aberdeen on May 2017, I was born into Celtic. I was standing in the rain in the trackside at Hampden Park while the Celtic supporters gave a stirring rendition of 'You'll Never Walk Alone' when the interviewer stated, 'This club have fallen in love with you and you have fallen in love with this club.'

I had to correct him and say I was born into a Celtic family and there was no growing into the club. I said then that there has only been pride and it's a huge honour to manage Celtic.

I look back at the men who have been in charge of Celtic, the likes of Jock Stein, Martin O'Neill, Davie Hay, Tommy Burns, Billy McNeill, among others, and you realise the legacy they left at the club. That was my intention, too, when I arrived in May 2016. Billy McNeill is an absolute icon, a man who has been a supreme ambassador for Celtic. He is one of the great figures who has inspired Celtic to become what it is today.

I met Billy for the first time on the Wednesday evening of 1 February 2017 when we played Aberdeen in a Premiership game at Celtic Park. I was told he would be at the ground and, naturally, I was eager to meet him. I made certain I didn't miss the opportunity. I was aware of his condition, but I have to say he was in good spirits. There was a twinkle in his eye, too. We won 1–0 and possibly it was written in the stars that a centre-back, Dedryck Boyata, should get the only goal of the evening with a header. Billy McNeill would have approved, I'm sure.

As I was gathering material for my autobiography, *The Road To Paradise*, I discovered an uncle had written a letter to Billy informing him he should sign his fourteen-year-old nephew. That was in September 1987, only four months after Billy had returned to Celtic Park following his spell in England. There was maybe a wee idea from others that I possessed some talent. I was fortunate enough to get into the Northern Ireland schoolboys' squad, while I also played for Ballymena United in the Milk Cup, Northern Ireland's top youth tournament. I was playing in a team and doing something I loved as I continued to hope for the call to tell me Celtic were interested. The Celtic scout for Northern Ireland back then was a guy called Dessy McGuinness and I'd always ask my dad on the way home from games if Dessy had been there.

It was only after I became Celtic manager I discovered my Uncle Kevin had sent the note to Billy McNeill, telling him about me and suggesting that Celtic should take a look. He was trying to do everything to get me into Celtic because he would have loved nothing more than that. Kevin was also a great fan of Big Billy and had hoped to arrange to meet him. Unfortunately, he never got to do that, but he received a lovely reply from Billy.

I got to Celtic some thirty years later than Kevin wished, but I can assure you it was well worth the wait.

In my childhood, Billy McNeill was the name that was always mentioned. If you look at him as a player, he inspired not just people at Celtic Football Club, but many a player around Britain, being the first captain of a British team to pick up the European Cup. Many players at that time would have wanted to have done that. You only get truly inspired seeing someone you know or are close to actually do it.

When Billy stood up in Lisbon and held aloft the trophy, I'm sure for many players in Britain it gave them a great source of inspiration to do the same and from that moment Liverpool won the European Cup five times and other teams and managers won it, too. Billy McNeill and his teammates, expertly guided by Jock Stein, were the trailblazers, they knocked down the barriers and showed the rest of the UK it could be done.

When I first came to the club, I said my duty as the manager was to fill the stand. One of the stands was named after the Lisbon Lions and Billy was their leader, so our objective, as players and coaching staff, was to inspire this team to entertain in order to get the stands full again as a mark of respect to those great figures of our past. The Celtic way has always been about enjoyment, fighting for the shirt, defending the culture of your club. So, every time you pull on your Celtic shirt, you have to play with confidence, play with aggression, tenacity, be optimistic that you can win every game and you've got to have enthusiasm before you even think about tactics.

When Celtic won that European Cup in Lisbon, many respected onlookers said it was a victory for football. Who could argue? Billy, of course, kept that tradition going when he was in charge before, during and after the centenary season which was a landmark year in the club's history and must have put him under awesome pressure while expectation levels would have been extraordinarily high. It is to his eternal credit he entered that crucial campaign with an attacking, adventurous outlook; he would stand or fall by playing the sort of football that is associated with Celtic.

I was too young to make the trip to Parkhead for games, so, the next best thing was the TV set and eagerly awaiting the Scottish football snippets on BBC Scotland. Even before the centenary team, I recall watching Celtic play at Nottingham Forest in a UEFA Cup-tie in 1983 which was televised live. Davie Hay was the Celtic manager and Brian Clough was the Forest boss. It was played in November on a frost bound pitch and ended goalless. I thought my team, Celtic, were unlucky. Packie Bonner was in goal and Paul McStay also played. If I remember correctly, McStay had a shot right at the end that just rose over the crossbar.

A year later, I did get the opportunity to watch them live when they played Finn Harps in a pre-season game in Ireland. I was taken to the game by some of my relatives and I recall it was a nice sunny day and it appeared everybody in the crowd – I later discovered it was around 5,000 – was wearing Celtic colours. I was excited and it was great to watch my favourites win 3–0 . It may just have been a bounce game to get rid of the summer rust, but try telling that to an eleven-year-old kid. A great memory.

But Celtic are all about such enchanting, romantic reminiscences, aren't they? Everyone has got a beguiling Celtic story. I will always remember Billy McNeill's team in that glorious and momentous one hundredth birthday year when he and his players answered the call to mark the occasion. I was asked by Celtic TV to name my Ultimate Celtic Eleven, but I could choose only one Lisbon Lion and just one from the current team. I hope Billy will understand, but Jinky Johnstone got my vote from the team that conquered Europe and Inter Milan in the Portuguese capital. I just could not see beyond the wee winger. My uncles had told me so much about him and I've seen some breathtaking footage of a unique player in action. Scott Brown, so influential, inspirational and important in the current line-up, was a shoo-in.

From the 1988 side, you won't be surprised to learn I went for Packie Bonner in goal, Roy Aitken in central defence, the peerless Paul McStay in midfield with Tommy Burns providing the balance on the left. The man I chose for the No.3 position may raise an eyebrow or two, but he is in my dream team on merit, I can assure you of that. Anton Rogan, signed from Irish club Distillery, was a real Celtic man who gave absolutely everything for the cause. In fact, I admired him so much I named my son after him. Outwith that era, I chose the redoubtable Danny McGrain at right-back, Paul Elliott, a gifted, elegant performer to partner Roy 'The Bear' in central defence with two guys who epitomised Celtic, Kenny Dalglish and Henrik Larsson, playing up front alongside Jinky. I don't think there would be too many goalless draws around when that team played.

Like Billy McNeill and other Celtic managers in the past, I understand what the club is all about and that gives you an extra edge when you are standing on the touchline on matchday. You are passionately involved in the team, you are eager and determined to see them put in a display that will earn a win in the proper manner for the supporters. It's not about a pay cheque, it's about your love for the club.

I was fortunate enough to witness the team going sixty-nine successive domestic games undefeated following my arrival. I was told that sequence beat the previous best of sixty-two which had been held by Willie Maley's Celtic team from November 1915 to April 1917. It was a little surreal to discover I had been involved in making fresh Celtic history.

It was also a little strange to become only the third Celtic manager to complete a domestic clean sweep of honours, as I did in my first season, and be placed alongside Jock Stein, who achieved the feat twice in 1966/67 and 1968/69, and Martin O'Neill in 2000/01. Of course, we repeated the domestic clean sweep in the 2017/18 campaign to become the first team in Scottish football history to do this.

It is simply a pleasure and an honour to be involved with such a great club. I know how Billy McNeill and others felt in being entrusted with the position and the hopes and ambitions of so many people worldwide.

It will never be underestimated what Billy McNeill brought to Celtic Football Club.

1

A Light in the Darkest Place

10.18 p.m., Sunday, 24 November 1963, Glasgow

In the sixties, the Saltmarket area at Glasgow Cross was a rundown district that had long since forgotten how to smile. Opulent in another century, the damp and decay now hung in the air, the stench clinging stubbornly to the location's undertone. Depression invaded every corner.

Running north towards the High Street was a row of dull, grey sandstone, three-storeyed buildings, propped up by a hotchpotch of characterless shops, selling everything from a cheap suit to a poke of chips, elbowing each other in the forlorn hope of a brisk passing trade.

The bleak facade served to disguise the deprivation and squalor of the narrow pock-marked entrances that led to the landings and the dingy single-roomed apartments of the tenements that huddled in the perpetual darkness of unsympathetic shadows. The sun never shone on the slums in this part of the city. The relentless poverty smacked you in the face with the force of a shovel. No one strode, everyone shuffled. A sad resignation had been forced upon the denizens of an abandoned place, the pall of resolute despair as palpable as it was unshakeable.

All of which meant very little to an eleven-year-old boy who shivered alongside his mother on an interminably cruel winter's evening as they awaited the number 37 corporation bus which would ferry them from the cheerless city centre to the sprawling housing scheme of Castlemilk on Glasgow's south side, some five miles and forty minutes away. Once again, they had undertaken the weekend visit to his widowed grandmother, the bulk of whose life had been spent in the virtual hovel she called home. It had been a solitary, cramped room with well-scuffed linoleum covering the floor. The humble dwelling place contained a two-ring gas stove, a kitchen sink situated below the sole window, the twelve moderate panes of glass rattling in the rotting wooden frames when the elements paid a visit, a compact rectangular table upon which a plastic tablecloth had taken permanent residence, a wrought-iron grate in a tiny hearth, a coal bunker, two fireside armchairs, a thinly-woven mat of indeterminate design in front of the fireplace, a double bed, a low-level old-fashioned wooden wardrobe and a chest of drawers, all in various states of decrepitude. Spotlessly clean, though.

The only adornment amongst the clutter was a mustard-coloured chalk statuette of Christ being helped from the cross at Calvary. A wireless provided the sole source of entertainment. A lone dangling bulb, offering a dim yellow glow, lit the apartment. The toilet, a dank closet bereft of natural light, was lodged on the outside landing and shared by three other families, all occupants of the first floor of the gloomy stairwell, secreted out of sight and up a close, hidden from the main thoroughfare.

For decades, it was all his gran had ever known. 'The only way I'll ever leave here is in a box,' she had mentioned often enough. The old lady hadn't required the qualities of a soothsayer to call that one accurately. 'I'll be happy with three score years and ten.' She received a bonus of two years.

Standing with a noble air in the midst of an island at Glasgow Cross was the Tolbooth Steeple. In another era, public hangings took place in this area. Near the top of the renovated 126-foot 17th-century stone-built structure was a large, square clock, with bronze Roman numerals and ornate hands set against a dark-blue background. On this particular evening, it peered down and informed the boy it had just nudged beyond the witching hour of ten o'clock; 'pub throwing-out time', as it was known. Not far from the imposing High Court building was his father's favourite howf, The Old Ship Bank. Located diagonally opposite the bus stop was The Empire Bar while the corner of Saltmarket and London Road housed the Tolbooth Bar. There may have been precious little money for life's essentials such as sustenance, but there had always been a sufficiency of ready cash among the working-class citizens for the purchase of strong ale and, if the illegal backyard bookies had paid out on a winner, a substandard whisky.

Each evening, the newspaper-seller would dutifully set up outside the Tolbooth Bar preparing to dispense with the first editions of Glasgow's favourite dailies, the broadsheet *Daily Express* and the tabloid *Daily Record*, both priced at 3d (three pennies in old money, just over one new pence today). Tory versus Labour in black and white every day. The corner patch was ideally positioned to attract criss-crossing trade. Hot off the presses, around 10 p.m., the rival journals usually arrived within five minutes of each other, the nightly race to see who would be first to get the news on the street.

The *Express* was printed at its city offices at 129 Albion Street while the *Record* was published at 67 Hope Street, running parallel with Central Railway Station. Back then, the printed word was the main, vital and vibrant vehicle of information. Television was perceived by many as an unaffordable extravagance while radio reception, in an abundance of locales, was annoyingly fickle.

The pubs emptied as minutes ticked their way into history. Straight lines were not keenly observed as imbibers lurched into the night. Some stopped to purchase a newspaper, a great percentage immediately bypassing the front page in their haste to view the sports headlines on the back. It was obviously of paramount importance to discover what was happening at Celtic or Rangers, far more pressing than the continuing threat of a nuclear war between the USA and USSR, each nation possessing enough firepower to wipe each other off the map and take the rest of the world with them.

It was another unremarkable, raw winter's evening in Glasgow, the Saltmarket undertaking its obligatory impression of a freezing and neglected concrete wasteland. The bloated, dark-tinged clouds, with the seemingly-perennial threat of a deluge, hovered menacingly overhead. Thin, cold rain never seemed far away. The youngster, suitably smothered in woollens in an attempt to combat the chills, put one foot on the road and craned his neck, peering up towards the High Street, a vain search for the welcoming sight of the number 37 bus which would have been journeying from the Springburn depot. 'No sign,' he said. The information had been greeted with a quiet sigh. His mother had long been convinced no bus in the city ever ran on time, especially the number 37 on a perishing evening on the Sabbath.

Her son wanted to talk of the excitement of attending only his second Celtic game at Parkhead the previous afternoon, 23 November. Politely, she feigned interest as she was enlightened as to how Celtic had beaten Kilmarnock 5–0 with a player by the name of John Hughes scoring three goals. This giant of a man was known as 'Yogi', named after the popular American TV cartoon character 'Yogi Bear'. The son imparted the knowledge that Celtic supporters would sing 'Feed The Bear' to encourage teammates to pass the ball to him. It transpired the aforementioned John Hughes was, in fact, the favourite player of her husband. The mother was told breathlessly about the virtues of a tiny, flame-haired outside-right by the name of Jimmy Johnstone, who also scored a goal. Johnny Divers – who was 'brilliant' – got on the scoresheet, too.

In his first visit to Celtic Park a fortnight earlier, the boy had seen 'his' team also claim five goals in a 5–3 triumph over Partick Thistle in another thrilling First Division encounter. John Hughes and Jimmy Johnstone had scored on that memorable occasion, too, but the player who had commandeered the spotlight was the centre-forward by the name of Stevie Chalmers who thumped three beyond goalkeeper George Niven. What an introduction to Parkhead for a young boy, the foundation of an unwavering lifetime love affair. This was entertainment Celtic-style, as he would grow to anticipate, appreciate, savour and, occasionally when things didn't go according to plan, bemoan.

Goals from Chalmers and Johnstone had the team with the iconic green-and-white hooped shirts ahead inside twenty minutes. In the whirlwind space of five minutes, Thistle fired three behind eccentric custodian Frank Haffey and Celtic, unbelievably, were trailing at the interval. A newspaper report the following day noted, 'The Thistle goals extinguished the triumphant singing from the terracing with the suddenness of a power cut.'

It took Celtic until the sixty-seventh minute to equalise when Chalmers struck and then Hughes – 'Big Yogi' – clattered in a thirty-five-yard piledriver that almost took the unfortunate keeper with it as the ball bulged the net. With four minutes to go, Ernie Yard, an eager centre-forward for the visitors, crashed a shot against the inside of Haffey's upright and, within sixty seconds, Chalmers had completed his hat-trick. Welcome to Celtic Park, young man, step aboard the rollercoaster, enjoy the ride.

His understanding mother knew when to nod at the precise moments as though she was digesting every indispensable morsel of information eagerly delivered by her son.

'Stevie Chalmers is as fast as a whippet.'

'Really?'

'Left-back Tommy Gemmell plays like an outside-left.'

'That's good.'

'Bobby Murdoch is a super passer of the ball.'

'Fine.'

'Jimmy Johnstone is unstoppable, he's really tricky. You should see the things he can do with the ball.'

'Maybe someday.'

The boy droned on.

And then something quite extraordinary happened. A shiny, sleek motor vehicle pulled over to park at the kerbside just in front of the bus stop. The driver swung open his door as he prepared to step out. An inky crevice of night-time Glasgow was instantly illuminated, a brilliant flash of sheet lightning couldn't have done a better job. The tall, fair-haired and immaculately-dressed individual said something to his impossibly-attractive, impeccably-coiffured blonde companion, instantly recognisable as his wife, before he gently closed the door. With a straight-backed, purposeful gait, the man, counting his change as he did so, moved towards the newspaper-seller. The boy, transfixed by the vision, noticed he bought both journals, shared a joke with the vendor and turned to head back to his gleaming mode of transport. Moments later, the automobile and its glamorous occupants swished out of sight.

The handsome gentleman could not have made more of an

impression on the young lad had he arrived on a Roman Emperor's bejewelled chariot, drawn by four ivory-white Arabian thoroughbreds while being announced by the tumultuous harmony of a brass fanfare and the shuddering clash of cymbals.

It was the first time I had come within touching distance of Billy McNeill.

2

Hand in Hand with an Honourable Man

Monday, 8 December 2014, Glasgow

I was aware Billy McNeill was being cursed with bad days as well as being blessed with good ones. The random fluctuation and hopelessness of the illness was challenged on a daily basis with the individual's usual doughtiness.

'Will you be able to make the book launch?' I asked as I checked my wristwatch: 10.06 a.m.

'Don't start without me,' came the remarkably jolly reply. Billy McNeill, obviously, was enjoying one of his better mornings.

I had been in touch the previous week to place the initial request. My new book, majoring on the Celtic managerial careers of Billy McNeill and Davie Hay – entitled *Caesar and the Assassin* – had just been published. Now it was time to go through the rigmarole of the required publicity for the tome. Peter Lawwell, chief executive of Celtic, had kindly agreed for the use of Parkhead for the promotion. The wheels had been set in motion for a noon presentation at the ground on Monday, 8 December 2014. Iain Jamieson, the club's PR boss, could not have been more helpful or courteous. I emailed my colleagues in the media, newspapers, television and radio, and a freelance photographer was notified too.

The only tricky bit was to ensure Billy McNeill and Davie Hay made an appearance.

I am fortunate enough to have known both these gentlemen for decades and I would unhesitatingly include them in my best friends' list. Not just for their Celtic connections, their allegiance or even for what they achieved at the club. Simply because both are such damn fine human beings. These are guys you want in the trench beside you when the flak begins to fly. They are undoubtedly men's men, both without a trace of conceit. Neither McNeill nor Hay could ever be accused of narcissistic tendencies.

Egos and arrogance, those two irritating imposters, have never been welcomed into the psyche of these luminaries. They hailed from working-class backgrounds and their success in football, on and off the field, had been the accomplishment of two human beings determinedly pushing themselves to the absolute zenith of their abilities in their chosen profession. They never cheated their teammates, the supporters or themselves.

Davie Hay informed me he had a prior arrangement on the day of the book's unveiling, but he had a window of opportunity which he would use to be at Celtic Park at midday. I was not in the least surprised by his magnanimous gesture. I knew with every confidence he would be there at the appointed hour.

Given the circumstances, I would have understood completely if Billy McNeill, in a delicate condition at the age of seventy-four, had declined the invitation. It would be another two years and two months before his family would go public to declare this legend's momentous and courageous struggle against dementia. I knew at the onset of the fragility of his health but, naturally, it had not been anything I deemed worthy of splashing over front pages of newspapers. For me, it was a private, family affair and would remain that way until his redoubtable wife Liz decided otherwise. And that, of course, had been the case on Sunday, 26 February 2017.

However, back in December 2014, I hoped Billy would be able to grace the occasion with his considerable presence. There would not be the semblance of pressure, I held the man in far too high esteem for that. If Billy had said no, he would have been free of coercion. With a fair bit of trepidation, I put in the call. Any fears I may have entertained were dispelled immediately.

'It would be a pleasure, Alex,' came the welcome response. 'I'll ask Liz to look out my best bib and tucker.'

We chatted for another ten minutes or so and, although a bit forgetful on occasion, it was clear Billy, mercifully, had been bestowed another good day. I realised, though, I would have to put in a check call on the morning of the launch. Situations could take an unexpected downturn through no fault of anyone's. Billy didn't disappoint. 'I'll be there,' he confirmed.

Noon rolled around at Celtic Park and Billy McNeill, along with his lifelong friend and former Celtic teammate Mike Jackson, had arrived some thirty minutes earlier. They sat upstairs in the Jock Stein lounge, sipping coffee and chatting with some of the Celtic Park personnel. Davie Hay arrived at the same time as my wife Gerda and me. The media were beginning to mill around in a room just off the main entrance. I looked at Billy and, unless you had known differently, he appeared in mint condition. Impeccably dressed, as ever, he smiled, 'Right, what time do we kick off?'

Fifteen minutes or so later, on the touchline at Celtic Park, I was flanked by two Celtic legends, Billy on my right and Davie on my left, as we posed for the images to promote the book. Billy grinned at the camera and whispered in my ear, 'The things I do for a free lunch.'

Once the publicity work had been taken care of and the photographer was satisfied, Davie departed for his scheduled assignment and Gerda, very helpfully, fetched her vehicle from the car park to give Billy, Mike and me a lift to the White Cart bar/restaurant on the south side of the city, about equidistant from where Billy and I lived. On a quiet Monday near the beginning of the month, the dining room was fairly tranquil, a welcome hiatus as the bar and kitchen staff prepared for the onslaught of the festive season. The four of us ordered bowls of piping hot Scotch broth and crusty bread to be followed by hand-battered fish and chips with garden peas.

A pleasant afternoon ensued and we chatted about everything from politics to ping-pong, majoring, of course, on football. I was always amazed at the colourful anecdotes Billy could produce. Just when you believed you had heard them all and he had exhausted his treasure trove, he would unwrap another marvellous reminiscence and, once again, you were spirited off on a magical carpet ride into unforgettable territory. In truth, I found Billy endlessly fascinating. Maybe the detail wasn't quite so sharp, possibly the delivery might not be quite as precise, but, as you would expect, Celtic's greatest ever captain could serve up a tale or two. With personal clouds dispelled, at least temporarily, he sparkled over his repast that afternoon, the raconteur of not so long ago.

Mike received a call on his mobile phone to remind him to pick up his grandkids from school; time had raced away, as usual. Billy was happy to stay in our company and Mike got in touch with Liz to inform her of the situation. I vowed to make sure a Celtic great would be home, safe and sound, between 5 p.m. and 6 p.m. Thankfully, Liz took me at my word. We whiled away the remaining hour or so – it was never a burden to spend time in this gentleman's company – and when it reached just beyond 5 p.m., we knew it was time to make a move. 'Have I got my keys?' asked Billy. Before he made his exit, Mike had told me to reassure Billy his house keys were in his inside coat pocket. I told him where they would be found. Billy fumbled a bit before they were located. He had looked just a tad anxious for the first time that day.

Gerda drove the car to the front of the eatery and I slipped into the back while Billy sat in the passenger seat. Our vehicle joined the traffic heading along the busy Ayr Road in the direction of Prestwick. Billy continued to chat away. 'Did you get everything you needed, Alex?' he asked, thoughtfully. 'Everything's good, Billy,' I replied. Eventually, Gerda pulled the car in at the side of the road opposite the Parkland Hotel and Country Club. I knew Billy's home was within five minutes walking distance. He eased open the door and said, 'Right, folks, I'm off now. Thanks for lunch. Good luck with the book, Alex.'

'Whoa there, fella,' I said as I scrambled out to follow him. There was no way I was going to allow him to cross the bustling A77 with cars nose to tail, commuters making their way home from work combining with others who had strayed into the chaotic traffic. We stood side-by-side, shoulder-to-shoulder, as we waited for a break in the flow of metal. Suddenly, without warning, Billy slipped his right hand into my left hand. It was a surreal moment. With hands linked, we threaded our way through the sluggish stream of vehicles and reached the opposite pavement without mishap. Billy turned, looked me straight in the eye and said, 'You were brilliant there.' I didn't know how to respond. I think I burbled something along the lines of, 'You weren't so bad yourself, Billy.'

He practically marched up the driveway of the smart detached family home, didn't bother looking for his keys, rang the doorbell and Liz answered.

'One Lisbon legend returned, as promised,' I said.

'And fed and watered,' added Billy. He looked again at me and said, 'Thanks, I enjoyed that.' And with that he walked up the steps leading to the front door and vanished down the hallway.

'Everything fine, Alex?' asked Liz.

'It couldn't have gone better,' I answered, truthfully.

I never once mentioned to Billy McNeill about the chilly winter's evening in the Saltmarket just over fifty-one years earlier when an eleven-year-old awe-struck novice Celtic fan had been briefly in his extraordinary presence for the first time.

MIKE JACKSON

Millions of people know the name Billy McNeill. But I would ask, 'How many people actually *know* Billy McNeill?'

The Celtic legend has been a great friend of mine since we first met in the summer of 1957. I was his best man when he married Liz in June 1963 and he would have been mine, too, if my brother Jim hadn't claimed the honour.

We came through the Celtic ranks together after Billy returned from a year with Junior side Blantyre Vics. I had arrived from Benburb and had been playing in the reserves while he was gaining experience in that rough, tough environment where old professionals were eager to let youngsters know who was the boss. I had the chance to sign for Manchester United, but when Celtic came calling there was only one team for me. And it was exactly the same for Billy.

He was more fortunate than me – they kept him and gave me the boot! The Celtic chairman Bob Kelly made all the decisions back then and if your face didn't fit, you would soon be heading for the exit. Paddy Crerand, Bertie Auld and yours truly had a few things to say about how things were being mishandled back in the early sixties and, one by one, we were 'invited' to leave the premises. They weren't so daft, though, as to sell my big mate. I doubt if the fans in the old Jungle would have tolerated that.

However, the true measure of a man as a human being is not determined on a green patch of grass on match day. On the field of battle anyone can be a hero to legions of fans, a *Roy of the Rovers* character who can do no wrong. They can score winning goals in Cup Finals and take centre stage for their country in vital international campaigns. That just means they have been blessed with God-given football skills. Away from the roar of the crowd and the adulation, they are mere mortals like you and me.

Let me give you an illustration of how Billy McNeill shapes up as a man. My mother, Sarah, passed away in October 1984. The funeral Mass was arranged for Holy Cross Parish Church in Crosshill, Glasgow, at ten o'clock on a Thursday morning. Billy was manager of Manchester City at the time and I realised they had an away game in that midweek. I thought the time factor would be against him attempting to turn up to pay his last respects. The match wouldn't have finished much before ten o'clock and it would have taken a good hour after that for the players to get showered and changed before they would be ready to get on the team coach bound for their old ground at Maine Road to pick up their cars and make their own way home.

I had worked it out Billy wouldn't have got to his house until around four o'clock in the morning, six hours before my mother's funeral. He would have been shattered. Would anyone have blamed him for collapsing into bed? Not me. However, this is Billy McNeill we are talking about. He took the opportunity to freshen up, shower and shave, put on a dark suit, white shirt and black tie before getting back into his car. He drove through the night to get to Glasgow later that morning. When the family and relatives walked into the church, Billy was already sitting in a pew. And that gesture is what makes this extraordinary man so special.

At the start of our everlasting friendship, some twenty-seven years earlier, I took one look at Celtic's latest recruit and thought, 'Thank God he's on my side!' I signed for the club just ahead of Billy and in one of our first bounce games I vividly recall this big, blond guy leaping about three times higher than anyone else to head the ball. He could run, he could tackle and he put so much energy into his football. He wasn't the best passer of a ball, so he kept it simple and, more often than not, would knock it onto a midfield player to hit the through balls. There was no larking around with Billy. He was there to train and attempt to be the absolute best he possibly could be as a footballer.

He demanded the same dedication from his teammates. Don't get the impression it was all work and no play for my pal. Big Billy embraced a night out just like the rest of us. Back then, we were aware the board didn't like their players socialising with each other. Big Billy, Bertie Auld, Paddy Crerand, John Colrain, an under-rated Irish centre-forward, and myself went around together and were known as the Rat Pack after the original Hollywood gang that was led by Frank Sinatra and consisted of actors, singers and comedians Dean Martin, Peter Lawford, Sammy Davis Junior and Joey Bishop. I remember the day we decided to copy the entertainers. As usual, we were in a restaurant and coffee shop named Ferrari's which was situated on Sauchiehall Street. It was a favourite haunt of the Celtic players for years.

We were shooting the breeze, mainly talking about football, when someone asked if we fancied taking in an afternoon movie. They were showing *Ocean's Eleven* at the nearby Odeon cinema. It was a 1960 crime caper about a mob of guys plotting to rob a Las Vegas casino and we decided to give it a look. We all enjoyed the film and afterwards someone suggested we should form our own Celtic version of the Rat Pack. I was nicknamed Dino after Martin because, although the boys will still tell you differently, I could hold a note and belt out a song or two. All these years down the line, friends still call me Dino!

Wee Bertie became Sammy D after Sammy Davis, who was a black Jew. Terribly politically incorrect today, of course, but Bertie had this dark growth and had to shave about twice a day. Paddy answered to Joey for comedian Joey Bishop and Colly became known as Oceans. Sinatra was a character named Danny Ocean in the title role of the movie and it stuck with Colly, who was a massive fan of the crooner.

Billy became Cesar after an actor by the name of Cesar Romero, who had a role in the movie as the gang's driver. Among us, Billy was the only one who had a car, a sky blue Austin A35, so that's where he picked up his original nickname. Of course, most of us came to recognise it as Caesar after the Roman Emperor as his career took off. Sounds a bit more respectful, too, but the original moniker stuck for many folk. Romero wasn't quite Hollywood box office and isn't remembered for too many starring roles. He's probably best known as The Joker in the *Batman* TV series of the sixties.

As the Rat Pack, with a certain Jim Baxter also in tow, we used to visit the Locarno Ballroom in Glasgow's Sauchiehall Street on a Tuesday or Saturday or, if we were flush, both nights. I lost count of the times Bertie, Colly, Paddy and myself were asked to go to the manager's office on a Monday morning. Apparently, there had been reports about some players enjoying wild nights on the town. Don't make me laugh. It only took a couple of lager and limes to get the lot of us pissed. Anyway, these were the days when they rolled up the pavements in Glasgow at ten o'clock. We were often asked to explain ourselves. 'The four of you were spotted drinking,' said Jimmy McGrory, who, to be fair, never looked too comfortable going through the interrogation process. Obviously, he had been put up to it by someone else.

Big Billy was never mentioned. 'Who were you drinking with?' the manager would enquire. 'How about the blond, six-foot-plus captain of the club?' we could have answered. Billy was spared these regular Monday morning meetings. Maybe he wore an invisible suit on a Saturday! Slowly and surely, though, the board offloaded Bertie, Colly, Paddy and myself. We were seen as expendable. Obviously, as I said earlier, my big mate wasn't. That was one decision they got right.

I was aware Billy was far from happy when he heard I had been moved on to St Johnstone in April 1963. Billy had been with the Scotland international squad for the game against England at Wembley – we won 2–1 with goals from honorary Rat Pack member Jim Baxter – and our captain was given some extra time off. While he was elsewhere, Bob Kelly made his move to get rid of me. I've often wondered if it was a coincidence my big mate wasn't around at the time. Remember, these were the days before mobile phones, Billy wasn't at home and I didn't have a number, so, unfortunately, I couldn't get in touch for almost a week. That was all the time that was required to get me out of Parkhead.

Two years later, Jock Stein returned and told me, 'You should never have left. Did you not realise I would be back one day?' My crystal ball must have been a bit faulty back then. You would have needed dynamite to get me out of Celtic if I had realised Big Jock was ever going to return.

A week or so after my switch to the Perth team, Billy and I were discussing the situation. My big mate was convinced I had got on the wrong side of Bob Kelly after I had related the story of a Wednesday night league game at Celtic Park during the time of the Home Internationals and Paddy Crerand was with the Scottish squad, so I half-expected to be playing in his position at right-half. I arrived at the park just after six o'clock and was met by my old schoolteacher John Murphy, who was instrumental in most of the boys from Glasgow's Holyrood School going to Celtic. He sent me and others such as Paddy, John Kurila and Charlie Gallagher to the club. I think he acted as an unpaid scout and for years he did the public address work at Parkhead.

Anyway, I met Mr Murphy – I could never call my former schoolteacher John – and he had just received the team to announce for the game. Sure enough, I was pencilled in to play at right-half. At six forty-five, Bob Rooney, our physiotherapist, came into the snooker room where all the lads congregated to relax and get ready before a game. According to Bob, I was now at inside-right, but, at least, I was playing, so I went in to get ready for the game.

I did all my usual preparations, had my rubdown with the oil and liniment and was knocking the ball about in the shower area. Then Bob reappeared. He told me to go and have a bath. I wasn't playing now, there had been another change made to the team. So, at six thirty I was right-half, at six forty-five I was inside-right and at seven fifteen I was out of the team altogether. I had given my dad a ticket for the game and told him I was playing. He was in the stand and wondered why there was no sign of his son when the team ran out. He thought I had taken ill.

Honestly, that is a true story and all too commonplace during the years I was at Celtic. Undoubtedly, Kelly would not have welcomed the retelling of that story, the main reason being he would have been the one meddling with the line-up. Poor Jimmy McGrory was the manager but didn't have a say in who would play for Celtic. A nonsensical situation.

I still laugh at the time Billy, Colly and I teamed up with three Third Lanark players, Matt Gray, Dave Hilley and Alex Harley. It was the summer of 1961 and we decided to embark upon a great adventure of going on a Continental holiday. Growing up, we would all have been used to our fortnight with the family on the Costa Clyde and the delights of Largs, Rothesay, Arran and Millport. This particular year, while we were all single, we decided to try the real thing, the Costa Brava, and ended up in Lloret de Mar.

A holidaymaker spotted us and asked if we wanted to take part in a game the following day. There would be a few extra quid in it for us, we were told. It was an actual game with a referee, linesmen and fans turning out to watch. We knew the Scottish Football Association had laws against registered footballers with clubs in Scotland taking part in such games. 'Ach,' said Billy, 'what harm can it do? Who's ever going to hear about it?' We all turned out, played at half-pace, received our payment and thought nothing more about it.

Billy and I stepped off the plane at the airport after our holiday to be confronted by some press reporters and photographers. They were asking for details about our game in Spain. Billy and I feigned innocence, so, too, did the Third Lanark guys. 'Must be some mistake, lads,' we said as we rushed for a taxi.

I got home and my dad didn't look too pleased to see me. He had heard about our involvement in the game and asked me about it. I wasn't going to lie to my dad. I came clean, but I added, 'They've got no proof. It's our word against theirs.' He produced a copy of that day's *Daily Express* and chucked it at me. Looking back at me was a team picture with Billy, me and the Thirds players all stripped and posing away naively. A helpful tourist from Glasgow identified us, took a few snaps and flogged them to the newspaper. We were in trouble.

The SFA fined us something like fifty quid each and, needless to say, Bob Kelly wasn't overly enamoured. Inside two years, I was on my bike. Thankfully, for Celtic's sake, Billy McNeill remained.

PAT CRERAND

Billy McNeill and I both signed for Celtic on the same Monday evening on 5 August 1957. I arrived from Junior side Duntocher Hibs while Billy came in from Our Lady's High School in Motherwell before being farmed out for a year to Blantyre Vics – and we have been friends through thick and thin ever since.

When we turned up at Parkhead we were met by the reserve team coach who would have a huge impact on both of us, a bloke called Jock Stein. The manager was Jimmy McGrory, the club's all-time highest goal scorer, but we soon found out he was manager in name only. The man who ran the team was the chairman, Bob Kelly. I'm not being disrespectful, but he knew nothing about that side of the game. And I mean nothing. McGrory was a genuine club legend because of his phenomenal goal scoring record, but, as team boss, he appeared to accept the situation and take a backseat.

On the night of our arrival, Big Jock had a word with Billy and me, but there were no grand speeches, just a firm handshake and he told us both he hoped we would have good careers as professional footballers. Obviously, that was the first time I had ever met Jock, although I had seen him often enough from the terraces. In 1954, for instance, I travelled with my mates on the Gorbals Celtic Supporters' Bus to Edinburgh to watch Jock captain the side and play at centre-half when the club won its first title since 1938.

I remember they beat Hibs 3–0 at a packed Easter Road with Neilly Mochan, who would later become a trainer, scoring two goals. I was in the crowd at Hampden a fortnight later when Jock again inspired the team to a 2–1 Scottish Cup Final victory over Aberdeen. So, I was quite thrilled to meet a Celtic hero who, unfortunately, had been forced to quit playing in 1956 with an ankle injury that left him with a permanent limp. He was only thirty-four. That was when he took over the role of looking after the reserves and the youths. No one could have forecast it at the time, but what a move that was in the right direction for the club.

As Billy and I left the ground that night, I was on a high. Jock Stein had actually shaken my hand! Billy smiled and informed me Jock had already visited his parents' house to tell them their son should sign for Celtic. Billy also told me Jock had said, 'If he's cheeky, can I skelp him one?' When we signed, I was eighteen, a year older than Billy. We first played alongside each other in the reserves and I knew immediately he would be a monumental success. He was in a different class from day one. I really mean that; his quality just shone through, even at that age.

What struck me immediately was his astonishing spring and his timing in the air. It was actually quite breathtaking. I had never seen anyone leap so high and, in all my years in the game, I never witnessed anyone who came anywhere near Billy's aerial prowess. He was unbeatable and, for me, that is one of the two qualities a top-class central defender requires, the other being the ability to tackle. Big Billy ticked both boxes.

When Billy signed, the centre-half was Bobby Evans, who had been a fixture in the team for about a decade, playing mainly in the old right-half position before settling into the middle of defence. He was also a mainstay in the Scotland international team. So, it looked as though Billy might have a fairly lengthy wait before making his first appearance for the top team. I wasn't one bit surprised when he made his debut just one year later. I had to wait another fifteen months before I got the nod to step up.

No one should be unduly surprised at the rapid rise through the ranks for young players back then. It was so typical of Celtic. Players just out of the Juniors were expected to fill in when a first-team player was injured or had left the club. Bobby Evans, who had captained the club when they beat Rangers 7–1 in the 1957 League Cup Final, left to join Chelsea in the summer of 1959 and that practically ensured Billy McNeill would be the first team centre-half for the foreseeable future. And then I stepped up to play in the No.4 position, which today would be called right midfield.

At that time, some of the Scottish journalists were calling the team 'Kelly's Kids' as a copy of what was happening at Manchester United where the side was known as the 'Busby Babes'. Looking at our nickname, you would have thought Bob Kelly was the manager and not the chairman. Matt Busby was team boss at Old Trafford at the time, so why weren't we called 'McGrory's Mites' or something like that? At United, Busby put his young players through an apprenticeship before making absolutely certain they were first-team material. That didn't happen at Celtic.

You knew you were getting near the top side when you were allowed to train with the first team. Jimmy McGrory was probably too nice to be a manager and I know that thought will be backed up by many who came through the ranks at Parkhead in the early sixties. He didn't get involved in tactics. He would instruct Billy to head the ball 'as far away as possible'. Me? I was told 'aim for the corner flag'. He reckoned if I passed the ball in that direction there should be a winger waiting. Not exactly revolutionary, was it?

But that's what we were brought up with and it didn't matter because we were playing for Celtic. Every now and again, the first team would play the reserves in a bounce game. After Billy and I had signed, we played in a few of these with Jock Stein taking the second string. I don't know who would be in charge of the top side because Jimmy McGrory never went anywhere near the training ground. We regularly won these matches, mainly because we were better prepared by Big Jock and were tactically aware.

I left my boyhood idols to join Manchester United in 1963. I didn't want to go, but it was obvious the Celtic hierarchy did not welcome someone in the dressing room having a say about how the club was being run. Bertie Auld was the same. And, of course, it wasn't long before he was shipped out to Birmingham City, although Bertie, like me, had no desire to leave the club. Mike Jackson was another who couldn't just sit there and keep his mouth shut. Mike was an excellent midfield player, but he didn't play as many games as he should have and you have to question why that was the case. Anyway, Mike's Celtic career was cut short when he was sold to St Johnstone.

Big Billy was obviously smarter than the three of us; he kept his own counsel inside the walls of Celtic Park. Outside, he was just as vehement as Bertie, Mike and me. The directors didn't like hassle, no one had an opinion outside the boardroom, it had to be their way or the highway.

I was surprised Billy did not join me at Manchester United. When I left, I was convinced he would follow me to Old Trafford. Matt Busby liked Billy, I knew that, and the United boss also realised what Scottish players would bring to his team. That was why he paid £115,000 to sign Denis Law from Torino in 1962, which was by far the British record transfer fee at the time. I believe Celtic received £43,000 for me – the biggest deal between English and Scottish clubs at the time – and something in that region might have been enough to tempt them to sell Big Billy. Would he have gone?

The mere fact he never played for any other club answers that. A journalist by the name of Jim Rodger, who worked for the *Daily Record*, was a Mr Fixit in these transfer deals. He was probably the first non-commissioned agent and this guy had contacts all over the place. When I married Noreen on 25 June 1963, I was amazed to receive a message from Pope Paul VI. It was no hoax. That wee reporter had connections everywhere! He was very friendly with Matt Busby and the Spurs manager Bill Nicholson.

I know he could have got Billy to the London club. They were looking for a centre-half in 1964 to replace the veteran Maurice Norman and Rodger could have put Billy and Nicholson together. Spurs' main scout in Scotland was a bloke called Eric Smith who had been a teammate of Billy at Celtic. If my big pal had been in the game purely for financial gain and not his overwhelming affection for Celtic, he would have been on his way to White Hart Lane. They would have put him on a guaranteed salary of £100 a week and I reckon that would have been almost four times what he was earning at Parkhead. There would have been a sizeable signing-on fee on top of that. But Billy refused to budge.

Like everyone with Celtic at heart, Billy was growing frustrated at the lack of success and the league was blown practically every season shortly after the turn of the year. They hadn't won anything since that 7–1 League Cup walloping of our old Ibrox friends in 1957. And then came the news Jock Stein was coming back to the club around January of 1965, although he didn't officially become manager until March. Typical of the man, he remained at Hibs until they found a replacement and as soon as Bob Shankly, brother of Liverpool legend Bill, was put in place, Jock moved back to Parkhead.

There was no chance of Billy leaving Celtic after that appointment. Bill Nicholson eventually paid big money to sign Welsh international centre-half Mike England from Blackburn Rovers. Mike was a good defender, but he wasn't in Big Billy's class. So, it could so easily have been Billy McNeill of Spurs if he hadn't been so committed to Celtic.

If I had known there was the possibility of Jock returning, I doubt if I would have left Celtic. Who wouldn't have wanted to work under his guidance? Mind you, I might never have won a European Cup medal if I had remained at Celtic because Bobby Murdoch was in my position when my old club conquered Europe in 1967. Bobby was a brilliant player, so I might have watched the game in Lisbon from the stand. I had to wait another year before I got my hands on one of those precious badges when I played in the United team that beat Benfica 4–1 at Wembley. However, it was no surprise to me when Celtic's fortunes took off under Big Jock.

Even during the days when Jock was manager of Dunfermline or Hibs, he was a regular visitor to Old Trafford for European games. He was always striving to improve himself. I recall he came down to watch Manchester United in a midweek game and we were chatting afterwards. He looked particularly happy with life. I asked him, 'Why the big smiles?' He grinned and said, 'Ach, you'll find out soon enough.' A few days later came the announcement Jock was the new Celtic manager and Jimmy McGrory was to be put in charge of the Press Relations at the club. I think that position would have been more suited to this genuinely nice guy.

Billy couldn't wait to phone me. 'Paddy, have you heard? Big Jock's back!' He was clearly excited and he made the valid point that it could only be good news for himself and the likes of Bobby Murdoch, John Clark, Jimmy Johnstone, Bobby Lennox and the younger players he had coached at reserve-team level. He would develop their strengths and work on their weaknesses.

There was no looking back for Big Billy when Jock Stein walked back through those old massive green doors at Celtic Park.

3

Billy in the Sun

Billy McNeill was still a part-time player when, at the age of eighteen, he made his Celtic first-team debut appearance against Clyde in a League Cup-tie at Parkhead on Saturday, 23 August 1958. McNeill had worked for the Lanarkshire County Council and then Stenhouse Insurance, a company based in Glasgow city centre, in his first three years at the club after joining from Junior side Blantyre Vics in 1957.

The future legend didn't expect his rapid rise to promotion, but Celtic manager Jimmy McGrory didn't have too many options at the time when club stalwart Bobby Evans, an experienced Scotland international of some repute, called off with an injury and his replacement, John Jack, a reliable, if unspectacular, back-up, was similarly afflicted. And, so, in front of a crowd of 39,000 supporters on a bright afternoon in the east end of Glasgow, Billy McNeill trotted out behind skipper Bertie Peacock, the Northern Ireland left-half, and goalkeeper Frank Haffey, making only his second appearance after his initial outing in a 4–1 win over Third Lanark at the end of the previous campaign.

Bertie Auld, who accompanied McNeill out of the Celtic Park tunnel to be cheered onto the park that day, has hazy recollections of Celtic's 2–0 triumph.

'Clyde had a good team in the fifties with individuals such as Harry Haddock, Tommy Ring and Archie Robertson in the line-up. We knew we would have to scrap to get anything from them – and so it proved. Going into the match, I was aware Clyde could go top of our section if they beat us. We were sitting on five points after three games – remember, it was two points for a win and one for a draw – and they were one behind. We were holders of the trophy, of course, following our win over Rangers in the final the previous year. The fans were still singing, *'Oh, Hampden in the sun, Celtic 7, Rangers 1'* at all our games. The manager must have had a lot of faith in Billy at that age to bring him in.

'Naturally, I took the pressure off him with the second goal. I started off looking after Big Billy and it was something I got used to in all our years as teammates! Seriously, I think Billy eased into the first team that afternoon. Even a blind man would have recognised his ability in the air. Bobby Evans, who played a lot of games at wing-half, was not tall for a centre-half and did most of his good work on the ground. So, it was a real change to see someone in our defence so dominant at dealing with crosses. It seemed prophetic we had a clean sheet in his first game.'

In those days, there was often a stampede for the news-stands or the vendors on street corners an hour or so after a game to catch up with the match reports and results around the UK. The main newspaper rivals were the pink *Evening Times* and the green *Evening Citizen*. Under the headline 'CLYDE DRIFT ON AS CELTS SCORE', here is the full assessment from the reporter from the former. Please note the misspelling of McNeill. The man at the match afforded him only one 'l'. Such is fame.

Bright sunshine and a new-look Celtic with teenagers Frank Haffey in goal, Billy McNeil at centre-half and Jim Conway at centre-forward brought the crowd in good numbers to Parkhead for the League Cup game against unchanged Clyde.

Both teams opened up at full throttle and all within the first three minutes a like number of commendable efforts from Conway, Ring and Coyle had slid just past with McCulloch and Haffey mighty pleased young men.

Then came three minutes of Clyde disaster. Conway's persistence forced a corner. Tully's cross drifted over and Sammy Wilson headed Celtic into the lead with a clean-as-a-whistle effort.

Three minutes later came further disaster for McCulloch, who was led off with a cut face and Haddock took over in goal. Just to complete Clyde's misery, Archie Robertson shot tamely past from the penalty spot two minutes later after Tully had pushed Coyle off the ball. To a cheer from the Clyde supporters, McCulloch resumed after a ten-minute quick repair job, with a plaster on his forehead. He was hardly back in goal before Conway waded past Finlay and Walters before placing the ball past from six yards.

Clyde celebrated with a neat attack which fizzled to a bad end when Robertson shot tamely at Haffey from open-sight range. Clyde were improving with every delightful football minute and Ring hurtled a right-foot shot inches past. The Clyde onslaught continued with a Herd shot which Haffey did well to clutch. The young keeper brought out every stop again thirty seconds later to fingertip a Ring volley to safety.

Such activity stung Celtic back into attack with Tully the maestro conducting the sweet rhythm of their all-in-a-line movements. Collins and Peacock almost knocked two Clyde defenders right of the park with piledrivers before Clyde's red shirts went charging back to bring danger to Haffey.

In the thirty-fifth minute, Celtic were in green and white paradise as Auld scored a magnificent second goal. Wilson gave him the ball in the clear and from twenty yards it hardly rose a foot as it flew past McCulloch, who had no chance.

Celtic's new-look team were certainly playing with spirit and excellent understanding against a Clyde team who, although neat enough in outfield, sadly lacked a killer's touch near goal.

Clyde resumed, still playing their precise football, in contrast to Celtic, who were moving the ball around in a much more purposeful manner.

Herd finally showed what was wanted with a fierce drive which slid inches over. Then Tully danced Clyde into trouble again with a balletic effort in which he gave Conway a perfect pass, but McCulloch brought off a fine clearance from the centre's cross. Celtic were playing with all the confidence in the Parkhead world, with young McNeil a steady pivot.

The pace was now slowing down with Clyde continuing to pattern-weave the ball into Celtic's goal area before undoing all their good work by ineffective finishing.

In contrast, Celtic were still a hard-hitting team with Tully and Collins a good wing, and Conway an 'up-and-at-em' centre giving Finlay a busy afternoon's chasing.

And with that report, a legend was born. Even if his name was spelled incorrectly.

BERTIE AULD

Billy McNeill began his Celtic career alongside me in a game against Clyde at Parkhead on 23 August 1958. I ended my Celtic career against the same opponents at the same venue on 1 May 1971. He came in as a winner. I went out as a winner. I think you can take it as read we shared a few memories in the thirteen years in between.

I'm exactly two years and twenty-one days older than my chum and I signed first time around from Maryhill Juniors in April 1955 while Billy arrived from Blantyre Vics in August 1957. So, I had a two-year head start on him and that gave me the opportunity to welcome our new centre-half into the first team. I had made my debut the previous year, but I couldn't call myself a regular in the top side. I played in six successive League Cup-ties up to the Final against Rangers on 19 October 1957 – and was left out of the line-up for Hampden. Neilly Mochan took my place at outside-left and smacked in two goals as Celtic walloped our old rivals 7–1. Oh, to have been on the field that day, but I could hardly complain when you look at the scoreline.

Neilly played most of the games wide on the left that season and every now and again Willie Fernie was switched from the right to wear the No.11 shorts. I was hardly a veteran when Billy prepared to take his bow in those green and white hoops. Bobby Evans was our regular centre-half and he also played there for the Scotland international team. He had been a mainstay in the team since 1948, so it looked like Billy might have a long wait before he was given a run in the team.

Evans had also captained the club to its Coronation Cup success in 1953 over Hibs, who were favourites for the trophy. Celtic won 2–0 and Evans had completely nullified the threat of the Edinburgh side's star forward Lawrie Reilly as well as making a telling contribution to the second goal, which was scored by Jimmy Walsh. He was the first Celtic captain to lift the League Cup, in 1956, and he was in place again the following season for the 7–1 rout. The fans idolised him.

That afternoon, though, Billy was clearly determined to make his mark. The single-mindedness that has followed him throughout his life was clearly evident. He would have been a new Bhoy to most of our supporters, but I had played alongside him a few times in the reserves and I had a good idea of how those fans would react to an eager eighteen-year-old central defender.

Bobby, who had converted from the old right-half berth to the middle of the rearguard, was not particularly tall, certainly under six foot. He had a mop of bright red hair and was a good passer of the ball, powerfully built and strong in the tackle. All eyes would have been on Big Billy against the Shawfield side. The supporters might have been intrigued, or even surprised, to note he was just about the opposite of their hero. Billy was around the six-foot-two mark, extremely lean and, of course, possessed fair hair.

Pre-Jock Stein, there were no in-depth team talks before kick-off. Jimmy McGrory was the manager, but we all knew it was chairman Bob Kelly who had the final say in team matters. It was farcical at times and occasionally you didn't know if you were playing until about half-an-hour before the game actually started. The senior pros, such as Neilly Mochan, who had switched to right-half on this occasion, Willie Fernie, Bertie Peacock and Bobby Collins, might have had a word of advice.

'Keep it simple, play it out the park when you're in trouble, nothing fancy', that sort of stuff. Charlie Tully, our irrepressible Irish outside-right, played that day, too, but he did everything off the cuff, so there would have been little requirement for his input for a rookie defender.

I recall my goal during Billy's baptism. I remember *all* my goals, I just wish there had been more of them! I accepted a pass as I came in from the old inside-left position and, fortunately for me, the defenders backed off. Had they forgotten my left foot was a magic wand? I hit the ball from about twenty yards and it flew wide of their keeper, a guy called Tommy McCulloch. Astoundingly, at the age of thirty-seven, he was still in goal for Clyde when I played my last game for the club in May 1971. Billy's first appearance concluded with a 2–0 triumph and I like to think I contributed to his first win bonus. Well, that's what I've been telling my big mate for years, anyway.

Bobby Evans, after recovering from injury, might have expected to walk straight back into the team. That was not the case, though. Bob Kelly had taken a shine to Billy and that was an 'open sesame' to the first team. Billy and I played the remaining five games in the League Cup, winning four against Airdrie (2–0), St Mirren (3–0), Cowdenbeath (2–1 and 8–1 in the two-legged quarter-finals) before losing 2–1 to Partick Thistle in the last four at Ibrox in front of a crowd of 45,000.

That would have been Billy's first major disappointment in football. We were looking to win the silverware for three successive seasons, especially after that 7–1 result the previous year. Theoretically, Billy McNeill was only three hours away from his first medal after a mere nine games – he had played three in the league – in senior football. As everyone knows, I was born and brought up in Maryhill and always had a soft spot for the Jags. I thought what a friend gets is no loss. Thistle were thumped 5–1 in the final by Hearts. Maybe they had used up all their good fortune against us in the semi-final.

I watched Billy grow in stature and become a proper Celtic man. It was an honour to be in at the start of his truly wonderful odyssey in green and white.

JOHN CLARK

No one took a blind bit of notice of Jock Stein and three of his European Cup-winning team as we waited for our buses at Parkhead Cross. To be fair, it was 1959 and Lisbon was a location on another planet light years away for the four of us, Billy McNeill, Jimmy Johnstone, yours truly and the manager who revolutionised football.

It was the start of an incredible journey for all of us. Jock was the reserve team coach who lived in Burnbank, Hamilton and we were three youngsters with stars in their eyes. I lived in Chapelhall and my bus was the number 44 that Billy, who lived in Bellshill, could share. Wee Jinky, who trained on Tuesdays and Thursdays as a provisional signing, lived in Viewpark in Uddingston and had to get a different bus. We would stand for ages talking about football until our buses finally arrived. Big Jock pulled rank even back then. No one was allowed to get on their bus until his arrived. 'I'm no' standing here on my own,' he would say. And no one argued.

Not one of us could have even begun to imagine what it would be like to play in a team that conquered Europe. That would have been beyond preposterous. Only sides such as Real Madrid won the European Cup. We would stand in a huddle on Tollcross Road, stamping our feet for warmth, as the grim chill settled on the east end of Glasgow on brutal winter evenings and we would discuss magical performers such as Di Stefano, Gento, Puskas, Kopa, Santamaria. These individuals played a brand of our chosen profession that was unknown to most of us. In truth, the only thing we had in common with these guys was that we kicked a round leather thing called a football about a park.

But there was a determination to at least succeed on the home front. That was a more attainable target; but even that was proving to be a momentous and insurmountable task. Celtic had slipped into the also-rans category very quickly after winning the League Cup with the memorable 7–1 triumph over old foes Rangers in 1957. Billy was already a regular in the top side by 1961, I had made my debut in October 1959, a year after signing from Junior side Larkhall Thistle, and Jinky would have to wait another four years before he would make his first appearance in the green and white hoops. John Fallon, our back-up goalkeeper to Ronnie Simpson all the way through the victorious European Cup run, would sometimes join our shivering little group at the bus stop on his way home to Blantyre. He came through into the first team around the same time as me.

We were all Celtic men; we knew how much success meant to the supporters. We felt it when we lost, trust me. We were all bad losers, Big Billy, in particular. I saw that all the way through his career, first as his teammate in defence and then as his assistant manager at Aberdeen for a year and then, of course, at Celtic. At the start, Billy was working in accountancy, but we all knew that was never going to be his occupation. It was an absolute certainty Billy McNeill was going to make it as a footballer. Just how big we could never have hazarded a guess, but the only way was up for my lifelong friend.

A quick glance at the league tables back then demonstrated the amount of work that was urgently required to turn things around at Celtic. At the end of the 1959/60 season, we were in ninth place in the eighteen-team First Division. Halfway was the best we could achieve. No disrespect, but even Ayr United and Clyde finished above us that year. The following season saw us rise to a heady fourth, but we were still adrift of Rangers, Kilmarnock and Third Lanark. Twelve months on, we showed more progress by achieving third spot behind Dundee and Rangers. At the end of the 1962/63 campaign, we were back to fourth while Partick

Thistle were third. A year later, Celtic replaced the Maryhill side in third position, but we plummeted again in 1965 as we limped in an unacceptable eighth. My goodness, though, we celebrated at the end of that term!

Bertie Auld has often insisted our Scottish Cup Final victory over Dunfermline that year was even more important than our European Cup triumph. I understand what he means. One had to come before the other and the 3–2 win over the Fifers at Hampden that sunny Saturday in April 1965 was a major breakthrough. It proved we could be winners. The stigma of being runners-up in the same competition in 1961 and '63 was removed. We had actually won some silverware to put in the trophy cabinet at Celtic Park. Of course, being Celtic we had to do it the hard way by coming back twice and how fitting was it that Billy McNeill should get the winner with one of his trademark headers?

Let me tell you, we all worked hard for that success. Yes, I know that was our job and, as professionals, we always gave 100 per cent. But everyone – and I mean *everyone* – went that extra yard to show Celtic players could again go up those Hampden steps, accept a trophy and show it to our supporters. None of that team had won anything before. Bertie had been on the club's books first time around when they beat Rangers in the League Cup Final, but he was with the reserves that particular Saturday. He had a four-year interlude with Birmingham City, had returned to Celtic and we still hadn't won a thing in his absence. I think that emphasises what that Scottish Cup victory meant to all of us. For the first time in our professional careers, we knew we could compete on a level playing field with anyone else in the country.

I remember Big Billy and I and all our teammates in the Hampden bath after the Cup presentation. We were all just so happy. Someone came in and informed us Kilmarnock had beaten Hearts 2–0 at Tynecastle and had won the league title on goal average, as it was then.

'Who cares?' said someone. 'We've won the Cup!'

Big Jock had just returned to Celtic the previous month and, when things eventually calmed down, he said, 'Now is our time to make history. This is our era.' He had said something similar before his first game in charge, a league game against Airdrie at Broomfield on 10 March. Wee Bertie scored five that evening as we won 6–0. Big Jock already had his eyes on Kilmarnock's newly-won First Division championship. And, of course, we were to take possession of the honour for the following nine years.

Billy and I had maintained our early friendship and I'm delighted everything clicked into place for us on the pitch. We had a great understanding in the heart of the defence, but it was never anything we worked on constantly in training, which may surprise some. It just came naturally. Billy's strength was in the air where he was just about immaculate. If I had a forte it was on the deck, trying to read situations and anticipating danger. Tommy Gemmell once said I was the best defender he had ever seen at jockeying an opponent. There might be some truth in that because I refused to dive into a tackle, I never sold myself. Tommy even went as far as to say if it was a two versus one situation with me holding the fort on my own he would have backed me every time. A lovely vote of confidence from my fellow Lisbon Lion. On the rare occasion this situation arose, I would simply try to force the nearest forward into where I wanted him to go and then got ready to cut out the expected pass.

I accepted my role in the team. I wasn't flashy, I had no airs or graces and was happy to work hard for the good of the team. We had enough quality in our line-up to keep the fans cheering. And then we had Billy McNeill at the heart of it all.

I roomed with him everywhere we went and I can now reveal it was like walking into a chocolate factory. He had sweeties all over the place. The guy loved his Milk Tray and all sorts of other confectionery. You could hardly move for the stuff!

It was absolutely no surprise to me when he went into management. He had his quickfire spell at Clyde before he headed to Aberdeen to take over from Ally MacLeod in 1977. Big Jock was behind that appointment. It wasn't long before my big mate was on the blower to ask me if I wanted to join him. How could I resist?

There's another thing you should know about Billy. I am convinced he was a frustrated Formula One driver. It was the same with Big Jock. They would get behind the wheel of their car and just take off. They always drove big powerful cars, too, normally top-of-the-range Mercs. I don't know if they were taking their frustrations out on the motorways as they hurtled along, but I was always thankful I did not possess a nervous disposition during the occasions I was a passenger.

When Billy contacted me about the assistant manager's job at the Dons, I wanted to get up there and find out a bit more about the place. He had moved to Stonehaven with Liz and the family and I didn't know the area. He arranged for me to drive up in my Austin Maxi, a sensible car and my pride and joy. Billy would wait for me at a certain point and then guide me to his new home. Everything was going well until Billy got onto a dual carriageway and must have forgotten I was behind him. Once more, he put his foot through the floor and I could just see his car disappearing into the horizon.

There was no such thing as satnav back then. I had a rough idea where he was located, so I drove along at my own pace. I came off the carriageway and was quite satisfied I was heading in the right direction when a car came flying out of a side street and crashed into my Maxi smack on at the passenger side. Once I had gathered my wits, I noticed the other vehicle was still embedded in my car. I raced round the side and there was an old chap, leaning to this side with his head against the window. I pulled open the driver's door and he practically fell out. I had to make sure he was conscious. I sat him back in the seat as gently as I could and thought I would have to phone an ambulance. Again, no such thing as a mobile phone back then. I hoped there would be a passer-by, but, unfortunately, the accident had taken place in a quiet area.

Eventually, the old lad came to, looked at me, focused and asked, 'Are you John Clark of Celtic?' I didn't think it was the time or place to remind him I had left Celtic some years earlier. Thankfully, Billy had double-backed, found me and we made the necessary arrangements after the police and ambulance guys had done their bit. Thankfully, the old fella was okay and he had just lost control for a moment. Just my bad luck for my car to be right in line for a direct hit. My car was off the road for ten weeks while the garage mechanics put it back together.

My wife Eileen and I hadn't found a place in Aberdeen and she remained in Holytown while I looked around. I was still with Billy and Liz, who had given me a room in their spacious home. One day, after I had just got my Maxi back from the garage, I drove to training and was back at the McNeills' in the early evening. Actually, I was on the phone to my missus when Billy burst into my room. He hadn't bothered knocking.

'Quick, come and have a look at this,' he ordered.

'What is it?' I asked, wondering why my mate was so agitated.

'You've just got to come and see this,' he said, with a fair bit of urgency.

I followed him down the stairs and we went out the front door and onto the driveway. 'There! Look!' he said and pointed to the parking area at the front of his garage.

His Mercedes had collided with my restored Maxi. Billy had reversed his car straight into mine at the exact spot where it had been hit by the old chap ten weeks earlier.

'Sorry,' said Billy, fairly lamely. 'I forgot you were still staying with us.'

The following day it was back to the garage, the owner of which must have seen me as his profit margin for as long as I remained in the vicinity.

I'm glad to say things got better in my year with Billy at Aberdeen. And, later on, at Celtic, too, of course. One thing was certain, life was never dull when Billy McNeill was around.

4

Heading for Something Extraordinary

Lou Macari couldn't bear to look. The minutes were crawling along at a painfully slow and agonising rate. He turned his back on the frantic events taking place on the pitch to focus his attention on the Hampden car park.

'I was fifteen years old at the time,' recalled the former Celtic player and manager. 'I had left Largs that morning on a coach with members of the local supporters' club to head for Glasgow. We were all thrilled and excited with Celtic due to play Dunfermline in the 1965 Scottish Cup Final. I had been seven the last time my favourite team had won a trophy. Trust me, gaining silverware that afternoon meant a lot to a wee boy from the Ayrshire coast.

'My nerves were stretched to breaking point throughout the game. When Billy McNeill headed in Charlie Gallagher's left-wing corner-kick, I was swept off my feet by my mates. When everything settled down, I just wanted the referee to blow for time-up and put us out of our agony and let us get on with our celebrations. I was told there was something like eight minutes to play. It felt like eight hours. We were so close to actually winning a trophy, something that had hardly been a common occurrence in the club's barren years.

'I just couldn't watch any more. I stood at the top of the traditional Celtic end, high up on the slopes of Hampden, and gazed down on the car park. I was still facing in that direction when the referee blew his whistle to signal the end of the game and I just felt so overjoyed and relieved. Everyone was hugging each other and it was just great to be a Celtic fan. Billy McNeill went up to collect the Scottish Cup and, one by one, the players were handed their winner's medal. And then they went out onto the pitch to accept the cheers of the followers who had been through so much but were united in joy that afternoon. It's a marvellous memory which has not dimmed with time.'

Macari and his fellow Celtic fans had every right to celebrate with vigorous glee at the national stadium on 24 April 1965. At long last, their favourites had emerged triumphant when the crunch had arrived. Too often, though, they had failed to rise to the occasion. They were runaway favourites to overwhelm Dunfermline, then managed by Jock Stein, in the 1961 Scottish Cup Final. They had been held to a goalless stalemate in the first game and collapsed 2–0 in the replay. A young Billy McNeill, then aged twenty-three, was inconsolable at the end of the game.

Two years later, Jimmy McGrory, the club's record goal scorer with 550 strikes from 1921 to 1937, once again led the team to the final of Scotland's blue riband competition. They battled their way to a 1–1 draw with fiercest foes Rangers to force another replay. Yet again, they weren't up to the task and disappointed in an abysmal 3–0 loss. It was torment for McNeill, who watched helplessly as his personal friend, Rangers' strolling minstrel Jim Baxter, took centre stage. The Fifer, with the educated left foot he labelled 'The Glove', sauntered through the encounter with the nonchalant air of someone out for an evening constitutional. This, though, was a Scottish Cup Final between football's ancient and fiercest foes at the national stadium with 120,263 frenzied supporters raising the decibel levels in the Mount Florida area of the city. Baxter, in that sort of form, was irrepressible.

Ralph Brand scored in the seventh minute and Davie Wilson doubled the advantage just before the interval. There was to be no Celtic fightback, alas, and long before Brand bamboozled a nervy Frank Haffey with the third goal with twenty minutes still to play, Baxter was strutting his stuff with embarrassing ease and arrogance against hapless opponents who couldn't get near him. During a lull in play, McNeill took the opportunity to have a word in his pal's ear. 'Right, Stanley,' – Baxter was nicknamed after the famous Scottish comedian – 'that's enough of that. It's tough enough for us out here without you making it worse.' Thankfully, Baxter displayed a compassionate side and eased off a tad.

So, it was with these grim memories to haunt them that some Celtic fans headed for Hampden for the grand finale against Dunfermline with optimism falling just short of that of the condemned man heading for the gallows, a game against the bookmakers' favourites who had already won 2–1 at Parkhead in the league earlier in the season. Celtic's two games before Hampden had ended in cringeworthy defeats, a landslide 6–2 loss at Brockville on 14 April against a Falkirk team that completed the campaign third bottom of the First Division and a 2–1 nosedive against Partick Thistle three days later at Parkhead. Hardly performances to instil confidence before the trek to the national stadium.

John Fallon took his place in goal behind Billy McNeill and John Clark with Ian Young and Tommy Gemmell on the defensive flanks. The keeper recalled, 'A lot of shrewd judges rated Dunfermline the best team in the country at the time. Kilmarnock won the title on goal average from Hearts, but the Fifers were only a point adrift at the end of the season. Many thought they had been unfortunate and would channel all their efforts into the Scottish Cup Final.

'Jock Stein had just returned the previous month to take over from Jimmy McGrory and things were changing drastically at Parkhead. He liked to play mind-games with other team bosses and, although we had been far from convincing against Falkirk and Thistle, he announced his line-up on Wednesday. Normally, a manager would wait right up until the last minute before his opposite number could see his chosen eleven. It was a wee bit of bravado from our boss, a show of confidence in his players. Billy hadn't played in the debacle at Brockville when we were 2–0 down in seven minutes and 4–1 adrift after twenty-seven minutes. He had been injured playing for Scotland and John Cushley was brought in for that match. Absolutely no disrespect to Cushley, who was a sturdy central defender, but he wasn't Billy McNeill.

'Billy played against Thistle the week before the Cup Final, but he still didn't look 100 per cent fit. However, he was determined to play at Hampden and thank goodness for his resolution. We knew it was going to be difficult against a very good Dunfermline team and we didn't help ourselves when they took the lead in the fifteenth minute. A ball came into the penalty area and I shouted to Billy to leave it. He duly followed my instructions, but, unfortunately, Ian Young was also in the vicinity and I bumped into him as I tried to punch it to safety. I didn't get enough on the ball to clear the penalty area and it came back to Harry Melrose who popped it into the net. There was no time for an inquest, we just had to get the ball re-centred and set about getting an equaliser as swiftly as possible.

'Bertie Auld duly obliged when a twenty-five yard shot from Charlie Gallagher clattered off the face of the crossbar, spun into the air and there was Wee Bertie racing in to nod the ball into the net from practically the goal-line. A few minutes from half-time, though, the Fifers scored again and I got a bit of stick. They worked a short free-kick outside our box and John McLaughlin, a big, powerful centre-forward, lashed the ball goalward. Alarmingly, my defensive wall parted. It simply opened up and his effort zipped low past my right hand. We had it all to do again.

'There was no ranting or raving in the dressing room at the interval. Big Jock was very calm, poised and reassured. He convinced us we would get an early goal and go on to win the game and the Cup. That's the way it turned out, of course. Bobby Lennox darted down the left wing before sending in a wonderful low cross and Wee Bertie was there again to ram the ball behind Jim Herriot for our second equaliser. Shortly after that, I pulled off a save of which I am still immensely proud.

'Dunfermline were stung into retaliation and their clever little outside-right Alex Edwards latched onto a pass on the edge of the box. Instantly, he controlled the ball and attempted to chip me. It was heading for the top right-hand corner of my net, but I somehow managed to stretch almost backwards to claw the ball out of the air and hold onto it. If Dunfermline had scored a third goal at that point we might not have been celebrating that evening.

'Afterwards, someone pointed out that no team had come back in a Scottish Cup Final after going behind twice. We managed it, but could we have come back a third time? Who knows? One thing is certain and that was the spirit of this team and, naturally, Billy McNeill was our on-field leader. He had the attributes to be inspirational. You took one look at him and you had to admire his stature. He stood out in a crowd, always commanding and possibly he got that from his father's army background. And, of course, he made his presence known that afternoon at Hampden when he timed his leap to absolute perfection to head in Charlie Gallagher's corner-kick from the left wing near the end.

'There's a photograph of me hanging upside down from the crossbar and I actually tried to get up to stand on it at the final whistle. However, my studs got caught in the net and I ended up in a heap at the back of the goal. Who cared? Celtic had won their first trophy in ages and Hampden was awash in green and white.

'I hadn't played in the previous Cup Final defeats against Dunfermline and Rangers, but Billy had and that must have made this victory all the sweeter.'

SIR ALEX FERGUSON

Billy McNeill hated playing against me. He could never cope with skilful centre-forwards. I faced the Celtic skipper with five different teams during my playing career: St Johnstone, Dunfermline, Rangers, Falkirk and Ayr United. Billy is on record as saying I 'made use of my flailing elbows to great effect'. You could say I played to my strengths!

I loved playing against Billy McNeill. We had a few good ding-dongs over the years, but let me say here and now Big Billy was scrupulously clean. In my playing days, there were at least half-a-dozen brutal defenders who wanted to boot you off the park. They wouldn't have lost a wink of sleep if they had put you in hospital with a broken leg. Billy, on the other hand, was the fairest of them all. Don't get me wrong, he could be a fierce competitor, but everything was done within the laws of the game. So, when we were in direct competition, we could roll up our sleeves and get at it. It was a man's game, after all. But I could go into challenges with Billy safe in the knowledge I wouldn't be visiting the A&E department at some hospital later that day.

Sometimes you wonder how futures would have progressed if you received a different bounce of the ball. Billy McNeill was the man who started Celtic on their silverware trail under the great Jock Stein when he headed in the winner against Dunfermline in the Scottish Cup Final at Hampden in 1965. I was the Fife club's top goal scorer that season and I would have been Billy's direct opponent if I had been playing. Manager Willie Cunningham dropped me for that game and I was far from happy with his decision. That's putting it mildly. I had missed a late chance against St Johnstone in the previous game that might have won the league championship for the East End Park outfit. Clearly, Cunningham thought I should have scored and I'm convinced

47

that can be the only reason I sat in the Hampden stand that day.

It was 2–2 with the clock ticking down when Charlie Gallagher flighted over the left-wing corner-kick and Billy simply rose to thump in a header and Celtic had won their first trophy in eight years. Don't get the notion I am saying I could have done something to stop Billy getting in that header. The Celtic man was the finest header of a ball I have ever seen, second to none. He was a big fella, of course, but his timing was close to immaculate. It was rare for anyone to get the better of him in an aerial duel. Maybe our keeper, Jim Herriot, could have come for the cross on that occasion, but if anyone deserved to score a Cup winner for Celtic back then it was Billy McNeill.

Four years after that game, Billy netted another goal in a Scottish Cup Final and it got me the boot from Rangers. I had moved to Ibrox for £65,000, a Scottish record transfer fee at the time, in the summer of 1967 as the Govan side prepared a determined assault on the newly-crowned European champions. As well as me, they brought in Morton goalkeeper Erik Sorensen, Dundee inside-forward Andy Penman and Dundee United winger Orjan Persson. We beat Celtic 1–0 at Ibrox in September with the Swede Persson claiming the goal and we managed a 2–2 draw at Parkhead in January 1968, but Celtic still won the league. They knocked us out of the League Cup in that campaign – mainly because one of our players didn't know the laws of the game.

We were drawn in a four-team group section – Dundee United and Aberdeen were in with us – and our first Old Firm encounter had ended 1–1 at Ibrox. Tommy Gemmell fairly blasted in a penalty-kick to give Big Jock's men the lead and then Andy Penman saw his spot-kick saved by Ronnie Simpson. Penman atoned somewhat when he hit a spectacular equaliser a couple of minutes from time.

A week later, we were at Parkhead and we were within fourteen minutes of a famous triumph: until we were awarded a penalty-kick. Willie Henderson had given us an early lead in front of an all-ticket crowd of 75,000. The place was heaving. There were only fourteen minutes left to play when I beat Big Billy to knock the ball into the path of our wee outside-right. With Billy out of position, his defensive sidekick John Clark had to come across to confront Henderson. He mistimed his tackle and sent Wee Willie sprawling. Referee Tiny Wharton pointed to the spot immediately. What were the odds of Celtic coming back if we had gone two goals ahead with less than quarter-of-an-hour to play?

Following Penman's failure the previous week, Kai Johansen stepped up to take the award. He strode forward and clattered the inside of the crossbar with his effort. That was bad, but it got worse. The ball bounced down and spun back into play. The Danish right-back then raced forward and got his head to the ball from the rebound. An obvious free-kick because you aren't allowed to touch the ball twice from a penalty without the opposition intervening. I was immediately behind Kai and if he had left the ball I would surely have scored with Ronnie Simpson out of position. Instead, he decided to have another go. I was raging. I wondered if the laws of the game were different in Denmark.

The League Cup was the first trophy up for grabs in my debut season at the club and I was determined to get off to a winning start. My mood wasn't eased when Celtic then scored three goals in the remaining minutes to dump us out of the competition. If I thought that had been unfair, it was nothing to the way I felt after the 1969 Scottish Cup Final against Billy McNeill and Celtic

I had scored goals against Jock Stein's team for St Johnstone and Dunfermline, but just couldn't get off the mark in the light blue of my boyhood favourites, my local team as I grew up in

49

Govan. I hoped for a change of fortune when we rolled up at the national stadium on a sunny April afternoon four years after I had been denied a Cup Final appearance by the Dunfermline gaffer.

Rangers had hit some excellent form on the way to Hampden and had turned over a very good Aberdeen side 6–1 in the semi-final. We went into the game as favourites in a lot of people's reckoning. Celtic had beaten us twice in the League Cup section back in August, but Rangers had won both league encounters. We triumphed 4–2 at Parkhead in the opening meeting and it was our opponents' first league defeat in over thirty games. And we took two more points off them in the New Year game at our place with a John Greig penalty-kick after Billy McNeill was judged to have handled a Willie Henderson shot on the hour mark.

Colin Stein, who overtook my record fee when he arrived from Hibs in November 1968 for £100,000, had been my main rival for the No.9 shirt. However, I knew I would be facing Billy McNeill that afternoon with Stein suspended. You can't help but wonder what might have happened if he had been free to be selected. In any case, manager Davie White, who had taken over from the man who bought me, Scot Symon, told me I was in and would lead the line. In the countdown to Hampden, we were discussing Big Billy's prowess in the air as we talked tactics and how to deal with his menace. Everybody knew the threat he posed when he came forward for set-pieces, so how were we going to attempt to cope with it?

Ronnie McKinnon was our centre-half, but he admitted he wasn't comfortable in a one-on-one confrontation with the Celtic skipper. Who was? In the end, it was decided I would man-mark Billy at the deadball situations. I was good enough in the air, but Billy McNeill was easily the best I've ever played against or witnessed. I took the kick-off in the Cup Final and exactly two minutes and twenty seconds later, I was required to re-enact the movement.

As luck would have it, Celtic were awarded an early left-wing corner-kick after Ronnie McKinnon had conceded as Bobby Lennox chased a throw-in from Stevie Chalmers. Lennox elected to take the kick and flighted it high into the box. I had seen Billy coming forward as he always did in these situations and he took up his usual position that allowed him a run at the ball when it dropped around the penalty spot. I was ready to get in position to make sure he did not get a clear header.

As the ball arced into the danger zone, Billy made his move. I was ready to make my challenge, but Willie Wallace ran across me at that moment and blocked me off. Billy was allowed a free header and he rarely passed up those gifts. I watched in frustration as he made perfect contact with the ball and sent a header gliding in at goalkeeper Norrie Martin's right-hand post. What a disaster for us. The first-half descended into chaos as we virtually presented Celtic with two more goals, taken by Bobby Lennox and George Connelly, and Stevie Chalmers completed our misery with the fourth after the interval. Rangers had gone into that game with so much hope, but, ninety minutes later, we had been shredded.

I should have anticipated what happened next. I was blamed for the crucial first goal. Billy later publicly said it was unfair I had been made a scapegoat. He made the point I was a centre-forward and did my best work at the other end of the pitch. Billy also asked, 'Where was their centre-half Ronnie McKinnon when I scored?' Kind words from a good opponent, but no one at Ibrox was listening. The finger of guilt pointed at yours truly and my two years at Rangers were over. Aye, it's a fickle old game, football.

I'm glad I did a better job of following Big Billy when I succeeded him as boss of Aberdeen in 1978. I began my managerial career at the relatively young age of thirty-two with East Stirling in June 1974 and that gave me a solid grounding of working at that level. I can remember a conversation I had with Billy who was out of the game at the time after quitting as a player. We were talking about management and I told him, 'Starting out in the lower leagues is fine for gaining experience, but it's soul-destroying and when the chance to better yourself presents itself, then jump at it.'

I left Firs Park for St Mirren in October 1974 and Billy had a couple of months at Clyde before taking over from Ally MacLeod at Aberdeen in 1977. Billy only spent one season at Pittodrie, but what a brilliant job he did. He brought in Steve Archibald from Clyde, and Gordon Strachan from Dundee, for a start. The Dons finished runners-up in the league and lost 2–1 in the Scottish Cup, beaten by Rangers on both occasions.

I could only describe as seismic what happened in the summer of 1978 when Billy McNeill took over from Jock Stein as manager of Celtic and my old teammate John Greig replaced Jock Wallace as Rangers boss. I had already left St Mirren and, while the world turned its attention on the Old Firm, I got the job at Aberdeen. Billy, naturally, would have been better equipped to deal with being a gaffer at his old club than John Greig at Ibrox. For a start, Billy had been away from Parkhead for three years and had some managerial experience at Clyde and Aberdeen. John was going straight from the dressing room to the manager's office. Tell me that's not seismic!

I looked at the great job Billy had done at Aberdeen and I realised he would be a hard act to follow, but, at the same time, I wanted to put my stamp on the team. That's only natural. I had noticed the two centre-halves, Willie Miller and Willie Garner, defended very deeply. Neither was blessed with a fabulous turn of pace, but they were excellent at anticipating danger in their penalty area. Their reading of the game close to their own goal was superb; Miller, in my opinion, was the best penalty-box defender bar none. However, I wanted them to defend further up the field. So, a bit of tweaking was required in that department, but there were no great changes.

Billy had given Alex McLeish his debut at centre-half during his season and I thought Big Eck, at only eighteen, was streets ahead of anyone else in the country. He could play in the middle of the defence or in central midfield. Big Eck was a first-rate all-rounder and he was a defender who could pass the ball without trying to put his laces through it all the time, like many who were around at the time. Steve Archibald was making astonishing progress and I could see he would be leaving us and stepping up at some stage. I wasn't surprised he had such a good career at Spurs, Barcelona and Scotland. In my first season, Archibald and Miller were different class. I changed Gordon Strachan's role in the team, too, and that seemed to have the desired effect.

Billy had left me with plenty to work with. The 1978/79 season in Scotland was certainly an interesting one. Billy won the big one – the league title – while John Greig took both the Cups. In fact, Rangers beat Aberdeen 2–1 in the League Cup Final and I missed the chance of some quickfire silverware at the Dons. We lost by the same margin to Hibs in the Scottish Cup semi-final and we finished fourth in the Premier Division. Another odd-goal defeat put us out of the European Cup-Winners' Cup at the second round when we lost 3–0 away to Fortuna Dusseldorf before winning 2–0 at Pittodrie. Thankfully, I would have more success with the Dons in that competition four years later.

I had several dealings with Billy over the years and, in fact, he bought Dom Sullivan from Aberdeen for £70,000 in October

1979. It was a deal that suited both clubs and the player, and he went to Celtic with my best wishes. I also sold Willie Garner to Billy in 1981 and he returned to Pittodrie three years later as my assistant manager. He was my No.2 for two years. Billy and I have never been too far removed in our football careers, but I can reveal we were even closer off the field – we used to live within a hundred yards of each other in our semi-detached homes in the Simshill area on the south side of Glasgow. The location wasn't too far from Hampden which might have been some sort of omen for Billy and me. Our families were very friendly and my boys, Jason and Darren, would often play alongside Billy's girls, Susan, Carol and Libby, in nearby Linn Park.

It would have been interesting to cross swords with my big pal in Manchester, but he had left City for Aston Villa in December 1986 by the time I arrived at United. However, we were in competition in a league game at Villa Park that ended 3–3. I gave a debut that day to a young goalkeeper by the name of Gary Walsh and what a doing he got from Andy Gray and Garry Thompson, the two big guys up front for Villa. It was a rousing encounter – well, that's one way of putting it. We met again on the last day of the season when we won 3–1 at Old Trafford and, unfortunately, Villa were relegated. Billy left the club a couple of days later.

And then look what happened. Twelve months later, Billy McNeill was celebrating leading Celtic to the league and Cup double in the club's centenary year. It was meant to be.

JOHN FALLON

The telephone call left me a little mystified. 'Billy McNeill wants to see you at the park,' was the simple message from my old teammate John Clark. As usual, there was no preamble from the quiet man of the Lisbon Lions team.

'What's it about, Luggy?' I asked.

'I'll let Billy fill you in with the details when you catch up,' came the even more puzzling reply.

Intrigued, I made arrangements to see my old captain the following day after training at Barrowfield. Billy had just returned as manager of the club in May 1978 and, as you would expect, had plenty on his plate to contend with, but he had taken the time to ask his assistant boss to get in touch with me. The call came right out of the blue and I spent most of the previous evening wondering why the new Celtic team boss wanted to have a chat with me. Somehow, I didn't think he would be asking me to look out my old goalkeeper's gloves. So, in a bit of a quandary, I made my way to Celtic Park to get my answer.

Billy was waiting to greet me and he ushered me into his manager's office. He went behind his desk and told me to pull up a chair. He was his usual charming self, the perfect gentleman. As a centre-half, playing directly in front of me, we had the odd disagreement, but nothing too serious to affect our friendship.

He smiled at me, that big, bright grin that could light up a room, and said, 'I hear you don't get in the front door here any more. Is that the case?'

Sadly, I had to tell my old skipper he had heard quite correctly. There was no welcome and certainly no admission at Parkhead for someone who had been on Celtic's books for just over twelve years, having signed from Junior outfit Fauldhouse United on 11 December 1958. That door was firmly closed behind me when I left the club to join Motherwell in February 1972. No one told me I had been barred. As usual, I went up to the entrance for the second leg of the European Cup semi-final against Inter Milan – the night Dixie Deans missed a penalty-kick in the shoot-out decider. The doorman stopped me and told me I wasn't getting in. He told me he was acting on orders. Whose orders? I had no doubt where they had come from – Big Jock.

'I still watch the games, though,' I told Billy. 'I pay in at the turnstiles. I'm a Celtic fan and I'll always support my team.'

Jock Stein's successor looked at me, laughed and pushed a ticket and a pass across his desk top. 'There you are, my friend. That'll get you back in the front door.'

The little pieces of cardboard that got me into the stand behind the directors' box were most welcome and the gesture was a typical act of kindness by a fine human being.

It wasn't one of football's best-kept secrets that I did not get on with Jock Stein. I don't think he particularly liked any goalkeeper and I'm told that came from his playing days. Like Billy, he was a central defender operating smack in front of the last line of defence, so there might have been a little animosity when a goal was conceded. Big Jock carried that on when he gave up playing to become a manager.

His man-management skills left a lot to be desired. He would give you a right sherricking in front of your teammates and he was always quick to blame the keeper for the loss of a goal. Remember Racing Club's winner in the World Club Championship play-off in Montevideo? No prizes for guessing who got it in the neck for that one. Not too many other people, including my teammates, with Billy among them, pointed the finger at me, but the Celtic boss did. Goalkeepers were always an easy target for Jock.

But, back in 1978, Billy had big boots to fill when he took over as manager from Jock Stein. Whether or not Jock and I sent each other Christmas cards, you could not take his achievements away from him. He was phenomenal for Celtic when he returned as team boss in March 1965. We hadn't won anything for years, but he changed all that. So, credit where credit's due, he turned things around in a remarkably short period of time and no one can ever take that away from him.

Billy was most people's choice to take Celtic into a new era and I was delighted when he got the job. I had known him since before we teamed up at Celtic as seventeen year olds – Billy is six months older than me – back in 1957. I played against him in schools' football when I was with St Bride's Cambuslang and he was at Lady's High Motherwell. I have to admit Billy stood out even then and it would be a few years later until I discovered his father had been in the army. He was always smart in his appearance, remarkably straight-backed and walked with a certain poise. And you could see immediately he was going to make the grade in professional football. Even as a kid, Billy caught the attention with his blond hair, height and stature. He was unbeatable in the air with his timing and ability to leap so high.

Billy signed professional forms at the club while I went to Fauldhouse before eventually catching up with him on the books at Parkhead. We played a reserve game alongside the legendary Charlie Tully who was in the twilight of a truly outstanding career. He had someone ghost-write a column for a newspaper and in one of his reports he stated, 'Fallon and McNeill, look out for these youngsters. I think they'll be big names in Celtic's future.' At least I was keeping good company!

I made my debut for the first team on 26 September 1959 when Bobby Evans wore the No.5 shorts. We drew 1–1 with Clyde at Parkhead and I kept my place for the next game against Arbroath at Gayfield. Evans was on Scotland international duty that day in a 4–0 win over Northern Ireland in Belfast and Billy, who had already had a few games in the top side, stepped in to take over. Coincidentally, John Clark made his first appearance that afternoon. We won 5–0, so it wasn't a bad start to our careers at Celtic.

JOHN HUGHES

I was with Billy McNeill when he celebrated his twenty-fourth birthday. I recall he was in considerable pain after sustaining a back injury six nights earlier following some robust buffeting from rugged Slovan Bratislava opponents during the first leg of the European Cup-Winners' Cup quarter-final at Parkhead on a raw Wednesday evening on 26 February 1964.

As expected, the confrontation against an unfussy Czechoslovakian team had given all the indications of settling into a fairly towsy affair mere moments after Belgian referee Valentin Triochal had blown to set the game in motion. The Czechs had no intention of putting on an extravagant show for the 55,000 fans in our ground.

We weren't in the least surprised when Slovan retreated immediately behind the ball and formed a human barrier in front of their keeper. In the previous round, we had rampaged to a 3–0 home first-leg triumph over Dinamo Zagreb, of Yugoslavia, a nation, like Czechoslovakia and other eastern European countries, which was a satellite state of the Communist Soviet Union.

Early on, I thumped a header against the crossbar following a Jimmy Johnstone right-wing corner-kick. In the end, Bobby Murdoch settled a nervy occasion by tucking away a penalty-kick in the seventieth minute after the persistent Stevie Chalmers had been sent spinning by a wayward challenge from a panicking defender.

However, the victory came at a cost. Big Billy complained afterwards of some discomfort in the base of his spine. As usual, he had been bumped and barged as he had made his way upfield to take his place in the opponents' penalty area when we forced a set-piece situation.

I got the same treatment. They looked at Billy and me, two

guys over the six-foot mark, and decided we would get their undivided attention. They would try to block your run, they would get a hold of your jersey and you would feel something sharp digging into your ribs when you were airborne, it could have been an elbow or a knee. We got similar treatment in domestic games, but our European foes seemed to be a little bit more adept at these things.

Billy had been sufficiently injured to fail a fitness test before the league game against East Stirling at Parkhead three days later. John McNamee filled in at centre-half and we won 5–2 against opponents who were relegated from the eighteen-team First Division at the end of the season. The race was on to get our inspirational captain fit to play in Czechoslovakia in four days' time.

On 3 March, the day before the return leg, his twenty-fourth birthday arrived and it wasn't one of his most memorable. He had been ordered to refrain from any unnecessary physical activity. And Billy wouldn't have been helped by the forty-mile coach trip from Vienna to reach the team's destination the previous evening. But he was passed fit to play in the tie that had an afternoon kick-off because Slovan's spartan ground did not possess floodlights.

Bob Kelly, our chairman, had a pale complexion at the best of times, but he would go even more ashen-faced at the mere thought of someone mentioning Celtic should shut up shop in any game. We were Celtic, after all, and we had a duty to entertain wherever we played. That was how he perceived it, anyway. We were a goal ahead, a hard-earned advantage from the first game, and had something to hang onto and protect in a tie that was delicately poised. We could have sat in, invited Slovan to come to us and we could have hit on the break. And we had players with pace to exploit Slovan at the back – Jinky, Stevie and myself. Simple enough tactics which were employed by so many successful teams in Europe back in the days when you did not get the reward of the away goal counting double in the event of a stalemate.

Yet again, the players were told that 'was not the Celtic way' and we would play our normal attacking game. So, we went onto the pitch in Bratislava against Slovan in a crucial European tie with exactly the same outlook as we would a game at Broomfield against Airdrie in a run-of-the-mill end-of-season league game. Crazy doesn't come into it.

I recall the playing surface being unusually good considering it was March and we had been informed there had been some severe frost in most parts of Bratislava. The ground staff must have worked overtime to get the game played which made me believe they were eager to get on with the job at hand and prepare for a place in the semi-final which was due the following month.

I believe the game had gone something like ten minutes or so when John Clark took a sore one from an over-eager Czech. Wee Luggy never stayed down, he saw that as a sign of weakness. But he writhed on the ground after that 'challenge', for the want of a better word, and I could clearly see he was in pain as he got back to his feet, helped by Neilly Mochan, our trainer. Remember, these were the days before substitutes. To me, Luggy was out of the game, but, as so often happened in these circumstances, he was stuck on the wing where he could be of nuisance value. Big Billy would have to play the remaining eighty or so minutes without his usual defensive colleague. Bobby Murdoch was pulled back from inside-right to play in the position and we just took it from there. It was all a bit haphazard and slapdash, but, astoundingly, it worked.

With only five minutes remaining, I collected the ball around the halfway mark and it wasn't in my mind to go for goal. I was probably a little surprised when Jim Kennedy shoved a short pass to me because the man known to everyone as 'The Pres' would normally put his foot through the ball and hoof it from one end of the pitch to another and we were invited to chase after it. On this occasion, for whatever reason, he knocked it to my feet. There was a quick thought to take it down the line in an attempt to waste time, try to force a corner-kick or a throw-in and give my teammates a chance to regroup and come forward.

I could have tried to hold onto the ball, too, and encourage my colleagues to join me in Slovan's half, but I could sense there were a lot of tired limbs out there. I actually lost control of the ball, but quickly got it back and then I simply picked up momentum. I was on the left wing when one of their players came across to put in a tackle. It was a bit of a half-hearted attempt, because he probably thought someone behind him would deal with the danger. I skipped past him and just kept going. I had a swift glance up and counted three defenders between me and the goal. They were spread apart across the park in a line. What they couldn't have anticipated was that I had made up my mind at this point that I was going to head straight for goal. I cut inside as another of the opposition moved to block me.

I dodged past him and suddenly you get an adrenalin rush in these situations. I realised there were now only two defenders in front of me and I was going full-tilt. No one was going to catch me and I was never easy to shove off the ball because of my strength and I could see the possibilities. A Czech came across to confront me. He could do one of two things; jockey me back to the touchline and wait for his colleagues to get back in numbers or go straight in and make a challenge in an effort to win the ball. He must have realised I was in no mood to be re-routed, so he chose the latter. He was just too late and I nicked the ball past him and kept going.

The last Slovan player between me and their goalkeeper must have been a tad unsettled when I raced towards him. I didn't wait for him to make up his mind about coming out to meet me. While he was still trying to sort that one out, I slipped the ball past him and chased after it as he tackled fresh air. Now it was me and Villiam Schroif. In these situations you do not even consider that the guy in front of you is a world-class goalkeeper. Simply put, he was just another bloke to beat if you wanted to score a goal. He came off his line as I took a moment to compose myself. I waited for him to commit, but he was too experienced to sell himself. He remained on his feet, I saw a vulnerable space and hit a swift shot. The ball flew beyond him and thumped into the net.

It was the strangest experience. Apart from my teammates and our backroom staff on the touchline, there wasn't a cheer to be heard in the vast, old-fashioned stadium. There were around 30,000 Slovan fans in the ground that day and they had been struck dumb. My goal certainly wasn't in the script. On this occasion, silence was, indeed, golden.

That goal was undoubtedly one of the best of my career and it took most of the headlines. That's normal for goal scorers; it's almost part of the job description. We get the applause and the sterling efforts of the guys at the back are often overlooked.

And that is my point exactly. I would never have been in that position to score that goal if it hadn't been for the outstanding and unselfish work done that afternoon by Billy McNeill and the boys in defence. We could have been about three goals down before I scored. The Czechs bombarded us, especially after the interval when they got a bit more desperate with the expected equaliser proving to be elusive.

They decided to go route one with half-an-hour or so to go and were launching the ball in and around our penalty box. But

Big Billy remained in control, stamping complete authority on the game. For me, it was easily one of his finest games for Celtic. The sad thing is that hardly anyone was there to witness it. These days, the match would have been beamed live throughout the world, but I don't even know if there were *any* TV cameras there that day. There's probably some grainy film gathering dust in a loft somewhere, but I have never witnessed any footage of that tie. Amazing, isn't it? A British club in a European quarter-final and it was largely ignored.

So, my old mate's immaculate and commanding performance against Slovan has hardly rated a mention in the club's folklore. You'll have to take my word for it, Billy was unbeatable in the air and on the ground that day. And he didn't complain once about being in pain.

That's what made Billy McNeill that little bit special.

BOBBY LENNOX

Billy McNeill was my hero. When you looked around the Celtic dressing room on matchday and you saw Big Billy, stripped and ready for action, you instinctively knew you had a good chance of winning. That was how important I rated our skipper, centre-half and on-field inspiration.

I first encountered the man who would mean so much to me as a teammate and a human being when I signed provisional forms at Celtic from Junior club Ardeer Recreation in 1961. There are only four years of difference between us, but Billy was already a first-team regular by the time I pitched up. Not only did he play in the top side, but he had already represented Scotland at full international level. However, there was never the hint of him looking down at eager youngsters coming in that front door at Celtic Park. Quite the reverse. Billy went out of his way to welcome everyone.

Remember, he was still a young man, too, when he accepted this responsibility. I'm fairly certain that was not his remit, but he took it on in any case. If the reserves had a midweek fixture and Billy was free there was every chance he would turn up before the game just for a blether with the boys. It meant so much to me on a personal level. You knew you were among friends and the club's biggest personality was going out of his way to help you settle in.

I was a foreigner at Parkhead – the only player in the Lisbon Lions who had been born outwith a thirty-yard radius of the club's ground. I was from that far-off place called Saltcoats and I was mixing with lads born in Bellshill, in Billy's case, or Glasgow, such as Ronnie Simpson, Jim Craig, Bertie Auld, Stevie Chalmers, or Uddingston, birthplace of my wee pal Jimmy Johnstone. Tommy Gemmell was born and reared in Craigneuk while

Willie Wallace was from Kirkintilloch. Bobby Murdoch hailed from Rutherglen, well within walking distance of Celtic Park. Me? I was from a place Wee Bertie was convinced no one actually lived, but just visited on their holidays.

I should have known Billy and I would click from my very first appearance in the Celtic first team against a very good Dundee side in a league game at Parkhead on Saturday, 3 March 1963. We were being held 1–1 with only five minutes to go when Billy headed in the winner. It was the first time I had ever experienced his exploits in the air at first hand and I never grew tired of them. Celtic's basic wage wasn't great back then, but the bonuses certainly helped boost it. I wasn't thinking of cash, though, as Billy rose above a posse of Dens Park players to get his head to a corner-kick and send the ball past their keeper, Pat Liney. I was so delighted to have marked my debut with a win.

It would be just over two years later until Celtic won their first trophy in eight years. As a fan of the club, that was a lifetime, believe me. Celtic had been in the doldrums and teams such as Rangers, Kilmarnock, Hearts, Dundee and Dunfermline appeared to be way ahead of us. It was the Fifers who provided the opposition when we made our way to the Scottish Cup Final in April 1965. Jock Stein had just arrived as manager and things were already changing. But no one could argue Dunfermline were worthy favourites to win the silverware that afternoon. They were miles ahead of us in the league and Celtic had picked up the tag as Hampden losers after failing in replays in the Final against the team from East End Park in 1961 and Rangers two years later. Many of our critics questioned our big-game mentality.

We trailed twice and came back twice with goals from Bertie Auld. And, it's well-etched in Celtic folklore now, Billy bulleted in the winner with a powerful header from a Charlie Gallagher left-wing corner-kick. Every newspaper the following day had a huge photograph of our captain's goal with a banner headline. One paper called it 'BILLY'S BUMPER' and another labelled it 'BILLY'S BEAUTY'. The image is of Billy rising above yours truly to knock the ball into the net with the Dunfermline defence, thankfully, in a bit of disarray. Billy told me he didn't like that image. 'Why?' I asked innocently. 'You're in it,' he answered with a straight face.

That victory meant so much to Celtic. With Jock Stein in charge, we turned a massive corner. Suddenly, we had self-belief. We could think of ourselves as winners. We were worthy opponents for anyone. Billy played his role perfectly. He slotted in to what Celtic Football Club had become. And he looked the part for a start. Tall, handsome and always immaculate, he became the players' spokesman. No matter where we went in the world, he was the guy who was to the forefront. He just seemed to be a natural leader and the mantle sat easily on him.

We all know what he contributed to Celtic's historic triumph in Lisbon on 25 May 1967 when we became the first British club to win the European Cup. Without his crucial intervention in the quarter-final against Yugoslavia's excellent Vojvodina we'll never know if we would have been celebrating in the Portuguese capital later that year. Billy headed in our last-minute winner that mist-shrouded March evening in the east end of Glasgow with Charlie Gallagher again providing the service with a corner-kick, this time from the right. If you watch footage of that memorable moment, you will see Charlie about to take a short kick to a teammate. A Vojvodina defender raced out to cover and that swayed Charlie's mind to put the ball into the mix. Thank goodness! Billy's goal took us into the semi-finals against Dukla Prague and the rest, as they say, is history.

And we came so close to winning it for a second time three

years later. Things didn't go according to plan against Feyenoord in Milan although I'm convinced I scored a perfectly good goal in the first-half which might have changed the entire complexion of the game. I scored as I came into the box on the left with a shot across the keeper that flashed into the net. It wasn't a bad effort, even if I do say so myself, but experienced Italian referee Concetto Lo Bello ruled it out for offside. TV pictures later showed I could have been played onside by three Dutch defenders, but when I actually reached and hit my shot I did look as though I was off by a good few yards. Big Billy used to say, 'You're too damn fast for your own good, wee man.' There were times when I couldn't argue.

However, there was real drama on the eve of the second leg of the semi-final of the competition at Hampden on 15 April and, given the magnitude of the occasion, it's amazing the club managed to keep it quiet. We had beaten Leeds United 1–0 in the opening tie at Elland Road a fortnight earlier when George Connelly scored in the early moments. In between those epic encounters, we lost 3–1 in the Scottish Cup to Aberdeen in a game wrecked by an awful refereeing performance from Bobby Davidson. He had never been a particular favourite of Jock Stein, the players or the Celtic support and during this display he cemented that reputation. However, unbeknownst to the public or the press, Billy McNeill had taken a sore one against the Dons. He soldiered on for a chunk of the game in a lot of pain, but that was typical of our skipper. I realised Billy believed if he betrayed an injury to an opponent he would be inviting his rival to play on a weakness.

However, Billy was in agony on Sunday once the injury really kicked in. Jock Stein was never one to panic, but he knew he was going into a monumental confrontation with so much at stake and he would not only be without his influential captain, but also his only recognised centre-half. Billy had been so consistent – and luckily free of knocks – that he had played in every single game that season apart from a 2–0 win over Airdrie back in October when George Connelly deputised. No disrespect to the Broomfield side, but you could have played me in the middle of defence against them and I'm pretty sure we would still have won. Leeds United in a European Cup semi-final with 136,505 fans in the national stadium was an entirely different proposition.

Don Revie's side relied on twin strikers Allan Clarke and Mick Jones with Scots Peter Lorimer and Eddie Gray on the flanks providing the ammo. Clarke's nickname was 'Sniffer' and that about summed him up. He played on the periphery and was always ready to pounce when an opportunity arose. His goal record showed he was quite good, too. Jones, on the other hand, was a battering ram of a direct centre-forward and he would have been the man lined up to face Billy. Big Jock wouldn't even have contemplated selecting a player who was not fully fit against someone such as Jones. We had a problem.

Monday came and went as we prepared for the game. Still no news about Billy. Tuesday morning saw all of the players seeking information on our skipper. 'We'll give him every chance,' was all we got from the manager. Of course, we fretted. Later that evening at the team HQ, we were given the news Billy had come through a rigorous fitness test. That news was greeted as enthusiastically among his teammates as our supporters celebrated a goal. We cheered to a man and Leeds were beaten there and then.

Thankfully, life wasn't always quite as tense when Billy was around. I recall an incident from our tour of the States in the summer of 1966 when we were in Bermuda. The players had gone through a light routine just to keep everything supple, some went for a walk, others read or played cards or simply sat around the pool at the hotel. I was in my room and wondered what Billy was getting up to a couple of flights up from my floor. I popped up to see my big mate and he was lying on his bed, dozing lightly.

I noticed he had a rather large book by his side. I picked it up and asked, 'Good book, Billy? Enjoying it?' He answered, 'Aye, it's a good read. Do you want to read it after me?' I smiled, crossed the room, opened the window and nonchalantly threw the book out. Billy suddenly bounced to his feet and looked apoplectic. He cried, 'What do you think you're doing?' Or words to that effect. 'All my cash and documents are in that book.' I looked out of the window and there were dollar bills flying around everywhere. Oops!

Incredibly, he still talked to me after my prank backfired. But that was Billy McNeill. I wouldn't have expected anything different from my big mate.

5

Awful at Wembley,
Euphoria at Hampden

Billy McNeill winced at the recollection. It should have been the realisation of a lifelong ambition when he was selected to play for Scotland for the first time on 15 April 1961. The fantasy had become reality when the envelope dropped through the letterbox of the McNeill household. It was clearly stamped Scottish Football Association and the message confirmed he had been named in manager Ian McColl's team to face England at Wembley.

'I had the misfortune to make the international debut from hell,' he would say later and repeat the scoreline, 'England 9 Scotland 3. It was the most humiliating result a Scottish side had ever suffered. It was one of the lowest points of my career and my first painful lesson of just how cruel sport can be. What was essentially a proud moment, playing my first international, turned out to be an absolute disaster.

'It was just one of those days when everything England attempted came off for them, while every mistake we made was magnified and punished in the most brutal fashion possible.

Incredibly, there was a stage in the game when we hauled England back to 3–2 after Davie Wilson, the Rangers winger, scored early in the second-half. Maybe that just made them angry. Bryan Douglas stole a couple of yards for their fourth goal when he moved the ball forward at a free-kick which shouldn't have been awarded in the first place. That restored England's two-goal advantage.

'We disintegrated after that and, with Johnny Haynes, scorer of two of their goals, and Jimmy Greaves, who notched a hat-trick, in outstanding form, England took us apart. I got some idea of how Custer felt at the Little Big Horn as opposing forwards bore down on us with ruthless efficiency. Frank Haffey, my Celtic teammate, was in goal and he admitted he did not have the best of games.'

The SFA selectors agreed with the Celtic custodian and he was removed from the team that faced the Republic of Ireland in a World Cup qualifier at Hampden the following month. In fact, Haffey, after two appearances, never represented his country again. Airdrie's Lawrie Leslie replaced him, but, more import-antly for Billy McNeill, the young defender had escaped most of the criticism of the Wembley fall-out and was again named at centre-half where he found himself playing beside his two good friends, Celtic colleague Pat Crerand and Rangers' Jim Baxter. On this occasion, in front of 46,696 fans, McNeill celebrated a victory with two goals apiece from Rangers' Ralph Brand and Arsenal's David Herd giving the Scots a 4–1 triumph.

A year after the agony of Wembley there was euphoria at Hampden when McNeill and Scotland spectacularly turned the tables on England when goals from Davie Wilson and Eric Caldow, with a penalty-kick, gave them a 2–0 victory. Billy recalled, 'Scotland had not beaten England in Glasgow since 1937, so to end a twenty-five year wait in the manner we did gave us all a wonderful feeling of pride and achievement. We effectively regained our self-respect and restored the fans' pride in the international team.

'Five of the team had suffered the humiliation of playing in the 9–3 defeat and that was probably the key to our success. We were fired up by the need for revenge and played like men possessed. Beating England had little to do with a game plan, but I think their players were taken aback by the ferocity of our approach. We fought for every ball and were so energised that we could have run and chased all day long.

'One report suggested we were Scotland's best team for twenty-five years and added that England were fortunate to hold us to two goals. Significantly, it was the first time for fifteen games England had failed to score. I have a host of happy memories of international football, but I think that was the highlight.'

Remarkably, McNeill, despite his phenomenal success at Celtic from 1965 onwards, only turned out in the dark blue of his country on another twenty-six occasions. In all, there were fourteen wins, ten defeats and five draws. He scored three goals for Scotland, one against Poland in a 2–1 loss in a World Cup qualifier at Hampden in October 1965, another against Wales in Wrexham during a 5–3 win in a Home International in May 1969 and he struck his last later that month against Cyprus in an 8–0 World Cup qualifying game in Glasgow.

Ironically, McNeill brought down the final curtain on his international career as it had kicked off eleven years earlier, with a defeat from England. Tommy Docherty had brought back the Celtic captain following a near-three-year hiatus – he hadn't played since a 3–2 World Cup qualifying defeat from West Germany in Hamburg in October 1969 – for the three games in the Home International tournament in May 1972. McNeill was at the heart of the defence that had registered two clean sheets in a 2–0 victory over Wales and 1–0 over Northern Ireland, but, with just a point required to win the Championship, faltered and lost 1–0 to England with Alan Ball scrambling the winner past Bobby Clark, of Aberdeen, in the first-half.

Five years and two days after proudly holding aloft the European Cup in Lisbon, Billy McNeill was allowed to concentrate on all matters Celtic.

1. HOME ARE THE HEROES

Billy McNeill holds aloft the European Cup along with Tommy Gemmell and Bertie Auld as the Lisbon Lions parade the trophy at Celtic Park on 26 May 1967 – the day after overcoming Inter Milan 2–1 in the Portuguese capital to conquer Europe. Also in the picture are Bobby Murdoch, John Hughes, Jimmy Johnstone and Willie Wallace.

2. THE CUP THAT CHEERS

Billy celebrates a Scottish Cup triumph with his teammates. Celtic lifted the trophy after a 2–0 win over Aberdeen on 29 April 1967, with Wallace getting the goals.

From back (left to right): Ronnie Simpson, John Fallon, John Cushley, John Clark, Charlie Gallagher, Joe McBride, Jim Craig, Billy McNeill, Willie Wallace, Stevie Chalmers, Tommy Gemmell, John Hughes, Bertie Auld, Jimmy Johnstone, Bobby Murdoch, with the silverware, and Bobby Lennox. Standing is Ian Young.

3. THE START OF SOMETHING GOOD
Billy (back row, second right) in the Scotland Schoolboys Under-18 team for a game against England at Celtic Park. The Scots won 3–0. Future Scotland international manager Craig Brown is seated extreme left.

4. SCOTLAND THE BRAVE
Billy with his international teammates before their 2–0 win over England at Hampden in the Home Championships on 14 April 1962.

From back (left to right): Alec Hamilton, Eric Caldow, Bill Brown, Pat Crerand, Billy McNeill and Jim Baxter; front row: Alex Scott, John White, Ian St John, Denis Law and Davie Wilson. The goalscorers were Wilson and Caldow (pen).

5. COP THAT!

Billy, flanked by two Portuguese policemen, proudly displays the European Cup after the epic 2–1 triumph over Inter Milan on 25 May 1967. Jock Stein's team became the first UK side to lift the coveted silverware.

6. PARADISE

Billy leads as the Celtic players parade the newly-won European Cup in front of their joyous supporters on a memorable evening in the east end of Glasgow.

7. FLYING START

Billy leaps with joy after scoring the opening goal in the 6–1 Scottish Cup Final triumph over Hibs on 6 May 1972. Dixie Deans, who netted a hat-trick, also celebrates. Not so happy are Easter Road defender Erich Schaedler and keeper Jim Herriot.

8. IN COMMAND

Billy clears the danger from Rangers attacker Alex MacDonald during the heat of a hectic Old Firm encounter.

9. THE FINAL FAREWELL

Billy is chaired by his teammates following his last appearance for Celtic, fittingly a 3–1 Scottish Cup Final win over Airdrie at Hampden on 3 May 1975. Kenny Dalglish (no.9) would take over from Caesar as captain of the team.

10. CHEERS AND CHEERIO

Billy does a lap of honour alongside keeper Peter Latchford and Harry Hood after the Scottish Cup Final triumph. Pat McCluskey, who scored the third goal via the penalty spot, and Paul Wilson, who claimed the other two, join in.

11. I'M IN CHARGE

Billy, with assistant manager Tommy Craig in the dugout, returned as Celtic's boss on 28 May 1987, after leaving for Manchester City on 2 July 1983. Coincidentally, his comeback was exactly nine years after he took over from Jock Stein in 1978.

12. EXTRA SPECIAL

Billy gives some last-minute instructions to his team as they prepare for another half hour in the Scottish Cup Final against Rangers at Hampden on 10 May 1980. The first 90 minutes ended in a goalless stalemate, but George McCluskey claimed the winner.

From back (left to right): Tommy Gemmell, Benny Rooney, Willie O'Neill, John Hughes, Bertie Auld, Joe McBride, Jim Craig, Charlie Gallagher, Bobby Lennox, Stevie Chalmers and Bobby Murdoch; front row: Jimmy Johnstone, John Fallon, Billy McNeill, Ronnie Simpson, Sean Fallon, John Clark and Willie Wallace.

13. THE LIONS ROAR AGAIN

It's Paradise revisited for Billy and his Lisbon teammates as they gather ahead of a gala occasion at Celtic Park. Also pictured are Jean Stein, widow of legendary manager Jock, and the game sponsor.

14. ALL SMILES

Billy, Tommy Gemmell, Jim Craig and Bertie Auld share a memorable moment with Celtic chief executive Peter Lawwell.

15. THE McNEILLS AT HOME:
Back row (left to right): Libby, Susan, Paula and Carol with Billy, Martyn and Liz in front.

16. THE GRANDCHILDREN
Back row (left to right): Gerrard, Michael, James, Matthew, Abby, Alexandra, Sean and Darcy.

17. HAIL CAESAR
The statue of Billy McNeill was unveiled at Celtic Park on 19 December 2015, a fitting tribute to Celtic's greatest ever Captain. It now has pride of place on the Celtic Way.

DENIS LAW

I think it would be fair to say Billy McNeill and I did not get off to the best of starts. We played alongside each other when he made his Scotland international debut against England at Wembley on Saturday, 15 April 1961 – a day and date that will haunt me forever. Do I have to repeat the scoreline? We lost 9–3 against our oldest footballing enemy and I have never watched film of this horrible ninety minutes. Why would I? I'm not a huge fan of horror movies.

I'm sure Big Billy will feel the same way. He was only twenty-one years old, had played just three seasons in the Celtic first team and had done enough to catch the eye of the Scotland selectors. By anyone's standards that was a fairly meteoric rise to representing his nation, especially in a key position in central defence where a solitary mistake can lead to a goal. Nine of our team that afternoon played their football in Scotland, so they could jump on a train and escape afterwards. My good mate Dave Mackay, who was with Tottenham Hotspur, and yours truly, at Manchester City, had to hang around and face the music.

I won't dwell on recollections of this match for rather obvious reasons. We got it back to 3–2 at one point and then it all fell apart. There's no way I would point the finger at our debutant centre-half, but just don't get me started on goalkeeper Frank Haffey, his Celtic teammate! Dave Mackay put it this way, 'The defence played crap, the keeper played double crap.'

After the game and the awful dawning of what we had just been put through, the Home Scots, Big Billy, his Celtic colleague Dunky McKay and Motherwell's Ian St John, Bert McCann and Pat Quinn, went in search of a backstreet London pub to drown their sorrows while Dave and I decided we needed to seek solace in alcohol elsewhere and we hoped to sneak into the

West End without anyone taking notice. We found a bar that was reasonably quiet – and then in walked half of the England team. There was no getting away from them that bloody day. However, I knew I would be seeing more of the fair-haired lad from Celtic, he had too much quality to let one dreadful result derail his career.

Later that year, in September, we teamed up again for a World Cup qualifier against Czechoslovakia at Hampden. We got it right second time around and on this occasion we emerged victorious 3–2 where I was fortunate enough to score two goals in the second-half after our visitors had taken the lead. Let me remind people just how good this Czech team was – it got all the way to the World Cup Final the following year and led a great Brazil side 1–0 at one stage before the South Americans came back to win 3–1. I also played alongside three of their players, Josef Masopust, Jan Popluhar and Svatopluk Pluskal, in the Rest of the World Select when we faced England to mark their Football Association's Centenary in 1963. That might tell you something of the quality of that nation at the beginning of the sixties.

And yet, we pushed them all the way. I genuinely believe guys such as Billy McNeill, Dave Mackay and his Spurs teammate John White, Manchester United's Pat Crerand, Jim Baxter, of Rangers, and Ian St John, who had joined Liverpool from Motherwell, were good enough to perform on the world stage. I have absolutely no doubt Billy McNeill would have shone at the highest level.

Alas, it wasn't to be. Scotland missed out in Chile in 1962, England in 1966 and Mexico four years later, but we managed to get to West Germany in 1974 where I played my solitary World Cup Finals game – a 2–0 win over Zaire. So, at least, I could say I was involved on international football's biggest stage. It's a platform where Billy McNeill deserved to perform. How good was Big Billy? He was a top man, on and off the pitch. A real gentleman and very good company. I didn't play against him too often, but I recall a friendly game at Parkhead in August just before the start of the 1966/67 season. My Manchester United colleagues Bobby Charlton, Nobby Stiles and John Connelly had won some sort of football trophy the week before, George Best was in our side and Pat Crerand was playing against his beloved Celtic. I was up front and Big Billy was at the heart of their defence.

Now let me make this clear just in case there is any confusion – I hated centre-halves. They got in the way of me and the goalkeeper and I had no time for them. They would kick me and I would kick them back. That was the matchday ritual. I expected no favours from them and they knew they certainly wouldn't get any from me. Big Jack Charlton and I had used to enjoy a fair old scrap back in the days when Manchester United and Leeds United were massive rivals. I had to laugh when Jack admitted he had a few of my shirts at home – the ones he had ripped off my back!

I might have been a Scotland teammate of Billy McNeill and we would share a beer or two after a game, but all bets were off when the referee blew to get the game underway. Afterwards, no problem and it was a case of 'where are we going for a refreshment?' But friendship went out the window when I was on the football pitch and Billy knew what to expect. We piled into each other that afternoon, no over-the-top stuff or anything like that, but we were two combative blokes playing against each other and I wanted to win for United and he wanted to do likewise for Celtic. I can say right now, Billy was scrupulously clean, which is not something I could have said about a lot of the defenders I faced back then.

His ability in the air? Just about unbeatable. I may not have been the tallest, but I knew I had a good spring and a reasonable sense of timing, so I scored a lot of goals with my head. I was quite good in the air and that was because I trained at home in Aberdeen as a kid with a ball of wool which was suspended on a string from the pulley. I could move it up and down and I had to strain all the way when it was at its highest. I practised every day until I became quite good. It may surprise you, though, to learn I never headed the ball in training. Colleagues firing one of those big, heavy spheres at me were wasting their time. After a few sessions early in my career, I thought, 'Stuff that. I'll go for everything in the air in an actual competitive game, but you can forget it in training. Who wants to spend all day sticking their head on a wrecking ball?'

Celtic beat us 4–1 that sunny afternoon in the east end of Glasgow and I could see Jock Stein had the makings of a very good side. I knew most of the lads from the Scotland team and Wee Jinky Johnstone was a personal favourite. Tommy Gemmell, too, a laughing cavalier of a left-back. Bobby Murdoch was such a fabulous passer of the ball and they had two strikers, Bobby Lennox and Joe McBride, who knew how to put the ball in the net. Big Yogi Hughes didn't play that day, but I was aware of his talents. And Billy McNeill was their leader. I was impressed with their performance because, although it was billed as a friendly, both clubs desperately wanted to get one over on the other. Managers Matt Busby and Jock Stein were huge friends, but there was genuine rivalry there, too. So, Celtic earned that victory.

However, I have to admit I did not believe they would win the European Cup at the end of that season. Who would have predicted that? Big Billy and his teammates were exceptional in Lisbon, you have to give them that. They won that trophy fair and square and no one who witnessed it will ever forget Big Billy going up to collect the Cup. How did I feel? I was envious! Okay, I was happy for my big mate, but I wanted United to be the first British club to lift that trophy and go into the history books. Celtic got there first and all credit to them. United won it the following year when I was stuck in hospital following a knee operation. I watched us beat Benfica 4–1 at Wembley on a TV at my bedside.

Billy McNeill got closer to that European Cup than I ever did and I can't think of a more deserving individual to become the first Scot to hold aloft that gleaming trophy. Pat Crerand might even agree!

JIM McCALLIOG

To any aspiring young footballer, Billy McNeill was the complete role model. When I was a kid growing up in the Gorbals, I couldn't get enough football. If I wasn't kicking a ball about in the streets around Caledonia Road, I was attending a game. I was a bit of a Clyde fan because Shawfield was only a short walk from where I lived, but I was a regular visitor to Celtic Park, Ibrox, Firhill, Hampden and Cathkin Park, home of the now-defunct Third Lanark. I never took a bus, I always walked.

You couldn't help but notice Billy when you watched Celtic in action. He was the leader, no doubt about it. On that pitch, he was very much the Celtic captain and he had a real commanding presence. He had that special something – a real aura about him. I never played against Billy because I spent all of my senior career in England, starting off as a seventeen year old at Leeds United before moving to Chelsea, then onto Sheffield Wednesday, Wolves, Manchester United and Southampton.

I played alongside Billy just once and I am sad to relate that it was not a winning occasion. It was at Hampden on 10 May 1967 in a friendly international against the USSR and the Scotland fans were already acclaiming us as 'world champions'. The previous month – 15 April, to be precise – we had beaten England 3–2 at Wembley when I was fortunate enough to score the winning goal on my debut at the age of twenty. I recall Celtic keeper Ronnie Simpson also made his international bow that wonderful afternoon at the age of thirty-six.

So, a crowd of 53,497 turned out at the national stadium to welcome home the heroes who had inflicted the first defeat on the English since they had lifted the World Cup the previous summer. Naturally, their title then passed on to us, according to a lot of our followers. Makes sense, doesn't it? Rangers' Ronnie

McKinnon was centre-half at Wembley, but Billy came in for the visit of the Russians. I felt as though I was playing in a Celtic Select line-up that evening. As well as Billy, Ronnie Simpson, Tommy Gemmell, John Clark, Jimmy Johnstone and Bobby Lennox started the game and Willie Wallace came on for Denis Law in the second-half.

To be honest, I shouldn't have been on the pitch at all and I would have missed my solitary appearance alongside the Celtic legend. I had sustained an ankle injury playing for Sheffield Wednesday and I should have withdrawn. However, I was still on a high after scoring that goal against Gordon Banks and wanted to keep my position alongside Denis. I don't think I did myself justice, but it was definitely a game to forget. Big Tommy Gemmell, a wonderful character, scored an astonishing own goal that night. There didn't look to be any danger when he received the ball and then he astounded everyone in the park when he lobbed the ball over our keeper into the net. Everything about it was perfect, except it was in the wrong net.

Tommy, of course, had a reason for his slight collapse in concentration. Afterwards he told the press, 'I looked up and saw an old guy in goal and presumed it was Lev Yashin, so I knocked the ball over him.' The Russian goalie that night was indeed the legendary Lev Yashin and, yes, he was a year older than Ronnie, who was known to his Celtic teammates as 'Faither'. Just before half-time a bloke by the name of Fedor Medved struck a second and that's how the game finished. Not quite as memorable as the previous international and not exactly how I would have wished my game alongside Big Billy to pan out.

I wasn't surprised to learn Billy and Jim Baxter were the best of pals off the pitch. One may have played for Celtic and the other for Rangers, their biggest rivals, but both were obviously strong, independent individuals who knew their own mind.

I could never imagine either of them ever allowing people to dominate them and push their beliefs upon them. When people talk about our win over England at Wembley that wonderful day in 1967 hardly anyone mentions my goal – they always go on about Jim's spot of keepy-uppy on the left wing as we ran our opponents ragged. Like Billy, Jim was a bit of a role model. And I must add Denis Law, as well.

When I joined up with Bobby Brown's players for that Home International encounter, I hardly knew any of the other players. There was Billy Bremner who had been at Leeds United when I had started my career at Elland Road and there was Eddie McCreadie, my old teammate at Chelsea. But I was the new kid on the block and Jim realised that. I'll always remember him coming over to me shortly after I had arrived. 'Come here, son,' he said as he draped an arm over my shoulder, 'we'll take care of you.' And they did. Hopefully, I repaid their generosity!

These characters were giants in the game: Billy McNeill, Jim Baxter and Denis Law. They were legends, but I will always remember how they looked after a wee lad from the Gorbals.

Later on, I was fortunate enough to meet Billy at many sporting functions. He always had that little gleam in his eye, a wee grin tucked away just below the surface. He was always the perfect gentleman, a charming, warm-hearted human being. And he wasn't a bad footballer, too!

6

Paradise Comes to Portugal

On 25 May 1967, in the Portuguese capital of Lisbon, the angels smiled down from the heavens on the day Celtic conquered Europe.

A noble Billy McNeill, the inspirational captain, with the sun dazzling on his blond hair, emphasising his physique, with his pristine green-and-white hooped shirt positively shimmering in the glow, held aloft the European Cup as he commanded the rostrum of the Estádio Nacional looking for all the world like Apollo ascending Mount Olympus.

Inter Milan, who had led through an early Sandro Mazzola penalty-kick, had been thrown to the Lions. Their defensive tradition dismantled, their suffocating tactics blown away, their masterly reputation devastated. Celtic, refreshingly entertaining, had put sparkle and gaiety back into the beautiful game.

A mighty first-time piledriver from Tommy Gemmell after the hour mark nullified the Italians' advantage and Stevie Chalmers diverted in the winner five minutes from the end.

Years later, Billy McNeill, reflected, 'To my mind, the greatest thing about our European Cup victory is that we did it in the Celtic manner. We always wanted to play with flair, adventure and style. We were determined for people to remember us for our attacking philosophy. I would like to think we managed that in Lisbon. It was a breakthrough for British football. It was marvellous for Scottish football. However, the main thing for everyone connected with the club, the manager, his assistants, the players and tea ladies, it was truly wonderful for Celtic Football Club.'

McNeill expanded on his memories. 'I've never had a tougher job than accepting the European Cup. It was the most stirring and exciting moment of my life. But I had to steel myself for it. I had just crossed the safety line into our dressing room at Lisbon after being swamped by the congratulations of our fans. My back ached with all the slapping. My jersey had been torn off as a souvenir. Now I had to go out and face them all again to collect the trophy.

'I put on a fresh jersey and, with assistant manager Sean Fallon and Ronnie Simpson giving me moral and physical support, I set off. The trophy was to be presented at the far side of the ground. It seemed there was just one way to get there – through the throng and right across the pitch. By the time we had made ten yards, Ronnie had got lost. Sean was on my left and around me was a posse of police. But the back-slapping, handshaking and general chaos never let up.

'We came to an obstacle – the six-foot-wide moat around the pitch. It was supposed to keep the fans on the terracing. Or, put another way, *off* the pitch. Some hope! Somehow, I made it to the other side. From there it was up the steps to the rostrum. The presentation was made by the President of Portugal, Américo Tomás. And it was only when I felt the magnificent three-foot-high trophy in my hands that the full impact of the moment came home to me – Celtic were European champions!

'I have to admit in the emotion of it all everything is a bit blurred. Also, I still had to get back to the dressing room. It was a bit easier than the first journey. This time we were led outside the stadium, hustled into a police car and whipped, siren wailing, through the crowds to the dressing room entrance.

'We had a bit of a job getting away from the policeman. It appeared he was determined to have his photograph taken with us and the trophy. But Sean and I eventually disentangled ourselves, dived for the dressing-room and got through the scrum unscathed – except for the fact I had lost my jersey again! It was only then that I got the chance to sit down and soak up the satisfaction of being captain of the Celtic team which had just won the European Cup.

'It may seem a strange observation to make, but Inter Milan scoring so early with Sandro Mazzola's penalty-kick was one of the best things that could have happened to us. It was their natural style to try to hold onto anything they had. They had a goal to protect and they seemed quite content to filter into their own half and do their best to keep us out.

'Although I was a central defender, it was not the way I was brought up to play football. It certainly wasn't the Celtic way. Our supporters wouldn't have tolerated that and, in any case, we all knew the fans deserved better. Those guys on the terraces were absolutely brilliant; they were our twelfth man. We never, ever took them for granted.

'I recall it was actually quite calm in our dressing room at half-time. There were no histrionics. Big Jock simply insisted, "Keep doing what you're doing and we'll be okay." He did make one telling observation, though, when he asked our wide men to think about pulling the ball back closer to the edge of the penalty box because Inter were crowding into the six-yard area as they tried to protect their goalkeeper. When you look again at our first goal, you'll see how good that advice was.

'Cairney was calmness personified when he came racing into the box onto Bobby Murdoch's pass. His cutback for Tommy Gemmell was just right and Tommy simply belted one of his specials high into the net. Sarti had no chance. Stevie Chalmers duly knocked in the winner with about five minutes to go and Inter Milan were out of it.

'They were a beaten team. If, by some chance, they had equalised, then the game would have gone into extra-time. Believe me, those guys didn't want to endure another half-hour of what they had already been through.'

SANDRO MAZZOLA

I remember well Billy McNeill's performance against Internazionale Milan in the European Cup Final in the Portuguese capital in 1967.

Helenio Herrera, our manager, went to Scotland to check on Celtic in person. He noted all their players, their strengths and their weaknesses. He told us of the Celtic captain and his ability in the air. To be honest, this did not worry the Internazionale players because we played our football on the ground. High balls, even at corner-kicks, would have been most unusual to our style of football.

However, Billy McNeill was, indeed, majestic. A very capable centre-half who played it very simple. When he got the ball he would pass it to his teammates in the middle of the park. We tried to put pressure on Celtic, but on this day we were not to be successful.

We were also informed to expect him to be hard, but fair. There were many defenders in that era who didn't perform with a lot of discipline. They were not too fussy about how they won the ball when they challenged an opponent. Billy McNeill, we were reassured, was not one of these players. It is always good for a forward player to hear this news.

When Helenio Herrera came back from watching Celtic, he also brought a tape with him.

The players watched the film of them in action and we weren't particularly impressed. I thought, 'These guys are mediocre.'

So, we possibly did not give them the full respect they were due. We had won the European Cup in two of the previous three years and we had beaten Real Madrid, the 1966 winners, en route to Lisbon. We were the favourites.

We believed it would be an easy game. That was the biggest

mistake we could possibly have made! When I scored with my penalty-kick early in the match, I thought that would allow us to slow the pace of the game and dictate the tempo. We did this every week in Italy.

The Celtic players would not allow us to do this. They refused to let us play our normal game. Celtic were superhuman and I have never known a team with so much energy. You could say they took us by surprise. However, we had no complaints about the result. They beat us fair and square. Billy McNeill has been a magnificent ambassador for Celtic for many, many years.

JIM CRAIG

There was a spring in Billy McNeill's step as he bounded out of the front doors of the five-star Palacio Hotel and skipped onto the Celtic team coach. Sitting in a seat beside the entrance to the bus was chairman Robert Kelly. He didn't smile a lot and he wasn't making an exception at this particular moment. Big Billy was grinning from ear to ear. 'Apologies if we made a bit of a noise last night,' said our captain. 'The boys let their hair down a little bit. I tried to make sure it didn't get out of hand.'

Kelly, stony-faced, glowered ahead and grumbled, 'I don't know what you've got to celebrate.'

Billy looked at the chairman and realised he was deadly serious. There wasn't even the faintest trace of mirth. Billy knew the club chief well enough not to bother talking him out of his sullen mood. That was Kelly, though. He thought Celtic should win *every* game. Billy shrugged his shoulders and moved up the bus to sit beside his teammates who were in a slightly more jovial mood. And why not? Celtic had just won through to the quarter-finals of the European Cup.

It was 13 November 1969, the morning after we had played the mighty Benfica, Eusebio *et al*, at the spectacular Stadium of Light in Lisbon and we had got through on the toss of the coin. By the way, that was the last time European's football bosses, UEFA, used that method to settle a tie when the teams were equal and goals away counting double didn't come into play. We had won 3–0 at Parkhead a fortnight earlier and had lost by the identical scoreline in the Portuguese capital. We were still locked at 3–3 on aggregate following thirty minutes of extra-time. Penalty-kicks would be introduced the following year, but this one would be settled by our skipper's skills at calling correctly between heads and tails.

At the end of the game, with the Benfica fans in an absolute fervour, the players of both teams were ushered to their respect-ive dressing rooms. Dutch referee Louis van Raavens asked for our captain to join him in the match officials' HQ , a small grey concrete room. Benfica's Mario Coluna was also summoned to take part on behalf of the hosts. A couple of UEFA officials were also crammed into the area. Nerve-wracking? You better believe it. No one said a word in our dressing room. It was similar in the Benfica room. Both sets of players were anxious to discover who was going to get through to the next stage.

It's a game of chance and hardly an ideal way to settle the outcome of three-and-a-half hours of football between the champions of Scotland and Portugal. Remember, these were the good old days when you actually had to win your country's championship to get into Europe's most prestigious competition.

The silence was eerie within the bowels of that massive stadium, but we could hear noises from the hysterical fans still in the ground. Inside, the referee's room all was quiet, too. And then there was this mighty roar. 'You beauty!' It was unmistake-ably our captain's voice. Only moments later, the door burst open and Billy came hurtling into the room. We were all jumping up and down, cuddling each other. We were through and at that moment that was all that mattered.

When things calmed down, Billy told us the match official from Holland had produced a coin and our fate would be decided by a spin and a call. Billy had the right to choose first after winning the initial toss. He had plumped for 'heads'. Van Raavens flipped the coin and it came down the way Billy guessed. Now he was put on the spot again. Did he want to call heads once more? Or would tails be more likely? I don't know how Billy felt at that moment, but the nerves of his colleagues were reaching snapping point. Billy went for heads again. The coin spun in the confines of the referee's room, came down and hit the floor, rolled and finally came to rest. Van Raavens, McNeill and Coluna raced to see how fortune would decide this epic encounter. Heads! 'You beauty!'

I played in both ties and if ever two games could be used as a barometer of success and failure in this sport it would be those confrontations. We absolutely hammered them in Glasgow. Big Tommy Gemmell raced onto a Bertie Auld free-kick to thunder an awesome shot from about twenty-five yards out that almost took the net away. Tommy could hit a ferocious effort, but I doubt if he hit one with more power than that one. The Portuguese were on the back foot right from the off and Willie Wallace and Harry Hood also scored to make it an emphatic three-goal winning margin. I am not exaggerating when I say we could have had at least two more.

Two weeks later, we were at their ground and it was a complete reversal of what had happened at our place. They flew out of the traps and Eusebio, who had been quiet in the first leg, responded to the hero worship of the home fans. He scored their first goal with a header and Jaime Graca added a second just before the interval. His low shot deceived John Fallon and looked as though it was going wide of his right-hand post, but it seemed to curl at the last moment, strike the base of the upright and ricochet into the net. Maybe Benfica had used up a large portion of their good fortune at that moment. In any case, all our hard work in Glasgow was dissolving in front of our very eyes.

They came at us in red waves, but we were fighting a brave rearguard action. The forty-five minutes came and went, but the referee had yet to blow for full-time. There hadn't been any injuries. Van Raavens refused to signal the end of the contest and then in two minutes overtime they equalised through a header from Diamantino. It was sheer bedlam as their fans swarmed onto the pitch, there were hundreds of them dancing around and then we were told the game was over. We didn't get a chance to kick off.

We were more than puzzled. Billy and Jock Stein attempted to find out if they had, in fact, scored before the full-time whistle had been blown. It was chaos. No one seemed certain if it was 3–2 on aggregate for us, or 3–3 overall and extra-time would have to be played. Our hearts sank when we were informed the Benfica equaliser had been the last touch of the ball mere seconds before it crossed the line. Now THAT is lucky!

Billy was brilliant in those extra thirty minutes. When you are looking for inspiration we didn't have to search too far. He stepped up to the plate. Big Jock had a quick word before the extra period and then it was over to Billy and his teammates. Our skipper was flawless, he was getting up and heading the ball about thirty or forty yards, Tommy Gemmell and I were tucking in to provide extra cover and Jim Brogan, in for the injured John Clark, was doing his bit, too. It was a bit frantic at times, but we managed to regain a bit of our composure and see it through. Maybe fortune favoured the brave in the end.

So, could you blame Billy for dancing out onto the Lisbon street the following morning to catch the team bus on our way to the airport? None of his teammates did. Maybe if our chairman, a bit of a perfectionist, had played that evening in the Stadium of Light, he would have known why his team's players believed they had every right to celebrate.

I had so many good times in the company of Billy McNeill, on and off the pitch. I recall a time when Celtic were on a trip to the States and we were in Las Vegas. Many of the players had gone to a Mass in the gambling capital of the world, Billy and I among them. As ever, the plates were passed around the congregation for donations. I checked my wallet and pulled out a couple of dollars, John Clark, standing beside me, did likewise. The plate was moved along our row, Billy put in his contribution and the bowl carried on its way. About a minute later, there was a bellow that shattered the serene atmosphere of the church. 'That was a one hundred dollar bill!' It was Billy. He had got his money mixed up and thought he was making a reasonable donation like the rest of us. 'That was a one hundred dollar bill,' he yelled again. Too late. The plate – and our skipper's sizeable financial gift – had gone. Billy always was a generous big guy.

I met Billy for the first time on 29 March 1961 when I was captaining Scotland Under-17 Schoolboys against England at Parkhead. I recall Rangers were playing a European Cup-Winners' Cup semi-final first leg against Wolves at Ibrox the same evening. Glasgow was awash with football fans, but they all appeared to be heading for Govan and not the east end of the city. I believe almost 80,000 took in that tie. It was a slightly more modest gate at the place where I would spend so many memorable years. Billy was already a Celtic first-team player at that time and he was brought into the dressing room before the match. He was obviously being held up as an example of what you could achieve in the game if you applied yourself.

We knew he, too, had played for Scotland at this level and clearly what he had achieved was something for us all to strive for and hope to attain. I remember him being a very down-to-earth chap, very approachable and if you had told me I would have been standing toe-to-toe with the big chap just over six years later and picking up a European Cup medal, I would have had you certified.

Because of my dental studies, I was a part-timer when I joined Celtic. Billy was most helpful from day one. I was always very much aware of him and what he was to Celtic Football Club.

WILLIE WALLACE

It wasn't often Jock Stein was left speechless. However, Billy McNeill managed it in Miami one evening in May 1968 as we prepared for a three-game end-of-season tour. To be fair, Billy did get a little assistance from me, Tommy Gemmell and John Clark in striking the Celtic manager dumb. I better start at the beginning to explain this near-phenomenon.

Big Jock had allowed his players some free time during a rest period to recharge our batteries before we were due to play AC Milan in New Jersey on 26 May, ten days after we had flown out to Florida from Prestwick, and again in Toronto six days later – we drew 1–1 and won 2–0 – and three days after that we were scheduled to be in Mexico City to face to Nexaca at the Azteca Stadium, where Brazil's memorable 4–1 World Cup Final victory over Italy would be staged two years later. We lost 3–2 and never got to grips with the altitude.

Before those games, though, we had landed in the sunshine island and looked forward to a little rest and recuperation before winding down the season. Jock gave us some latitude, but he was a real stickler for routine and demanded his players adhere to his timetable. If you attempted to pull the wool, you invariably found yourself lapping a track long after everyone had packed up, showered and gone home.

One early afternoon, four of us decided to go fishing on one of the local tubs. Tommy was a huntin', shootin', fishin' type of guy at home and he fancied a day trying to catch marlin. We made our way to one of the small harbours in Miami and hired a pokey little vessel, nothing too elaborate, because we reckoned we were only going out for an hour. What could go wrong? The crew consisted of the captain and a young deckhand. Billy, Tommy, John and I got on board and, of course, Big TG had brought along some 'supplies'. Obviously, he reckoned fishing for marlin might be thirsty work.

Would you believe the young deckhand was from Dundee and also a Celtic supporter? That was good enough for Tommy. He delved into his traveller's bag and presented the lad with a bottle of best malt. 'There you go, son, don't drink it all at once,' said our big mate. 'Are you sure, sir?' asked the kid, holding on grimly to his precious gift. 'You're welcome, son,' said Tommy with that big Danny Kaye smile. 'Just keep us safe out there in the middle of the Atlantic. Okay?' The boy almost saluted.

The four of us set up on deck and were rigged out with fishing rods and the boat cast off. Tommy was the only one taking it seriously. Billy, John and I just chatted away and had a sip of some of what Tommy had thoughtfully provided. It was very pleasant, I have to say. The sun was shining, the sky was blue and cloudless and there was hardly a ripple on the shimmering ocean as our wee fishing boat floated in the general direction of where the captain assured Tommy was the best spot for marlin.

We put our feet up, four guys without a care in the world, all thoughts of playing at Broomfield on a freezing December evening well and truly banished from our thoughts. Time tends to zoom along in these perfectly serene circumstances, doesn't it? We were gliding along for a couple of hours or so when Billy stirred. 'Shouldn't we think about heading back at some point?' 'Ach, stop worrying,' was our response, 'we'll be back in plenty of time.' Famous last words.

Billy sat back in his chair and relaxed. About an hour later, three of us were close to dozing off when Tommy broke our reverie. 'I think something's wrong,' he said. 'I'll go and see the captain and tell him it's about time we made a move to return to Miami.' My pal was away for about five minutes when he came back, his expression displayed he was clearly concerned.

We looked up. Billy was first to speak. 'What's wrong, TG? You look a bit alarmed.' Tommy could be a bit of joker, but on this occasion all three of us were aware he was deadly serious. 'The captain's done in the bottle, he's out the game, totally drunk, blotto, slumped over the steering wheel,' he said. 'No one's in charge of the boat.'

The four us made a very quick dash to the top of the vessel and, sure enough, the skipper was well and truly plastered. At his feet lay the empty bottle of malt Tommy had presented the deckhand. Where was the Celtic supporter from Dundee? We went downstairs and the lad was sound asleep in his bunk. We shook him awake and hastily told him of our predicament. Apparently, the captain had sneaked into his cabin, relieved him of his gift from Tommy and had emptied the contents of the bottle in one sitting. No wonder we couldn't rouse him.

'You'll have to take over, son,' said Billy. The kid informed us, 'I've never sailed a boat before. I just clean up after the captain and the anglers.' We peered out and could see nothing but the Atlantic Ocean. It was around this point I thought I could detect a little bit of panic from my pals. The kid went upstairs and headed for the bridge. He checked around, picked up some charts, looked thoughtful and said, 'I know where we're headed.' We chorused, 'Where?'

I'll never forget the lad's answer. 'Cuba,' he said.

'CUBA?' we shrieked.

'Aye,' he said, 'it's not too far away.' He pointed straight ahead.

'Turn this bloody thing around,' said Billy. 'Just aim us in another direction.'

The kid said, 'I'll do my best, Mr McNeill.'

He began pulling at the steering wheel as Billy and John, not too gently, removed the captain from his seat, carried him outside, took him downstairs and dumped him in his cabin. The guy was so far gone he hadn't a clue what was happening. He never said a word.

'That was a really good malt,' Tommy wistfully informed us all. Thankfully, the young Dundonian managed to steer a steady course and navigate us back in the direction of Miami.

Eventually, we returned to the team hotel and, as you might have guessed, Big Jock was waiting for us. We had broken his curfew and he wasn't too pleased.

'Okay, you lot,' he said sternly. 'You're two hours late. Where have you been?' He looked at the club captain for an answer. There was a stony silence. 'Well? I'm waiting,' Jock practically barked.

Billy cleared his throat and answered, 'Cuba, boss.' A moment later, he added, 'Or, at least, as near as dammit.' Big Jock was struck dumb for the first time in his life.

I can recall another occasion when Billy was forced to face the manager on a delicate matter. Celtic were due to take the players to Bermuda for a wee jolly and one of the wives thought it would be a nice gesture if the club decided to take them along, too. As our captain, Billy was our mouthpiece. A few of the players fancied the idea, but one who shall remain anonymous told me, 'There's no way I want my missus along while I'm having a good time in Bermuda.' I think he fancied a break from his other half. Billy, though, was persuaded to put the proposition to Big Jock.

'Oh, really?' asked the manager, who could do sarcasm with the best of them. 'You want your wives along, as well? A wee family holiday at the club's expense? No chance. If that's the case, the trip's off.'

Billy left Jock's office and relayed his reaction to the players. 'So is the tour on or off?' one of the players enquired.

'I'm not sure,' answered Billy.

About thirty minutes later, Sean Fallon came out and told us

Jock wanted to see us in the dressing room. We all filtered in. He looked at us.

'Right, here's what's going to happen,' he said. 'If you want your wives to go to Bermuda, the trip is off. If you don't want the wives to go, the trip is on.'

Big Jock never encouraged debate. He put up his giant right paw, 'We take the wives and it'll be a circus. They'll all be checking out each other at breakfast, looking at what everyone else is wearing. They'll turn it into a fashion parade. It's not going to happen. Take it or leave it.'

He grinned and added, 'I'll let you tell your wives they're not going.'

And then he shuffled out of the dressing room into the corridor and I'm sure I heard him cackling as he made his way back to the manager's office.

Poor Billy got lumbered with all sort of stuff as the players' spokesman. However, there was a clear bond between Jock and Billy. I know some players thought Billy got preferential treatment when the manager was having a go if he wasn't happy after a performance that didn't satisfy him. Everyone was fair game, apart from Billy. But what a few of them wouldn't have known was that Billy would get a call to see Jock in his office afterwards and he would be criticised in private. Jock obviously thought the club's captain deserved to keep his dignity in the dressing room, but Billy got a boot up the backside like the rest of us when Jock was displeased.

I was fortunate in my football career because my captain at Hearts before I moved to Celtic in December 1966 was a bloke called John Cumming and he, too, commanded respect. He played in the old wing-half position and made over 600 appearances for the Edinburgh club, won every domestic honour and was selected nine times for Scotland. He was a one-club man and played for the team that meant so much to him. He was

Hearts' mirror image of Billy. I still find it astounding that such a fine and accomplished player as Cumming only won nine caps for his country. It's the same with Billy, who was selected only twenty-nine times for Scotland.

Obviously, we had an awful lot of good central defenders around when Billy played. As a matter of fact, Rangers' Ronnie McKinnon played at the same time and he won just one fewer than his Old Firm counterpart. I find it unfathomable that selectors back then would choose McKinnon ahead of McNeill on twenty-eight occasions, unless, of course, my teammate was injured. I've often said it helped your international career if your team's shirt colour was light blue. Let's leave it at that.

I played against Billy a few times when I was with Hearts and recall some great duels. When we faced Celtic back then we were ordered to keep the ball on the deck. We reasoned Billy was so good in the air it was pointless slinging in high crosses. We believed we would have more chance of success of playing passes on the ground, but then you encountered John Clark and his anticipation was uncanny. So, we knew it was never going to be an easy ride against Celtic no matter which tactics we used. Everyone accepted Billy was just the best in the air but some have said he wasn't the best passer of the ball. Maybe that wasn't his strength, but he more than made up for it in other ways.

However, I'm not sure my big buddy would have appreciated a team talk from Jock before one particular game shortly after I had joined.

'Okay, you guys,' said The Boss, looking at some individuals in his defence. 'Don't mess about today. Just make sure you give the ball to the guys who can play.'

It was Big Billy's turn to be speechless.

EDDIE GRAY

Billy McNeill was a tremendous leader of a fabulous Celtic team. I grew up in Glasgow watching the club and have never hidden my admiration of Celtic. If Don Revie hadn't persuaded me to join Leeds United in 1965, then who knows if I might have gone to my boyhood favourites? Fate decreed otherwise.

I played against Billy several times in the late sixties and early seventies. I recall a challenge game being moved from Celtic Park to Hampden to accommodate the crowd. The official attendance was given as 75,110 for the pre-season match that was played on a sunny Saturday afternoon in August 1968. What an amazing turn-out for a friendly with nothing but pride at stake. Tommy Gemmell gave Celtic the half-time lead with a blaster of a penalty-kick past our keeper, Gary Sprake. However, we turned it around in the second period and won with goals from Johnny Giles and Peter Lorimer. The game was played in a proper manner between two teams who had obvious respect for each other. The managers, too, Big Jock Stein and Don Revie, were friendly rivals. Both demanded victories on all occasions and you could see they had a lot of time for each other.

I was at Hampden a year later when Celtic played Rangers in the Scottish Cup Final on 26 April. Leeds United had already won the old English First Division and we had a blank Saturday before we were due to play Liverpool at Anfield the following Monday. So, I headed home to take my place alongside over 132,000 spectators at Scotland's national stadium. I will never forget Billy McNeill giving Celtic the lead in about two minutes with one of his trade-mark headers. Bobby Lennox flighted over a left-wing corner-kick and the captain's timing was absolute perfection, as usual. He rose above everyone to make contact with his head and the ball soared beyond Rangers keeper Norrie Martin who didn't stand a chance.

That goal from Billy has always stuck in my memory bank. It was a good day to be a Celtic fan. Goals from Wee Lennox and George Connelly had Big Jock's team 3–0 ahead at the interval and Stevie Chalmers completed the scoring with a fourth.

I had a slightly more active role when I returned to Hampden just under a year later. This time it was the second leg of our two epic European Cup semi-finals against Celtic. My goodness, what a night that was! The stadium was rocking, the atmosphere was absolutely electric. I had never heard anything like it. The official crowd was given as 136,505, which is still a record for a European game. Years later, I was talking to Billy about that incredible evening and he told me he was convinced the attendance was closer to 170,000. It was an all-ticket affair, but there was obviously no stopping some determined supporters from getting into the ground. I think a few stadium walls were scaled that night.

Once again, the tie was played in the correct spirit of football, two teams who acknowledged each other's many qualities. It was a real battle, no quarter asked or given by two sets of players who were used to winning. Defeat for either of us was not an option. Our skipper Billy Bremner was, like me, a Celtic fan, but there was no sign of favouritism during that confrontation. Wee Billy was really friendly with another little redhead, Jinky Johnstone. They got on well during their days with the Scotland international squads and it must be said both were fiery characters. As you would expect, there was no old pal's act that night. Wee Billy clattered into Jinky early in proceedings, but there were no hard feelings. Jinky was like Billy; a tough and resolute wee individual who could take the punishment.

We went into that game after losing the first leg 1–0 at Elland Road. George Connelly scored in the second minute and we just couldn't get back into the match. Big Billy played really well. He was up against our Mick Jones, a big and strong centre-forward who would challenge for everything in the air and on the deck. There was no way through for us, but our manager told us afterwards he still believed we would win the tie. All we had to do was beat Celtic in Glasgow in front of over 120,000 of their own fans!

I took notice of a quote from Jock Stein in a Glasgow evening paper where he mentioned me. He said, 'Remember last time I said one flash of brilliance would win the game in Leeds? Well, who's going to do it this time? Eddie Gray for them? Or Jimmy Johnstone or John Hughes for us?'

Wee Billy Bremner must have sent shock waves through the supporters when he fired in a right-foot shot from about thirty yards and it soared into Evan Williams' top right-hand corner of the net. It was only the fourteenth minute and, suddenly, it was 1–1 on aggregate and we had a chance. It was still 1–0 at the break, but Celtic equalised within two minutes of the restart with a header from John Hughes and there was no stopping them after that. Gary Sprake had to be helped off after an accidental clash with Hughes and then another of my Scottish international teammates, Bobby Murdoch, blasted in a second beyond substitute keeper David Harvey. All that was left following a pulsating, never-to-be-forgotten encounter was for us to congratulate Billy McNeill and his players and wish them all the best in the European Cup Final.

Disappointingly, Celtic did not conquer Europe for a second time as they had done against Inter Milan in Lisbon on 25 May 1967. Another of my cherished memories is of Billy holding aloft that massive, gleaming trophy with the sun shining down on him. It's such a marvellous image of a player who epitomised Celtic Football Club.

Billy McNeill has been such a legendary figure in the club's history, a wonderful ambassador and it has been an absolute privilege to know the man.

7

The Last Hurrah

'Regrets?' smiled Billy McNeill. 'I've had a few.'

I half-expected my lunchtime companion to regale me with an impromptu version of the Frank Sinatra classic 'My Way', which, when you think about it, wouldn't have been totally inappropriate.

The Celtic fans celebrating the 3–1 Scottish Cup Final victory over Airdrie on Saturday, 3 May 1975 didn't realise they were witnessing the last performance from skipper-supreme Billy McNeill. The thirty-five-year-old icon had decided to get out at the top after serving eighteen years and making 790 appearances for his one and only club. It's maybe just as well the supporters in the 75,457 crowd hadn't a clue about their captain's momentous decision. It may have taken a day or two of encores from McNeill before the fans dispersed.

At least, now a loyal servant might have some spare time to visit his version of Fort Knox and count his medals, all twenty-three of them and, remember, he won the sum total of zilch in his first seven years as a top-team mainstay. Not bad for a late starter.

McNeill collected nine league championships, seven Scottish Cups, six League Cups and, of course, the coveted European Cup. He also picked up twenty-nine international caps, turned out nine times for the Scottish League and made five appearances as a freckle-faced youth with the Under-23s.

Any regrets? 'Actually, I do,' answered McNeill. 'I think I quit playing a bit too early. I felt fit enough to go on for at least another year, maybe two. I discussed it with Big Jock and he thought I should go out a winner. I took his advice. On that occasion, I wish I hadn't.'

This train of thought is in stark contrast to the one made by McNeill only days after his sudden decision. Then he went on record with, 'I do not regret my announcement to retire from football. I only hope the timing of it did not detract in any way from the team winning the Scottish Cup, that was the last thing I intended. Naturally, like everyone else at the Park, I was disappointed we did not make it ten-in-a-row in the Scottish League.

'But even if we had won the league championship it would not have changed my mind, I would still have quit playing. I always said that when the training began to seem difficult then I would know it was time to give up and I must be honest and say I have found it hard at times in the last season. I have also had a succession of niggling injuries and they have taken longer and longer to clear up. This is something that no amount of training can help. I reckon it is just one of the burdens any footballer faces late in his career.

'Also, I have business interests outside football at the stage I really have to devote all my time to. So, I could not think of a better time to bow out than now, when I know myself I have made the right decision. Naturally, I was glad it ended in a successful Cup Final, a game in which I feel I played well. But I was not fooled by that game. I think I have enough experience and ability and the old Cup adrenalin pumped through to help me.

'I have been fortunate that the happier days in my career at the end of it all far outnumbered the disappointments that come to any footballer.'

Jock Stein had an interesting take on his skipper's decision to put away the football boots. 'Billy has been the cornerstone of the team for such a long time, a player I have known personally since he was a schoolboy and I was coach at Celtic Park. His departure is the end of an era for he has been a wonderful example as a player and as a club captain for so many years. But I said at the time of his retirement that I felt he had made the right decision and I am sure Billy knows that too.

'When Celtic won the Scottish Cup in 1965 and we then swept on to even greater success, Billy McNeill was twenty-five years of age and an experienced, established international player. If a young player eventually takes over, he will play his own game, do things his own way and that is how it should be.'

A week before the Scottish Cup triumph, Jimmy Johnstone played in the final league game of the season, a 2–1 defeat against St Johnstone in Perth. It was the last time the famous green and white hoops would adorn his 5ft 4in frame and it was hardly the fitting end to a scintillating career for a born entertainer who had thrilled the world with his exclusive box of tricks. The winger, at the age of thirty, took his skills across the Atlantic to enthral a whole new appreciative audience at San Jose Earthquakes in the North American League. He left with a similar medal haul as his skipper; nineteen in all. He won nine leagues, four Scottish Cups, five League Cups and, of course, the precious prize from Lisbon. It's impossible to mention his name without smiling at the legacy he left behind. Wee Jinky was a complete one-off.

Johnstone, voted the Greatest-Ever Celtic Player by the

supporters, also left at the same time as his big buddy. Stein was not quite so charitable in his send-off speech for the winger. 'I feel he has climbed too many mountains with us,' remarked the manager. 'The challenge for him has gone, the spark can be rekindled elsewhere, just as Bobby Murdoch did so successfully with Middlesbrough.

'It is better he gets a new challenge now at thirty years of age, when he can still make something of it, rather than hang around until he would be of little value to any new club. I once said that no player during my time as Celtic manager has caused me more trouble. I do not withdraw that remark. There were many occasions when I leaned over backwards to help him and yet at times we seemed to move from one crisis to the next with him.'

In a slightly more mellow vein, Stein added somewhat wistfully, 'Yet it is also true to say that, just like the fans on the terracing, there was no player who could give me such delight when he was on form than the wee redhead.'

There was no sign of Johnstone, though, for a curtain call with McNeill on that emotional day in the south side of Glasgow.

Billy McNeill, for the last time ever, led out the Celtic team alongside Airdrie skipper Derek Whiteford on a fine May afternoon in 1975. Referee Ian Foote blew to begin the confrontation and McNeill, and not too many others, had the knowledge his Celtic career had only another one-and-a-half hours to go.

In the fourteenth minute, nerves were settled when Paul Wilson expertly headed a cross from Kenny Dalglish beyond keeper Davie McWilliams. In two incredible minutes just before the break, the Broomfield part-timers glimpsed glory only for it to be snatched away in quickfire fashion. Right-winger Kevin McCann followed up with a blistering drive high into the net after two efforts from teammates had been blocked. Celtic replied by racing down the pitch and forcing a left-wing corner-kick. Bobby Lennox swung it in and Wilson was unmarked to dash in and head a second goal.

Eight minutes after the turnaround, Lennox was sent tumbling in the box and the match official had no hesitation in pointing to the penalty spot. Pat McCluskey drilled the award wide of the diving McWilliams.

At full-time, Billy McNeill raised his arms to the heavens and accepted the cheers of the joyous fans – just as he had done ten years earlier against Dunfermline. In the space of a decade, he had started – and ended – an era.

SIR KENNY DALGLISH

Billy McNeill picked up the ball and handed it to me. 'Here, Kenny, you take it.' You could say I was more than a little surprised. It was the first game of the season, a vitally-important League Cup-tie against Rangers at Ibrox, I was making my Old Firm debut, there was a sell-out all-ticket crowd of 72,500 packed into the ground and we had just been awarded a penalty-kick in the seventieth minute.

John Hughes – 'Big Yogi', to the Celtic fans – had been brought down in the box by their centre-half, Ronnie McKinnon, and referee Bill Mullan immediately pointed to the spot. I didn't think for a moment I would be given the responsibility of having to convert the award. Let's face it, there were a lot of players wearing hooped jerseys with far more experience than me. I'll always remember my immediate response to Billy. 'Get lost,' I said.

It didn't stop Billy from continuing to thrust the ball at me. 'You take them for the reserves,' he insisted.

'Aye,' I said, 'but there are more photographers behind that goal than fans who turn up for reserve games.' Billy was insistent – and I learned that day he was a very difficult customer to argue with.

Celtic had guys on the pitch such as Wee Jinky Johnstone, Bobby Murdoch, Big Yogi and Bobby Lennox who were veterans of this fixture, but the Celtic captain chose to entrust me with the kick. What could I do? I placed the ball on the spot and noticed one of my bootlaces had come undone. I knelt down to sort the problem, but I was accused of gamesmanship and attempting to play mind games to unsettle their keeper, Peter McCloy. I hadn't even thought of that. I had a loose bootlace, start and end of story.

I stepped back, looked up and knew exactly where I would place the ball. I struck it sweetly enough with my right foot to the keeper's left, McCloy took off in the opposite direction and the Celtic end behind the goal simply erupted in joy. We had been leading with a goal from Wee Jinky, scored just three minutes beforehand, and I had just doubled our advantage. We weren't likely to throw away that advantage at the home of our greatest rivals and it was the perfect way to kick off a campaign.

In the midst of all the bedlam of one of these frantic derbies, it didn't occur to me the faith and confidence Billy had shown in me, a twenty-year-old Old Firm rookie who had hardly been a first-team regular the previous season. He really had the courage of his convictions and I will be forever thankful for that.

I suppose I came to most people's attention when I played in a testimonial match for a Kilmarnock stalwart, a big centre-half called Frank Beattie. It was on a May evening at the end of the 1970/71 campaign and a couple of our players, Davie Hay and Jim Brogan, were away on international duty and Wee Jinky was injured. Jock Stein sent a strong team to Rugby Park in recognition of the Killie player's seventeen-year service at the club.

We won 7–2 and I managed to score six goals – Bobby Murdoch got the other – with three coming in an amazing eighteen-minute spell near the end of the second-half. Billy was playing that evening and might have seen something in me. I was fortunate enough to keep my place in the team when we started the new season.

On 31 July 1971, we played a game at Parkhead against Dumbarton in a competition that was known as the Drybrough Cup. We won 5–2 and on this occasion I collected four goals, three coming in eight minutes. Four days later, I hit three in a 4–2 victory over St Johnstone in Perth in the semi-final. We lost 2–1 to Aberdeen at Pittodrie in the Final on a day when Jock

Stein went for youth and fielded me, Davie Hay, Vic Davidson, Lou Macari and George Connelly.

A week later came my big moment at Ibrox and, a fortnight later, I was back at the home of Rangers for another League Cup-tie. Parkhead was under construction at the time and Hampden had been seen as the reasonable alternative ground to host the game, but Queen's Park were also getting work done on their ground at the same time, so the Scottish League stepped in and ordered the match to be played in Govan again.

It was goalless at the interval, but I got the opening goal three minutes after the turnaround and Tommy Callaghan and Bobby Lennox added two more as we won convincingly by three goals to nil. Billy McNeill's insistence that I take that penalty-kick had undoubtedly given me a wee boost in confidence.

We knew we had another trip to Ibrox coming up, this time on league business, but before that we hammered Clyde 9–1 at Parkhead where Billy and I both got on the scoresheet. I reckoned he was picking up some hints in the art of finishing! Bobby Murdoch had already scored when I netted in the seventh minute and the Celtic captain added a third shortly afterwards. Poor Clyde. Bobby Lennox added two more before half-time and Big Jock was never one to tell us to take our foot off the gas. Lou Macari, with two, and Tommy Callaghan took the tally to eight before Wee Bobby completed his hat-trick.

Seven days later, I was trotting out for a third time at Ibrox. As everyone knows, I saw a lot of Rangers when I was a schoolboy and, in fact, my back bedroom looked out on to their training ground. Their South African centre-forward Don Kichenbrand was probably my first hero and I liked players such as Ian McMillan and Jim Baxter; two guys who knew how to pass the ball. But, for whatever reason, there was never any interest from them in me. So, there I was again playing on the pitch and at the stadium I had visited so often. With Big Billy there for inspiration, could I complete the hat-trick?

Remarkably, I did score again as we won the league game 3–2 after trailing 2–1 at half-time. Lou Macari had given us an early lead, but they came back to turn things around. I equalised following a left-wing corner-kick and then I set up the winner a minute from time with a flick into the box that was headed in by Wee Jinky, of all people. Inside the space of a month, I had played three games at Ibrox, won the lot and scored in all of them.

I had heard all about the atmosphere and tension of these derbies. The reserves would mingle with the first-team players during the pre-season. Billy might have been the captain of that fantastic team, but he always took an interest in the youngsters. He was never intimidating and was always sympathetic to the cause. Even back then, Billy was an outstanding servant to Celtic, on and off the pitch. He did so much for the club that no one would ever hear about. Nor did he look for plaudits. He just went about his business as a thorough professional. For instance, when I lived in Netherlee, on the south side of Glasgow, he would give me a lift to training every day. Wee Bertie Auld also helped out, too, because I didn't have a car at the time. These little things were all hugely appreciated and done without fuss.

My wife Marina and I used to babysit Billy's girls, Libby, Susan, Paula and Carol and son Martyn. We got on well and he could not have been more helpful in so many ways. I was in his car on the day of the Scottish Cup Final against Airdrie in 1975 when he took me by surprise again.

'This is going to be my last game, Kenny,' he said.

'Not before time!' I joked and then I realised, just like at Ibrox four years earlier, he was deadly serious.

'No, the boots are getting put away after this one. That's it for me.'

Just like that – the end of a glittering era for one of the most famous players in Celtic's history.

In that season leading up to the Hampden Final, Billy, at the age of thirty-five, had hardly been injury prone. He missed only six games, with Roddie MacDonald taking over on five occasions and Frank Welsh on one. But it was obvious he had made up his mind and I don't think for a moment it would have been a decision he had made lightly. He would have discussed it fully with his wife Liz and the family. There will have been major factors, of course. The league had been blown and Celtic finished in third place, which would have hurt Billy after winning the title for nine successive years. All these things would have weighed on his mind.

Remarkably, the press never got a whiff of his retirement, everything was kept inside the dressing room. Naturally, there was no one at Celtic who was going to allow Billy McNeill to go out as a loser. Airdrie may not have been one of the game's most glamorous names, but they could make life difficult for you. They were a big, tough team. We were the holders after beating Dundee United 3–0 the previous season, but we all knew strange things could happen in these sort of high-profile games.

We didn't require reminding of the afternoon when Billy McNeill was injured and missed the League Cup Final against Partick Thistle. His worth to the team was emphasised again when we lost 4–1 after trailing by four goals at the interval. There was no way we were going to allow Airdrie to stage an unexpected and unwanted action replay.

We won 3–1 with two goals from Paul Wilson and a penalty-kick from Pat McCluskey and the only flutter was when Airdrie equalised briefly with a fine effort from Kevin McCann. Billy, as he had done on six other occasions, went up to collect the Scottish Cup. Amazingly, a decade earlier, Billy had scored the winning goal against Dunfermline to lift the same trophy and end the barren years for Celtic. Somehow it seemed so apt that his last action as a player would be to triumph once again in the competition at the national stadium.

That wasn't the end of the surprises, though. Jock Stein didn't give anyone a hint of who would be Billy's successor as Celtic captain. There were a few contenders, of course. Danny McGrain, for a start. We came back from our summer break and Big Jock summoned me. He was never one to mess about, so he cut to the chase.

'I want you to be the new Celtic captain,' he said. My initial reaction was to say something like, 'What an honour, Boss.' And then you realise the big shoes you have to fill.

Somehow, though, it seemed inevitable Billy McNeill would return to Celtic. Although he had businesses to run, it was obvious football – and the only club he had ever played for – were in his blood. After a couple of months at Clyde, he moved to Aberdeen to succeed Ally MacLeod who had taken over as Scotland international manager in time for the 1978 World Cup Finals in Argentina. Big Jock would have charted Billy's progress closely. He had left as Celtic's reserve coach to become boss at Dunfermline and then go to Hibs before coming back to Parkhead in March 1965. So, Billy was taking a similar detour back to the east end of Glasgow.

I had joined Liverpool the year before Billy returned to Celtic, but it would have been interesting to play during his reign as manager. I'm sure he would have had a surprise or two for me!

PETER LATCHFORD

I can still vividly recall the first time I saw Billy McNeill. I was fourteen years old and living with my family in Birmingham. There used to be an evening TV sports programme that wrapped up the football news on ITV. It was hosted by former England international skipper Billy Wright and dealt mainly with what was going on in the Midlands.

However, on the evening of 25 May 1967, it gave us a very brief clip of Celtic winning the European Cup. Honestly, the footage wouldn't even have lasted a full minute. Obviously, the programme editor had never heard of Celtic. To be absolutely honest, I didn't bother too much with Scottish football either. But I watched with interest as this good-looking blond bloke, with a pristine green and white shirt, hardly giving anyone the impression he had just played a game of football, held up this enormous, gleaming trophy in beautiful sunshine. Honestly, he looked as though he had just walked onto a film set.

I thought to myself, 'He must be some player. He's won that Cup all on his own! Where's the rest of the team?' Normally, at trophy presentations, you have the entire line-up, the skipper accepts the award, waves it to the fans and then it gets passed around the other players. But this guy called Billy McNeill, apparently the captain of a Scottish team called Celtic, was being handed the silverware all on his lonesome. There wasn't a mention on the show that the other players were in the dressing room and the fans had invaded the pitch in Lisbon at the full-time whistle that heralded a British club winning the European Cup for the first time. I could never have believed I would one day bump into this character. And when I say 'bump', I mean it literally.

I signed for West Brom as a teenage goalkeeper a couple of

years later – my brothers Bob and Dave had joined Birmingham City – but things weren't quite going according to plan. So, when I got the chance to move to Celtic on loan in February 1975, I decided to give it a go. I didn't reckon I would remain in Scotland for the rest of my life. I thought I might be in Glasgow for a month or so and then return to the Midlands and try to get a regular place in the Hawthorns first team. It didn't quite turn out like that.

I heard the tale Jock Stein had been looking for a new keeper and he had asked his friend Don Revie, the former Leeds United boss, who was by then in charge of England, for a recommendation. I had made a couple of Under-23 appearances for my country, both goalless draws against Poland in 1973 and Wales the following year. Revie must have taken notice of me at some point and put in a good word.

The initial deal was until the end of the season, but, after only a few weeks, Jock Stein wanted to make the move permanent and he paid something like £25,000 for me in July that year – a couple of months after I had played in Billy McNeill's last game, the 1975 Scottish Cup Final against Airdrie when we won 3–1. I had turned out in a bounce game against Clydebank on a Tuesday before I made my debut against Hibs at Easter Road on a cold Saturday afternoon on 22 February. Billy was injured and missed that game with Roddie MacDonald at centre-half. It wasn't the most auspicious of starts for me and we lost 2–1. The press guys, thankfully, were kind to Celtic's new goalie and said some nice things about my overall performance. Jock Stein must have been relatively impressed, too, because I remained in the team for the last twelve games of the campaign, three in the victorious Cup run.

A week after the loss in Edinburgh, I played behind Big Billy for the first time when Partick Thistle provided the opposition. I don't know if anyone realises this, but all goalkeepers hate centre-halves and all centre-halves hate goalkeepers. It's just a football trait. Jock Stein had been a central defender and it was clear he was not a fan of the last line of defence. I'm sure if he could have devised a system that allowed a team to play without a keeper he would have gone with it. Ronnie Simpson told me he believed Jock thought all goalies were a necessary evil. Billy's thought process might have gone along similar lines to his manager.

Okay, I was the new guy in the team, but I couldn't change my style overnight. I liked to try to control my penalty area; those high balls were mine. That's the way I had been played since my schooldays and I had been encouraged to dominate that eighteen-yard box at West Brom. What I hadn't realised was that Billy had attacked those crosses for years. European Cup-winner Ronnie was a class act, but he wasn't that tall for a keeper, so he would often stay on his line and it was Billy's remit to go for everything in the air. He had a free rein in our box when it came to defensive headers. Needless to say, there were a few clashes as I ventured into traffic and Billy was jumping for the same ball. On some occasions, he gave me more grief than the opposing centre-forward!

I used to call him all sorts of names under my breath, but I don't think he understood my Brummie accent. Perhaps that was just as well for me because Billy was a big guy and could certainly look after himself. On that particular afternoon against the team I had been told were nicknamed the Jags, we won 3–2, but I didn't cover myself in glory when I allowed a long-range free-kick to sail over my head for a freak goal. Billy didn't look too impressed with his first close-up view of his club's new shot stopper, but I was bailed out when my mate Kenny Dalglish thumped in the equaliser against Alan Rough and Harry Hood conjured up a fabulous last-minute winner with a twenty-yard free-kick that ripped high into the top corner. Thanks, guys, for sparing my blushes in my debut performance at Parkhead.

There may have been a bit of friction between Billy and I on the pitch, but, off it, he was a perfect gentleman. In fact, he was great to me when I first arrived, but I got to discover he possessed a dodgy sense of humour. Coverage of Scottish football on television across the border was practically non-existent in the sixties. I really didn't know an awful lot about Celtic and there certainly weren't any snippets in the newspapers. As you would expect, there was an overload of news from the local clubs in the Midlands editions and if someone sneezed at West Brom, Birmingham, Wolves, Aston Villa, Coventry or Walsall, then we got to know about it. Whatever was going on in Scotland stayed in Scotland.

So, it was nice to meet a friendly face when I first turned up at the club. Billy put himself out for me and that was much appreciated. I can't say the same about his directional sense. He never helped me out with place names, either. I would look at somewhere called Milngavie and attempt to pronounce it.

'Milngavie,' I would say. 'Is that right, Billy?'

He would smile and nod, 'Yeah, Peter, spot on.' How was a stranger in Scotland expected to call it 'Mullguy'? After all these years, I still don't get it. When I was looking for a place to stay, I would locate an address and ask Billy for the quickest route so I could go and view it. Very helpfully, he would map it out for me. I would set off for Bishopbriggs and end up in Coatbridge or Greenock. Alas, there was no such thing as satnav back then and I had to take the word of my captain.

I would come in for training the following morning to be greeted with, 'Did you find East Kilbride okay, Peter?'

'Strangest thing, Billy,' I would reply, 'no, but I did end up in a place called Cambuslang.' Through it all, he kept a straight face.

'Don't know how that could happen, Peter, I thought my instructions were spot on.'

By the time I found a place to settle down, I had blown a fortune on petrol.

It was marvellous to spend some time, however briefly, on the pitch with such a legendary footballer. It didn't take me long to catch up with the history of Celtic Football Club, their heritage, their great managers and players and, of course, their truly magnificent supporters. It was an honour to bump off Big Billy a few times in his last game at Hampden when he went out in style with a Scottish Cup triumph. Airdrie were a big, determined team and we had to work hard to win 3–1 that afternoon. No one in Celtic's colours that day would have given their skipper anything less than 100 per cent for him and the club. The man deserved to go out as a winner.

Three years later he was back as our manager. It was such a quick turnaround. I remember his first day at training following his return. He gathered the players around him at Barrowfield. John Clark, his assistant manager, was standing to his left and Danny McGrain was on his right. Big Billy looked at me, Danny and a couple of other players he played alongside.

'This might be difficult for a few of you,' he said, 'but I'm your boss now. I'm not your teammate, I'm your manager. We've got to get this sorted out right from the start. You now address me as boss, manager, gaffer or even Mr McNeill.'

Billy stood there, at pains to make this point. He went over it a couple of times to drive home the message. No one was to be left in any confusion about his title.

After what felt about half-an-hour of this message getting drummed into the players, the manager looked around his players, nodded and said, 'Right, anyone got any questions?' Danny piped up, 'No, I think you said everything that was needed to be said, Billy.'

Our new boss was struck dumb as the rest of the players fell about in gales of laughter. Danny just didn't get the joke. I know he will tell this story a bit differently, but this is my memory of that moment and I'm sticking by it. Danny, by the way, is a tremendous unconscious comedian and I mean that in a nice way. He'll say something and crack me up and he hasn't a clue why I think it is so hilarious. Having said that, he was one helluva right-back and, at his peak, certainly one of the best, if not *the* best, in the world.

You may be interested to know I did eventually catch up with the entire footage of Celtic winning the European Cup in Lisbon. And, yes, Billy McNeill was the master of all he surveyed that evening. I will always remember that first glimpse of the great man. Quite unforgettable.

HARRY HOOD

I know for a fact Jock Stein never even hinted to any of his Celtic players to go out and injure a member of the opposition. However, the club's legendary manager did let his players know that he expected them to win their tackles and never shirk a challenge. 'Win your personal battle and the team will win the war,' he said often enough as he sent his troops into action.

I think Billy McNeill must have taken the instruction from his boss to heart on 1 April 1967 when Celtic were due to take on little Clyde in the semi-final of the Scottish Cup. Back then, I was at the part-time Shawfield outfit and, as you would expect, getting to the last four of the national competition was a real thrill for all of us. I wanted to savour the occasion. We were seen as upstarts and mere cannon fodder before our opponents booked their place at Hampden later in the month en route to winning the silverware. Who could blame anyone for writing us off?

The bookies had us at 5/1. Celtic had already won the League Cup, were top of the league, were piling up impressive results on a weekly basis and, on top of all that, were in the European Cup semi-finals.

As we are all aware now, they were on their way to a historic campaign, but Clyde hoped to produce a shock result when we took the field that day. We could only hope Big Billy and his mates might take their eye off the ball. I had played against them in January at Parkhead and we were doing reasonably well to be drawing 1–1 at the interval after Joe Gilroy had wiped out an early strike from Stevie Chalmers. Charlie Gallagher gave Celtic the advantage again when he scored ten minutes or so after the turnaround, but we were still in the game up until the seventy-second minute. Then we were hit by a whirlwind and conceded three goals in as many minutes with Chalmers, Tommy Gemmell and Bobby Lennox on target. So, we had been warned what to expect at the national stadium three months later.

There was the usual banter with Big Billy leading up to the match; we were already friends and our families were close. Any thoughts of an old pal's act by my chum in the heat of a semi-final went out the window after something like seven minutes! We were involved in a collision as we went for the ball and I was left writhing on the pitch in agony. I can tell you Billy was a big item. I thought, 'Wow! If Billy can hit a mate like that, how does he treat the enemy?'

I was in a fair bit of pain and then I realised blood was seeping through my boot. I had to have nine stitches inserted in the wound at half-time. The manager, Davie White, who later became boss at Rangers, asked me if I wanted to come off. Was he joking? I'm playing in a Scottish Cup semi-final and I don't know if I would ever get the opportunity to be involved in such a big game again. There was no way I was sitting on the sidelines for the second half, especially with the score at 0–0 at half-time.

That's the way it ended, too, which was a fair talking point among those who had given odds on us bothering to turn up at Hampden. That meant a replay the following Wednesday, but there would be no appearance from yours truly, Big Billy's tackle had made sure of that. I could hardly walk and there was no way I could kick a ball. So, when the second game rolled around, I was in the stand. This time Celtic made no mistake and won 2–0 with early goals from Bobby Lennox and Bertie Auld. A couple of years later, Bobby, Bertie and Big Billy were my teammates when I joined Celtic in a £40,000 deal, which was a fair amount of money in 1969. Funnily enough, I never mentioned our semi-final clash to my new skipper.

I have to say Billy went out of his way right at the start to make me feel welcome at Celtic. I think he saw that as one of his duties as club captain. I really appreciated him putting himself out on my behalf. Immediately, I realised what he meant to Celtic and what Celtic meant to him. Billy was in charge of the dressing room; he was the buffer between Jock Stein and the players. I didn't envy him the role. Let's face it, who wants to be put in charge of around twenty adolescents?

More often than not, if someone had a problem they would talk it over with Billy. Again, he accepted that as part and parcel of him being the team leader. He was the main reason for the great camaraderie that existed among the players at the time. Billy McNeill was a lot more than just an exceptional centre-half.

I was quite quiet in a dressing room, which was maybe just as well because I would have required a loud hailer to be heard above some of my Celtic teammates. Bertie Auld and Tommy Gemmell weren't exactly shy and retiring. When things got a little rowdy, Billy would say, 'Right, lads, that's enough of that.' It would get the job done and sanity would be restored. As I found out rather painfully in that semi-final, Billy was a fierce competitor, but he was a first-class teammate out on the field when the going got tough.

He was tall, had the chest jutting out and looked every inch the team's inspirational captain and some people may have misconstrued that as arrogance. They would be completely wrong in thinking along those lines. Billy McNeill was never conceited or full of himself; he was far too well grounded for that sort of egotistical outlook. What I would say is he was confident. And, believe me, that is a necessary commodity playing in front of many thousands every matchday for one of the most famous teams in the world. Big Jock would have us well prepared for a game and say all the right things before kick-off. After that, Big Billy took over when we were out on the pitch. He was a thorough professional and it was a joy to play alongside him.

Actually, I could have been his teammate at Celtic about five years earlier than I did. I came into the Clyde team for the first time around in 1962 at the age of eighteen. I was enjoying my football and there were tales that Celtic – remember this was before Jock Stein – liked what they saw. They did make a move and I turned them down. Why? Money. That's the simple and honest answer. I was part-time at Shawfield while working as a sales rep. I was picking up £26 per week. Celtic offered me twenty quid and I was informed there would be no signing-on fee. Six pounds was a fair amount of cash back then and I couldn't afford to take the drop. So, I stayed at Clyde and eventually moved to Sunderland where my time was ravaged by injuries. I missed an entire season with a double hernia.

Nine months after my move to the Wearside outfit, I played in a pre-season friendly against Big Billy and Celtic in August 1965. Celtic had won the Scottish Cup at the end of the previous campaign and everyone was excited about a new campaign. There was a good turn-out at the old Roker Park ground and it was estimated something like 10,000 Celtic fans were in the ground. I think the crowd was given as something in the region of 35,000 and it certainly looked as though there were more than half the supporters wearing green and white colours that afternoon.

It was also the Sunderland debut of Jim Baxter, Billy's old Rangers mate. As I would later discover, the Celtic captain never did his pals any favours. He was superb that day and John Hughes – 'Big Yogi' to the Hoops followers – was unstoppable. He ran amok and scored two goals as we were turned over 5–0. I was beginning to query the wisdom of my choice of football clubs. I returned to Shawfield in 1966 and came back onto Celtic's radar in 1969 when Jock shelled out his biggest-ever fee at the time to persuade me to make the short trip to Parkhead. They made it worth my while on that occasion.

That's when I really got to know and appreciate the true values of Billy McNeill. The supporters would see this immaculate player go through his defensive routine during a game while adding a crucial goal or two along the way, but there was another Billy McNeill away from the spectators and the cameras. And that was the guy who always made sure new players to the club were given a warm welcome. He made me feel immediately at home at Parkhead. In my time there, Billy made himself available to greet every new arrival.

Maybe it's a small point, but I believe it simply underlines one of the many qualities of Billy McNeill.

8

Going to the Dogs

Billy McNeill wondered why his Clyde players had suddenly stopped training midway through a routine at Shawfield. One minute, they were exercising, following his instructions and the next they were standing absolutely still, rooted to the spot and looking for all the world like exhibits at Madame Tussauds.

As part-timers, McNeill could only work with his playing staff on the evenings of Monday, Wednesday and Thursday. The first two sessions had gone well without a hitch as the manager got to know his players and they were introduced to his methods. This was Thursday, though, and things were different at the ground on this particular night. Robert Harvey, a thoughtful midfielder, recalled, 'Obviously, no one had told Big Billy Thursday was a greyhound racing night. The dog track would be open for business later that evening. Before that, though, he wanted to put us through our paces.

'Then, midway through training, there came the announcement, *"Can all players stop moving as a dog trial is about to start?"* We were used to it, of course, but clearly no one had tipped off our new manager. If you moved during a trial, the greyhounds would chase you. They would see movement and go for it. As soon as the announcement came over the tannoy, we remained stock still. Billy stood looking at us, just a bit baffled by our actions or, more accurately, inactions. Then the hare was released, whizzed around the dog track and the greyhounds chased after it. A few minutes later, the trial was over, it was safe for us to move again and we resumed training. Welcome to Shawfield, Mr McNeill, and the world of part-time football. It must have felt like light years away from what he had been used to at Celtic.

'And goodness only knows what he thought during his first game in charge, a league match against Alloa at Shawfield. It was being played on the same day as the Grand National at Aintree. The ball went onto the dog track for a throw-in to Clyde and Arthur Grant, a very under-rated winger, had to climb over a fence as he went to retrieve it to take the shy. As Arthur picked up the ball, there was an announcement over the tannoy, *"Red Rum has just won the National"*. Arthur obviously had a few quid on the horse. "Ya beauty!" he exclaimed and, in his excitement, made a mess of the shy and the referee awarded a foul throw to our opponents. This was right in front of the home dugout where Billy McNeill was sitting. He looked a little mystified.'

Billy McNeill had been out of football since ending his playing days in the 3–1 Scottish Cup Final triumph over Airdrie on 3 May 1975. However, no one was overly surprised when he returned to the game, although his choice of team may have raised a few eyebrows. McNeill saw it this way, 'Initially after I quit playing, I quite enjoyed the freedom of concentrating on my various business interests and I also aspired to become a TV and radio pundit as spectating at matches struck me as being somewhat less stressful than calling the shots from the touchline. But my time with the Celtic Bhoys' Club had whetted my appetite for a more direct involvement in the game, so, when Willie Dunne, the Clyde chairman, asked if I would be interested in managing his club, it seemed like a good idea.

'Frankly, some of my friends thought I was mad to take on such a challenge, because Clyde didn't have a penny to their name, but I knew the Dunne family well and I also realised that I would gain valuable experience of how the other side of football operated from a board of directors who were both knowledgeable and fair-minded. I also came into contact with Steve Archibald for the first time. I could see straight away Steve had the potential to make it big and his subsequent success with Aberdeen, Tottenham Hotspur and Barcelona proved me right.

'But Steve was very nearly anonymous when Clyde were drawn against Celtic in the Glasgow Cup. Because of a colour clash, I was forced to ask Umbro to rush through a fresh set of strips, but when they arrived one jersey was minus its number, so I had to dash to a local sports shop to buy the figure eight. My wife was kind enough to get out her needle and thread and Archibald was none the wiser, but, knowing Steve, he would not have been best pleased had he taken the field as the only player without a number.'

Harvey, who played in the game, which Celtic won 4–2, recalled, 'We put in a good performance that afternoon and I believe that was the game where Steve Archibald showed he had the quality to step up a level. He really got stuck in and looked a class act. In fact, it was 2–2 with about seven minutes to go and Celtic were toiling a little. Then Jock Stein changed things when he put on substitute Johannes Edvaldsson for Andy Lynch, moved Tommy Burns to left-back and brought Kenny Dalglish into midfield. Edvaldsson could play at centre-half or centre-forward and, on this occasion, the Celtic manager pushed him right up front. He was involved in the two goals that flattened us when he set up Kenny and then Brian McLaughlin.'

Archibald reflected, 'Yes, I played okay that day. I was in the middle of the park and got a lot of the ball. I wouldn't say I bossed the game or anything like that, but I would like to think I contributed to our cause. Even in such a short space of time, Billy McNeill had raised our levels of awareness of what could be achieved, individually and collectively. I had always trained hard and I worked on my fitness.

'Dom Sullivan, who went on to have a good career with Aberdeen and Celtic, was at the club when I arrived and he was the guy who always led from the front. In training, he was the fittest bloke around. It became my target to keep up with him. When we went running, Dom was always the leader of the pack. I reckoned it was a test for me to try to keep pace with him. And that's what I did. If Dom could do it, so could I, that was my belief.'

McNeill's sojourn at Shawfield didn't last too long. Two months later, he received a phone call from Jock Stein. He was on his way to Aberdeen.

STEVE ARCHIBALD

The first time I clapped eyes on Billy McNeill I realised I was in the company of someone special, even if the surroundings weren't quite in keeping with the moment, which will be etched in my memory for all time.

I'll never forget the day in April 1977 when Billy turned up at Shawfield after taking over as manager of Clyde. There was this absolute soccer legend standing in our scruffy, wee dressing room introducing himself and talking to the assembled players, many, if not all, in total awe.

The first Briton to hold the European Cup in his hands as captain of that great Celtic team in 1967 was chatting away to us and it was a magical experience for all the players, especially me as a part-timer at the age of twenty wondering what the future in the game held in store. It was fantastic to have someone that famous so close to you.

Billy always had that aura and presence about him, the straight back and the chest puffed out. I never once saw him slouch. He could simply be walking around Shawfield during training or going about his business, but he was always ramrod stiff. It made you proud to be in his company, he made you feel somehow significant just to be around him.

I will never forget what he did for me at Clyde and, later on, Aberdeen. I was disappointed on the day he left Clyde to take over at Pittodrie and succeed Ally MacLeod. No one at the club wanted to see him leave, he had such an uplifting and dignified air about him and that got through to everyone on the staff. Billy McNeill had a magnetism about him. He was always immaculate, shirt and tie, well-pressed suit, polished shoes. He was the epitome of professionalism and we all benefited from that, even if it was for an all-too-brief interlude.

At the time he said his farewells, I had no idea what was going to happen for me. I didn't have an inkling Billy would come back to Clyde to pay £25,000 – a lot of money for my old club – and take me to Aberdeen in January 1978. The day before the deal, Craig Brown, his successor at Shawfield, told me to get ready to travel up north. It appeared the transfer had just about been done and dusted and all that was required was my signature on the contract. There was never going to be the remotest chance I would say 'no' to Billy McNeill.

That move transformed my life and my career. I was delighted he had that much faith in me and it matched my complete trust in him. He was a top-notch manager and he helped me make the transformation from part-time to full-time. I appreciated he would sit down with me every now and again and say all the right things. He was a marvellous man-motivator. He put me on the right road in those little moments he took time off to ask me how things were going, was I settling into the area, all that sort of stuff.

There were more experienced players at Aberdeen, Scottish internationals such as Willie Miller, Joe Harper and Bobby Clark among them, but they gave Billy the same total respect he had received from the lads at Clyde. I always called him 'Boss', I would never have thought about addressing him as Billy. One quick glimpse at what he had achieved in the game told you he deserved the respect that came his way.

Later in my career, I was fortunate enough to be brought into the Scotland international set-up when Jock Stein, Billy's former Celtic boss, was in charge. Immediately I was struck at how similar Jock and Billy were in their methods and man-management skills.

It was obvious Billy had picked up a hint or two from Big Jock, especially in one-on-one situations. Billy would take you to the side and say, 'We're playing so-and-so on Saturday and they've got such-and-such a player. You're a lot better than him, go and show everyone your qualities.' So, I wasn't in the least bit surprised when I was pulled aside by Big Jock before my international debut against Portugal at Hampden in March 1980.

It was a crucial European Championship qualifier and a must-win situation. 'You're in the team tonight because you are the best at what you do,' encouraged Big Jock. I could have been listening to Billy McNeill! It must have worked – I scored my first goal for my country and we won 4–1.

I am aware Billy said some extremely kind things about me during our four months together at Pittodrie and, trust me, they are reciprocated. He set me up; his enthusiasm for being a winner was addictive and once again he left far too early in our careers. I was beginning to wonder if I was a jinx!

Billy McNeill never once disappointed me. I was sad when he left Pittodrie to go to Celtic, but you could say that was always going to be his destiny. Billy McNeill and Celtic are synonymous with one another.

And I'm sure that's how The Boss would have wanted it.

CRAIG BROWN

By his own admission, one of Billy McNeill's best-ever signings was Steve Archibald. Billy was aware of the player's qualities during his brief stint at Clyde before moving to Aberdeen in the summer of 1977. I took over from my long-time friend at Shawfield and it wasn't long before McNeill and Archibald were reunited at Pittodrie. But, as ever, there is a story behind any transfer. And Billy almost lost out on Archibald for the most bizarre reason.

I had a spell as assistant manager at Motherwell in 1974 before accepting the Clyde position. Very quickly, I got to know how a part-time club works. I was combining my duties as a lecturer at Craigie College in Ayrshire while running the Rutherglen side and I thought we were doing quite well in the first few months of my tenure. We were top of the old Second Division and I was hopeful of promotion. Then along came a couple of directors who informed me the club was facing financial struggles and I would have to sell one of my best players. There was little point in protesting, I knew exactly what I was getting into when I agreed to follow Billy.

My two best players were Steve Archibald and Joe Ward. Steve was a wonderfully talented and exceptionally versatile player. I knew I could trust him in any position in the team and he wouldn't let me down. He even played in goal against Queen's Park at Hampden when goalkeeper John Arroll sustained a broken leg. Billy had played him as sweeper and in midfield and he looked a natural in both positions. I didn't want to lose a player of his calibre, but I reckoned he might be the best bet to bring in the much-needed money.

Joe Ward was a big, strong centre-forward who was also well equipped to make the step up a couple of divisions. Every team needs a goal scorer and Joe was our main threat. Albeit reluctantly, I got in touch with every single manager in the Premier Division to let them know our situation. Basically, they could have their pick so long as they had the cash to back their interest. Dundee United boss Jim McLean watched Steve in a league game against Raith Rovers and was clearly unimpressed.

'He'll never be a player,' was his verdict. Alex Stuart, manager of Ayr United, didn't quite agree with the Tannadice gaffer and liked the look of Archibald. Unfortunately, they didn't have the sort of cash we required and I told the directors we might have to do some bartering with the Somerset Park side. Alex Stuart's team was struggling at the time in the top flight and a player of Steve's undoubted quality would have given them a huge boost.

The Ayr United boss assured me his club could only go to £15,000 for my player and they would offer one of their squad in part-exchange. Once again, I relayed the message to the Clyde board. They had hoped for something in the region of £25,000, but there was no way the Ayrshire club could raise that amount.

I was a little surprised Billy McNeill did not come in straight away for Archibald. I knew he rated the player, but he had only been at Pittodrie for five or six months, so, possibly, he was being fair to the playing staff he had inherited from Ally MacLeod. In any case, he had brought in Gordon Strachan from Dundee in November for a sizeable fee with midfield player Jim Shirra added to the deal. Whatever the reason, Billy did not come in with an offer for Steve at that stage.

So, that left us with Ayr United, the offer of a £15,000 cheque and A. N. Other. The Clyde board decided to accept the money and it was left to me to haggle with Alex Stuart for the player who would be the makeweight in the switch. I always had a high regard for Jim McSherry, a busy, hard-working midfielder who had the happy knack of being able to contribute a goal or two.

Everything looked set for Steve to go to Somerset Park and show what he could do in the Premier Division and for McSherry to move to us. And that is where fate stepped in to scupper the deal. When the proposed transfer was put to McSherry, he made it clear he wouldn't be part of any such transaction. 'I'm no' playing at a dog track,' was how he put it rather forcibly and it was back to the drawing board for me.

Intermittently, I had kept in touch with Billy and at the turn of the year, with the Dons going well in the league, he made contact to see if the situation at Clyde had changed. I told him it was still exactly as it had been a couple of months earlier; the club was still in need of money and all of my players were for sale.

'Okay,' he said, 'I'll give you £20,000 for Steve Archibald.' I wasn't having that and I told him, 'You know he is worth more than that, Billy. Make it £25,000 and you could have a deal.' He told me he would discuss it with Dick Donald, his very likeable chairman at Aberdeen. I updated my directors and you could sense the relief a cheque of that amount could do for everyone connected with the club. Billy got back to me and we had a handshake over the phone. Everyone was a winner in this move. Clyde received a fair fee for their player, Billy was delighted with his acquisition and, as you would expect, Steve didn't need too much persuasion to give up his job as a car mechanic to go full-time at Pittodrie.

On the day of the transfer, I recall the weather was dreadful with heavy snows and there was no way Steve could drive north to go through the signing formalities. I made sure he was on a train heading for Aberdeen before anyone changed their mind. I was happy for Steve because he had been a thorough professional at Clyde and worked hard in training. I had every confidence he would be a success at his new club, but I couldn't have predicted him joining Barcelona as Diego Maradona's replacement in 1984. That would have been a bit of a stretch.

And whatever happened to Joe Ward? He moved to Aston Villa in 1979, but made a quick return to Scotland with Hibs and then had a brief stint at Jim McLean's Dundee United. He moved down the leagues after that.

I was delighted Billy had a relatively successful season at Pittodrie, second in the league and runner-up in the Scottish Cup wasn't at all bad for someone in their thirties in his first full season as a manager. I wasn't one bit surprised, either, when Billy gave it all up when he got the call from Celtic a year later. Billy and Celtic were meant to be together. In fact, I came close to joining Billy at Celtic after we had played alongside each other in the Scottish Schoolboys' side. You took one look at this poised and assured centre-half and knew he was destined for great things in the game. The only club he ever talked about was Celtic, no other team mattered to Billy.

He lived in Belshill when I was in Hamilton and we would go into training together on the number 64 bus. A lot of clubs looked at Billy as a youngster, but they were wasting their time. Simply put, he was Celtic mad. We played together in the Scotland Under-18 side against our England counterparts at Parkhead and we won 3–0. We had a very useful team with players such as Billy Little (Aberdeen), Dave Hilley (Third Lanark) and Brian McIlroy (Rangers) in the ranks.

As things turned out, Billy did sign full-time for his beloved Celtic after a short stint in the Juniors with Blantyre Vics. I headed across the Clyde to sign for Rangers from Coltness United. I injured my knee and it didn't work out for me at Ibrox, but Bob Shankly signed me for Dundee in 1960. Bob, brother of Liverpool legend Bill, liked my tenacious style and soon gave me a role in the first team to 'sort out' opposing players who could be troublesome on match day. That became my strength. My major asset was to identify the opposition's key man and make sure he didn't make a telling contribution to proceedings for the next ninety minutes.

I recall playing against Celtic's classy Willie Fernie and I was told to get out there and keep him quiet. Not the most flamboyant role within a team's structure, but I was okay with the manager's instructions as long as it was for the good of the team and we got a reasonable result.

I also remember playing against Bobby Lennox when he made his debut for Celtic in March 1962. I was in the old left-half position that afternoon in the east end of Glasgow and I seem to recall Bobby receiving a smashed nose during his first game. We led 1–0 with ten minutes to go when Celtic equalised through Frank Brogan and then a tall, fresh-faced centre-half scored the winner shortly afterwards. Billy McNeill timed his run from about twenty yards to absolute perfection and just took off to get his head to a corner-kick and send the ball past our keeper Pat Liney.

Dundee won the First Division title that season and we had some excellent players such as Alan Gilzean, Ian Ure, Bobby Wishart, Gordon Smith, Andy Penman, Alec Hamilton, Alan Cousin and the like. I made nine appearances and qualified for a medal. However, as Big Billy's star continued to rise at a meteoric rate, I was bedevilled by persistent knee injuries. I had two years at Falkirk and, following five operations, was forced to quit at the age of twenty-seven in 1967, the year my former Scotland Youth teammate helped Celtic win the European Cup and every other competition they entered in a memorable season.

My managerial path led me to the Scotland international team, first as caretaker boss for games against Italy and Malta in 1993 and then as my own man. One of the most onerous and exacting tasks was putting a squad together, especially for World Cup and European Championship Finals. You knew you would have to disappoint some players and, naturally, that was never anything to which I looked forward with any great enthusiasm. However, it was part of my job to select the best players for the task in front of us. I always tried to do this face to face instead of by phone, text or letter. No such meeting would have taken place with Billy McNeill. At the peak of his powers, the Celtic captain would have been one of my first picks. Which country in the world could have afforded to overlook such quality? I note he was capped a mere twenty-nine times during his lengthy career. If I had been around at the time, I think it is safe to say he would have added to that total.

I have a lot of admiration for that man, even if Billy never let me forget he thought I was 'one of the dirtiest players in football'. Mind you, he said it with a smile.

9

Nearly Man in the North East

It takes a big man to confess to an error. It takes an even bigger man to acknowledge a monumental blunder. Billy McNeill held his hands up following his one year at Pittodrie in the 1977/78 season.

'I admit to making a catastrophic mistake in not signing Steve Archibald straight away when I became manager of Aberdeen,' he remarked with refreshing honesty. 'Had I done so, I believe we would have won the Scottish Cup and maybe the Premier Division title.

'Steve was this very interesting character who could play centre-half, left midfield, outside-right or centre-forward. I was so impressed, in fact, that when Jock Stein asked if we had any players at Clyde capable of doing a decent job for Celtic, I urged him to sign Archibald. I knew Clyde were in desperate need of funds and had no hesitation in recommending Archibald. I admitted that I wasn't sure what the player's best position was, but Jock had already seen him play and wasn't entirely convinced. I also got it wrong.

'I was embarrassed at having left Clyde so early and, as a consequence of my discomfort, I delayed making a move for Archibald. By the time I did pluck up courage to approach Clyde about signing him, he was already Cup-tied. If only I had made my move for Archibald the moment I took over at Pittodrie. I'm convinced he would have made the difference between us finishing second to Rangers and achieving the double.'

Considering he was still wearing managerial L-plates, McNeill's solitary season at the Dons can only be viewed as a success. They missed out on the championship by two points to Jock Wallace's Ibrox side. They actually beat Rangers in three of their four Premier Division confrontations, but four draws, two apiece, against Clydebank and Ayr United cost them dearly. Interestingly, they were three places higher than Celtic in the Premier Division final placings and seventeen points better off. In the Scottish Cup, they toppled 2–1 to Wallace's side in the Cup Final at the national stadium where their performance was far removed from doing themselves justice.

The Cup Final was played on 6 May – twenty-two days later Billy McNeill was installed as Celtic manager, succeeding his mentor, Jock Stein.

It had been the Celtic legend who had instigated McNeill's move to Aberdeen a year beforehand. McNeill said, 'I received a telephone call from Jock Stein one day. "How do you fancy the Aberdeen job?" he enquired. It didn't take me long to say yes. Such a move represented rapid promotion for someone whose experience in management was so limited.'

McNeill agreed to meet Dons chairman Dick Donald at the Wheel Inn at Scone in Perthshire for initial talks. He went on, 'It turned out to be a relatively short meeting because Dick preferred to come straight to the point. It was only when I returned home that it dawned on me that I hadn't even asked what sort of salary

I would be on or the duration of any contract. Later, when I breached the subject, there was no need to haggle. The chairman told me the salary was £10,000 a year and added, "As far as the contract is concerned, you can have what you want, Billy. Three or five years – the choice is yours." Not surprisingly, we struck up an instant rapport and our relationship remained warm until the day Dick died in 1993. I never did sign a contract, largely because I had complete trust in the man who had considered me a worthy successor to Ally MacLeod.'

McNeill, though, accepted it was time to return to his spiritual home when the call went out. 'I simply couldn't say no. Jock Stein again acted as the middle man and when Dick Donald was made aware of Celtic's approach, he realised that the pull of a return to Celtic Park would be too much for me to resist and didn't even try to persuade me to stay at Pittodrie.'

It was only later McNeill discovered the reason the Aberdeen chief had stepped aside. 'I was told he had said to a good friend, "Billy has been a Celtic man all his life and he might never get another chance to manage the club. He is entitled to go back to Celtic and I am not going to try to stop him".'

Wisely, Dick Donald realised it was futile to stand in the way of fate.

GORDON STRACHAN

My last game for Dundee was on 26 October 1977 when we were well and truly thumped 6–0 by Queen of the South in a League Cup-tie at Dumfries. A few days later, Billy McNeill signed me for Aberdeen. I will be forever grateful he took a chance on me. I also owe a debt of gratitude to Mike Jackson, who was the Palmerston side's manager that fateful night.

Tommy Gemmell was boss of the Dens Park club at the time and, thankfully, he had kept in touch with his fellow-Lisbon Lion after both their playing days had ended. Big Tam, by his own admission, had been told by Dundee chairman Ian Gellatly that the club urgently required £50,000 or the banks would close the gates. The club was on the brink of financial upheaval and the manager knew he would be forced to sell one of his players. I realised he rated me highly – he had made me captain at the age of nineteen so that might tell you something – and he would have known Billy McNeill was looking for players as he wanted to put his stamp on the Dons squad he had inherited from Ally MacLeod in the summer of 1977.

Big Tam later told me he had put in a call to his Celtic pal to tell him of Dundee's perilous situation. He also told Billy, 'We need £50,000 to stay afloat. I know you like the look of Gordon Strachan, but you're not getting him for that kind of money. We both know he is worth a lot more than that. You're a friend, but you're not getting bargains at this club.'

The matter could have ended there and then. However, according to Big Tam, Billy asked for time to think about it. The Aberdeen manager was reminded by his chum that time was not an ally of Dundee Football Club and he would need an answer within twenty-four hours. Billy promised to get back to him and, thankfully, he was as good as his word. However, there was a problem – Aberdeen would only go to £50,000 for me and Big Tam didn't want to let me go at that price.

The Celtic legends put their heads together as they searched for a compromise. Big Tam liked the look of Jim Shirra, a midfield player who wasn't getting a regular game at Pittodrie. Dundee were in the First Division back then and it wasn't exactly an arena that welcomed ball-playing artistes. Shirra was a terrier in the middle of the park and Big Tam admitted he enjoyed 'the way he snapped into tackles'. Would Billy be prepared to part with Shirra to make up the deal? Billy rated his player in the £35,000 bracket, so, in effect, he would be getting me in a deal worth £85,000. Billy talked to his board and I was delighted when I received a call from him shortly afterwards to tell me everything had been given the go-ahead.

I wasn't aware of it, but Mike Jackson was a close friend of Billy since their early days at Parkhead. On the evening we were totally embarrassed in Dumfries, Aberdeen beat Rangers 3–1 at Pittodrie in the competition, so there was no scope for Billy to look at me in person. He telephoned Mike the following day to enquire how I had performed. Let's face it, the Dons boss would have been forgiven for believing there was no one in a Dundee strip against Queen of the South who could have possibly done a turn for his team. Mike was extremely kind in his assessment of my display, I'm glad to say. He informed Billy I had been the only Dundee player who had kept going while his team were basically running amok. Mike thought I was worth a risk and said so.

Actually, that was my normal game. It was always alien to me to chuck it when things weren't going my way. It just made me more determined to try to turn things around. I could be in a team that was losing 3–0, 4–0, 5–0 or, indeed, 6–0, but I would still be going flat out. Throw in the towel? Never! As a matter of fact, I've often talked about that game in Dumfries to motivate players and to make sure their heads don't go down when they're on the receiving end. My advice is always, 'Get those sleeves rolled up and get out there and do something about it.'

The meeting with Billy went well and there were no problems with the contract negotiations. I wish I could say I hit the ground running at Pittodrie, but, unfortunately, that was far from being the case. I struggled to find my form at my new club. I wasn't helped by the fact I sustained a nasty ankle injury in training even before I had kicked a ball for the first team.

I had only been married to Lesley for about five months when the transfer went through and we had to make an adjustment in our lives. We looked for a new home in Aberdeen we liked and could afford and that led to time living in a hotel. It wasn't ideal for a new player, at the age of twenty, who wanted to show his new manager he was well worth the money he had spent on him. The more I tried, the more I struggled. I felt like the poor guy in quicksand – the more you thrashed around, the quicker you would sink.

Billy wasn't slow to give me a rollicking, either. He had paid good money for me and he wanted a return. I understood that. He could rip into you, but, listen, that never harmed me. I was aware he wasn't criticising me – or anyone else, for that matter – because he liked the sound of his own voice. Simply put, he wanted what was most beneficial for me and the team. That made a lot of sense to me, so I didn't take anything personally.

Billy made it abundantly clear that the only thing that mattered to him was winning; second best would not be tolerated. If you take his couple of months with Clyde out of the equation, Billy was a young manager trying to prove himself with a club in the top league in basically his first full season. He had been used to triumphs, titles, cups, glory and adulation at Celtic as a player and there can be little doubt that a lot of Jock Stein's influence had got through to him. He was out to prove himself and he let everyone know it.

I remember coming on as a substitute in a game against Partick Thistle at Firhill shortly after I had signed. The team had been toiling and Billy hoped I might have had an immediate impact. So, there I am on the right wing with no one near me as the ball is rolled in my direction. I've already got my head up looking for a teammate who is in a dangerous area where I can drop in a cross or slide in a pass. I took my eye off the ball and the bloody thing trundled under my foot and out of play. I'll let you fill in the blanks from the bellows that came from the Aberdeen dugout at that precise moment. I think you can take it that none of them were complimentary. The decibel level rose rather sharply for a few seconds in the west end of Glasgow.

I recall another incident when Billy got his view across rather pointedly. The Scottish Football Writers Association had initiated a Player of the Year award in 1965 and, ironically, Billy won the accolade. In my first season at Aberdeen, the Scottish Professional Footballers' Association decided to follow suit and have its own ceremony. Naturally, you couldn't vote for a player from your own team, so I sat down with my colleagues as we sifted through candidates we thought were worthy of the honour. We talked it through, weighed up the pros and cons, strengths and weaknesses and so on. Eventually, we decided on who should get the vote from Aberdeen.

Billy got to hear the name of the individual. He came into the dressing room. 'You really think this guy is the best player in Scotland?' he asked, somewhat menacingly. It was fairly obvious he wasn't quite in sync with the evaluation process of his playing staff. 'Anyone who picks this character won't be playing on Saturday.' We knew he wasn't joking, our manager was deadly earnest. I believe we had a rethink.

Back on the football pitch, I wanted to show Billy I was worth the money he had paid for me. Genuinely, I was desperate to do well for both our sakes. I was in and out of the team, but I played in all our Scottish Cup-ties up to the semi-final. Billy had signed Steve Archibald from Clyde a couple of months after he bought me. Steve had played for the Shawfield side in the competition and that made him ineligible, so I got the nod for Cup-ties. I was a substitute when we beat Partick Thistle 4–2 in the semi-final to book a place in the Final against Rangers. Naturally, I hoped to be involved on the big day, but the nearest I got to the pitch that 6 May afternoon was the Hampden stand.

Billy named his team following a training session the day before the big game and I wasn't included. I was disappointed, but, of course, you have to go with your manager's decision, although that logic doesn't help at the time of such an announcement. It was an unfortunate day for the Dons as they lost 2–1 to end Billy's first season empty-handed. It also turned out to be his last season as he took over from the great Jock Stein at Celtic that summer.

Alex Ferguson moved in at the Dons and that was an experience, too. I recall a game against Billy's Celtic at Pittodrie on Saturday, 27 December 1980. Both teams were battling it out at the top of the league. We won 4–1 and really turned it on that afternoon. Central defenders Alex McLeish and Willie Miller both scored following set-pieces from me to give us a two-goal advantage at the interval. Any hopes of Celtic salvaging something were blown away a minute into the second-half when Walker McCall scored a third. I made it 4–0 with a penalty-kick before Charlie Nicholas got a consolation effort.

It was a bit of a landslide victory and Billy must have been hurting like hell. I knew how he reacted to a defeat and this would have been a sore one for him. I played quite well, even if I do say so myself, and one particularly well-informed newspaper reporter noted, 'Gordon Strachan was virtually unplayable and gave a majestic performance.' Who am I to argue with that assessment?

I passed Billy on the touchline as I made my way to the tunnel at the far end of the ground. He must have been fairly distraught, but he managed a wan smile and said to me, 'You played not too badly, wee man'. I knew if I hung around long enough, I might get a compliment from Billy at Pittodrie!

Underlining the benevolent qualities of Billy, and he has many, he turned up at my house with his wife Liz later that evening. I think he was spending the weekend with friends they had met when he lived in Stonehaven during his year at Aberdeen. My son Gavin had just turned two four days earlier and the McNeills took the trouble to come over to my place with a gift for the kid. That is class, my friends.

As our careers developed, I moved to Manchester United in 1984, a year after Billy had joined Manchester City following his departure from Celtic. He must have wondered if I was stalking him! We might have been rivals in the city, but we became quite friendly. We met at a lot of functions and I got on great with him. We talked about our days together at Aberdeen and he only had nice things to say about me. I thought he must have been talking about another Gordon Strachan!

When I look back, I realise Billy instilled many good habits in me at a young and very impressionable age. I always had a hunger and desire to make the very best of my ability and he helped push that along. Very quickly, I realised that when you were about to go onto that big green area, with crowds of around 60,000 scrutinising your every move, you would discover your true self. It was up to you how you coped with the pressure, how you dealt with the expectations of your manager, your teammates and your team's supporters.

It wasn't a bad grounding. Billy McNeill took a chance on me. I will always remain thankful to that man.

ALEX McLEISH

I had been told to report to Pittodrie on 1 January 1978 to experience the atmosphere as the Aberdeen first team prepared for its league meeting with Dundee United twenty-four hours later. I was twenty days short of my nineteenth birthday and had yet to make my debut. Billy McNeill had taken over as Dons boss from Ally MacLeod the previous summer and had decided to give his reserve centre-half a little taste of what he might expect in the future.

I walked in through the main doors and was surprised to see Billy waiting for me. 'Happy New Year, boss,' I said, full of the joys of the festive season.

'Happy New Year to you, too, Alex,' Billy replied and added quickly, 'You're playing tomorrow.' That stopped me in my tracks. The manager didn't have a reputation as a practical joker, so I realised in an instant I would be facing the Tannadice side in the fixture between the teams who had been named the New Firm as serious challengers to the domestic domination of Glasgow's Old Firm of Celtic and Rangers.

It was one of Aberdeen's biggest encounters of the campaign and already it was a 25,000 sell-out. And I was going to make my first appearance for the Dons only two years after being signed by Billy's predecessor from Glasgow United. Billy took me aside and informed me two of the top team's central defenders, Willie Garner and Bobby Glennie, had been disciplined for breaking a curfew. They were suspended and I automatically stepped into the breach. The manager had only been at the club a few months, but already he was determined to show who was boss and, at the same time, show a lot of faith in a rookie teenager with no first-team experience.

I didn't get a chance to think about my sudden and unexpected elevation. I went straight out for training and was given preparation on what to expect from the United forwards the following day. Billy, as a former centre-half, passed on a lot of hints as he worked with me. By the time kick-off came around the next day, I was more than ready for the fray. I lined up alongside Willie Miller for the first time and could never have thought we would one day be colleagues in an Aberdeen team that would beat Real Madrid and win a European trophy.

On this particular afternoon, I was more concerned about what the men from Tayside had to offer. I thought I coped quite well and we kept a clean sheet, which was my priority. In fact, we won 1–0 with a goal from Ian Fleming, so it was a great day all round and a wonderful way to greet a new year.

I have to admit, with the folly of youth, I was convinced I had shown enough to be a shoo-in for our next game, which was against Ayr United at Somerset Park five days later. However, that's where Billy showed his shrewd management qualities. Once more, we had a private chat and he pointed out Garner and Glennie had served their punishment and were back in the squad while I would be dropping back into the reserves. The boss could have left it at that, he didn't require to give me an explanation. However, that's not Billy McNeill's style. He took the time to tell me the reason behind his thinking. Yes, he had been more than pleased with what he had witnessed from his young defender against difficult opponents, but, with an eye to the future, he had no intention of rushing me into the first team. His plan was to ease me in, pick my games and do his best to reduce the pressure on me.

So, I returned to the reserves, but I can tell you I started to play with a lot more confidence following my outing in the top side. I had also been reassured by my boss he believed I had first team potential and it was just a question of remaining patient, biding my time, working hard in training, listening to the boss and things would naturally fall into place. That was the way it played out, but Billy McNeill was not around to see it. I worked with him for just that one season and then he left to return to Celtic in the summer of 1978. Alex Ferguson came in and moved me into a central midfield position for a while before I eventually settled in at centre-back alongside Willie Miller.

I can reflect now on how good Billy McNeill was in giving advice on one-on-one situations. He even worked on the way I headed the ball. Big guys can just throw themselves at crosses and there is a chance they might make contact with their head and the ball could go anywhere. However, that was never enough for Billy and, given the career he enjoyed at club and country level, he might have had a fair idea of the proper method on how to attack the ball in the air. There is little point in jumping aggressively, simply clattering into the opposing forward and knocking a clearance up the park. Referees, even back then, were prone to award free-kicks to the attacking team while punishing the defender. It's not a new phenomenon.

You might have won your header, but you now have to defend a free-kick twenty-five or thirty yards from your goal. Billy showed me how to avoid being pinned by an experienced centre-forward, who would back into a defender and make life difficult. Some, clearly, were looking for the award of a free-kick and doing their best to force an awkward challenge the match official would misinterpret as a foul. Billy emphasised the need for anticipation, positioning and timing and I took it all on board. Playing in central defence became a whole lot more than simply clearing your lines. I've got a lot to thank him for and I was fortunate to be given that sort of guidance so early in my career, even if it was for only a formative year.

Billy McNeill, as we all know, was a winner, but, first and foremost, he was a gentleman. He detested defeat, but he accepted some losses with sportsmanship. A reversal for Celtic would have wounded him, but he never let his opponents witness that hurt. Billy always displayed dignity and he suffered a few times at Pittodrie when I was there.

On his first return in a league match in October 1978, I was at centre-half in the Dons team that won 4–1. Ironically, two of our goals were scored by Steve Archibald, who had been brought to the club by Billy from Clyde. Another of our star performers that afternoon was Gordon Strachan, another of Billy's purchases, my wee mate signing from Dundee.

Although we only had that solitary year at Pittodrie, I kept in touch with Billy over the years. He made many friends in his short spell at Aberdeen and I got to know Liz and the family well during his frequent visits back to Stonehaven. He became pals with a bloke called Charlie Rettie who, along with his wife Ruth, owned a guest house in the area where a few of the young players stayed when they first arrived at the club. During a couple of these meetings over the years I got the impression there was only one club that could entice Billy away from his new life in the north east of the country – and that was Celtic.

I was intrigued on one occasion when Billy told me he was convinced I would make a name for myself after watching me on my debut against Dundee United. Well, as I've always said, you only get one chance to make a first impression. He also revealed Ally MacLeod had predicted with a fair degree of confidence I would play for Scotland in the future. He got that right – seventy-seven times, to be precise!

I was extremely fortunate my first three managers were Ally, Billy and Alex Ferguson. These guys knew their football and, in their different ways, were determined to succeed. Moving from Glasgow United and training with the Dons' first team squad for the first team with Ally in charge was eye-opening. He was such an infectious, bubbly character and that enthusiasm got through to his players. He loved to talk and the press dubbed him 'Muhammad Ally' for rather obvious reasons. All this was part of a teenager's education as I tried to make my way in the game.

Not a lot of people will know that Billy once admitted making a mistake over yours truly. I was coming out of contract at Aberdeen at the end of a season and there were a few stories doing the rounds linking me with other clubs. There were a few nibbles, but nothing that persuaded me they would be a better option to what I had at Pittodrie, so I agreed an extension. Much later on, Billy confided to me, 'I boobed. I should have come for you.'

Now had Billy McNeill made that move at that particular time, I think I could be right in saying there is every possibility my career might not have panned out in the manner in which it did.

10

Pittodrie Despair,
Parkhead Delight

Billy McNeill was only eight Premier Division games into his Celtic managerial career – and he was furious. In the previous seven outings he had guided the team to six wins, interrupted by a 1–0 loss against Hibs at Parkhead. On a crisp October afternoon at Pittodrie in 1978, he had just witnessed a 4–1 collapse against former club Aberdeen.

Jock Stein's successor made no attempt to disguise his disappointment. A few days later, he still hadn't calmed down as he reflected, 'I was very, very angry. What I had watched was unacceptable. It was a dire performance and, on a personal level, it was a sore one. However, it was not about me – it was about Celtic Football Club and its supporters. I watched as the players trooped in, got cleaned up and prepared themselves for the trip back to Glasgow. I wanted to detect the mood in the camp. I wasn't about to start throwing teacups around.

'However, I would make certain I would have my say on the coach on our return. I went to the front of the bus and got their attention. "Do you think displays like that will be tolerated by anyone at this club?" I asked. "Do you want to remain Celtic players? If that's the best you can do, there is no place at Celtic for you." It went on in a similar vein most of the way back to Glasgow.

'I wanted them to have a good look at themselves and, at the same time, be honest with themselves. That was very important. Did they think they were good enough to play for Celtic? Obviously, I was looking for a response. I wanted the players to know how much Celtic meant to me. I was determined to get across all the good things Jock Stein had instilled in me. I had a clear vision of what I desired for the club and what I hoped to achieve. I couldn't accept Celtic teams playing like that in front of the best set of supporters in the world. If the players didn't know what it meant to pull on that green and white jersey before the game at Pittodrie, then they certainly did by the time we reached Glasgow.

'I had been tasked with managing Celtic and all that entailed. My eyes were wide open when I agreed to take the job. I wanted to hear those Celtic fans singing again, I wanted Celtic Park to be rocking and the supporters watching a team worthy of the name Celtic. I sensed the support wanted me to do well. I knew they were on my side and I had to prove worthy of that backing. There had always been an affinity with me and the fans as a player, it was reassuring it was still there as a manager. I had realised that the previous season, when I returned for the first time as manager of Aberdeen. I wondered how they would receive me in the opposite dugout from Jock Stein. You've no idea how I felt when they started singing my name. That was a truly amazing experience.'

McNeill's desire was imposed upon his players as the campaign unfolded. The team collected enough points to see them climb the table.

'I didn't expect us to be in this challenging position and I still say if we make it to Europe next season we will have done very well, all things considered,' announced the Celtic gaffer. That was for public consumption, inside the dressing room was a different matter. Murdo MacLeod said, 'He wanted that title, you can be sure of that. All season he had driven us towards it.'

The Monday evening of 21 May 1979 rolled around; the absolute moment of truth for Billy McNeill. The situation for Celtic was clear cut; a triumph over title holders Rangers would take the Premier League championship to Parkhead. A win or a draw would suit the Ibrox side, who still had two more games to play against Partick Thistle and Hibs. That being the case, McNeill, on his return, would have to settle for second best. McNeill was never comfortable with that mantle.

The manager recalled, 'I talked to the players as a team unit before the game. I didn't pick out individuals as I didn't think that would be fair. Jock did that every now and again, particularly with Jinky, but, then, he was exceptional, world class and could handle anything thrown at him. On this occasion, I just wanted to remind the players what we had all been through to get the club into this position. We were ninety minutes away from winning the league.

'I reminded them, "And listen to that crowd. That's your fans out there. They're worth a goal of a start." I sensed a very determined mood in the camp.'

The scramble for tickets had been made more frantic with a union strike keeping TV cameras away from Parkhead. A thriller of epic proportions was, sadly, never witnessed by millions. As kick-off time approached, Celtic Park throbbed and pulsated as a capacity attendance of 52,000 frenzied fans, engulfed in expectation, crowded into the arena. They were about to embark upon a crazy rollercoaster ride of high drama.

In the ninth minute, Rangers were a goal to the good after Alex MacDonald had knocked one wide of Peter Latchford. There was no change in the scoreline by the time the interval arrived. Ten minutes after the turnaround, McNeill must have feared the worst when his side was reduced to ten men. Johnny Doyle had foolishly become involved in a scuffle with MacDonald and the referee unhesitatingly banished the Celt. The winger heaved with sobs as he ran off the pitch.

Remarkably, Celtic drew level midway through the half as Roy Aitken surged forward to turn a close-range effort beyond keeper Peter McCloy. In the seventy-fourth minute, McNeill saw his side take the lead. George McCluskey rifled a low drive into the net. Two minutes later, it was 2–2 with Bobby Russell striking an eighteen-yarder past the helpless Latchford. Rangers sat in, obviously more than satisfied to take a point. Celtic, driven on by McNeill from the touchline, had other ideas. Six minutes were left when McCluskey fired in a dangerous angled effort from the wing. It was an awkward one for McCloy. The beanpole custodian parried the ball up and away, where it ricocheted off the inrushing Colin Jackson into the net. The minutes ticked down.

Midfield powerhouse MacLeod recalled, 'I picked up the ball in midfield. I knew it was late in the game, but I didn't know how late. There was a pass on to either side of me with teammates breaking forward. I just kept going. In an instant, I knew I was going to shoot, there was no chance of me passing. I thought to myself, "Hit this as hard as you can and, even if you miss, the ball will go away into the Celtic end and it will waste time."

'But I struck the shot really well and it went high and dipped over the keeper's right hand into the top corner. I still had no idea how long there was to go. We all geared up to go again when the referee blew for time-up seconds after Rangers had kicked off. I must have been the last Celtic player to touch the ball that evening. It was my best-ever night in football. I had a few memorable ones, but nothing ever touched that. No team could have stopped us even when we were down to ten men.'

McNeill enthused, 'The boys deserved it. It was simply fantastic. I have never seen a game like it. When George McCluskey scored to make it 2–1 for us, I just couldn't believe it. Then they came right back. One minute you're up there, the next you're down here. My players would climb a mountain and then find there was another waiting for them. Our ten men did extraordinary things. To score four goals in just over half-an-hour with only ten men against Rangers was just incredible. Unbelievable.

'John Greig was one of the first to congratulate me and I really appreciated that. He was as proud a Rangers man as I was a Celtic man and he must have been hurting, but he still sought me out to shake my hand. A great gesture from a genuine sportsman. I was overjoyed for my players and even had to persuade Johnny Doyle to go out there and take a bow. He didn't want to go because he thought he had let us down. Eventually, I threw him onto the pitch! All of my players, including Johnny, were heroes.'

Davie Provan summed it up succinctly, 'We couldn't have celebrated any more if we had won the European Cup that evening. That's how sweet it was.'

DANNY McGRAIN

Billy McNeill had a rare evening off when I made my first appearance for Celtic in a League Cup-tie against Dundee United at Tannadice. I came on as a substitute for Harry Hood in a 2–2 draw on Wednesday, 26 August 1970. I was nineteen years of age and I got twenty-five minutes' worth of action on Tayside. The result was academic as Celtic had already qualified from their section. So, the captain got a rest while George Connelly played in his place.

However, Billy returned three days later when I was given the nod for my full debut against Morton in a league game at Parkhead which we won 2–0. Billy was to remain a teammate all the way through to his last game, the 3–1 Scottish Cup Final victory over Airdrie on a sunny May afternoon at Hampden in 1975.

Over those years, I almost always referred to my colleague and captain as 'Big Man'. That stopped the day Billy walked back into Parkhead as manager on 28 May 1978.

I remember it well. Billy knew a lot of the players and, in fact, had been in the same Cup-winning side as myself, goalkeeper Peter Latchford, left-back Andy Lynch, midfielder Ronnie Glavin and winger Paul Wilson, who scored two goals in the Celtic great's last performance as a player at the age of thirty-five. On the first morning he took training, Billy gathered the players around him and delivered a simple speech. 'You can call me boss, manager or gaffer,' he said. Fair enough, I thought. I never called him Big Man again, not even when we were out socially and in company.

The boss was putting down a marker immediately. Things had changed in the three years he had been away from the club. He was no longer a teammate, the club's most famous captain. He was now in charge and he wanted total respect from the players right from day one. Billy always had that commanding presence and aura about him, whether it was on or off the park. He was a born leader, so it was easy to gain the esteem of everyone right away. It may have been just a little strange having spent so many years playing alongside him, but that was then and this was now and Billy McNeill had returned to take over from Jock Stein and do a job for a club that had won nothing the previous season. He wasn't going to hang about to get his message across.

It had been an entirely different situation with Big Jock. I was still in my teens when I first met the Celtic manager. He was already a giant in the game; a team boss who had led Celtic to their European Cup success in May 1967. He had every right to be revered. Never once did it cross my mind to call him Jock. He was always Mr Stein to me, even when I was a seasoned Scotland international player in my thirties. It would have been totally alien for me to address him as Jock. Like Billy McNeill, the admiration and recognition he received had been earned. Maybe Mr Stein could give you stick, but it was forgotten outside the dressing room. He taught me so much.

And it was Mr Stein who made me captain when Kenny Dalglish left for Liverpool in August 1977. And it was Kenny who had become skipper when Billy retired from playing. When I was told I was following these two iconic figures, I realised it was such an honour. I was captaining a team that had won a European Cup and was renowned throughout the world. Billy McNeill succeeded Jock Stein in the full knowledge of what was expected of him. He had been boss of Second Division Clyde for just over two months when he took over at Shawfield on 1 April 1977 before he moved to Aberdeen on 14 June the same year for a full season. He may only have been at Pittodrie for one campaign, but he managed to put his stamp and authority on the club in such a short space of time after replacing Ally MacLeod.

Billy was most unfortunate not to win silverware at the Dons. The club finished as runners-up in the Premier Division with fifty-three points, only two adrift of Rangers and, remember, these were the days when you only got two points for a win. They also lost 2–1 to the Ibrox side in the Scottish Cup Final on the last day of the season on 6 May. Someone at Celtic must have been taking note of Billy's achievements because he was named our manager shortly afterwards. At Aberdeen he had shown that he was not afraid to bring in youth – much like Jock Stein and the Quality Street Gang – and one young player who benefited from his brief stay up north was a rookie centre-half by the name of Alex McLeish.

Billy McNeill may have been new to the management game, but clearly he was going to stand or fall by his own decisions. On that first day of training, he gave us a broad outline of what he was looking for from his players. I can't remember his exact words, but he left us in no doubt that he expected us to be winners and to be proud to be Celtic players with the greatest supporters in football. As my on-field colleague, Billy had always stressed the importance of the Celtic fans. He had come into the team in August 1958, a side that had won the League Cup the previous year by beating Rangers 7–1 at Hampden. However, that was the last piece of silverware won by the club until Billy McNeill headed in the Scottish Cup winner against Dunfermline in 1965. So, he could appreciate the backing of followers who hadn't had too much to celebrate over a fairly lengthy period, but still turned up in numbers to cheer on their favourites.

I took Billy McNeill for granted when I first came into the side. I hasten to add I mean that as a compliment. Automatically, you knew you could rely on him. For instance, if anyone outjumped him it was a double-take because that didn't happen too often. As anyone who saw Billy in action will tell you, he was virtually unbeatable in the air. His timing was incredible. I swear he could jump so high that he had snow on his hair when he came back to the ground. So, with a guy like that around to protect your goal, it allowed others to take care of their own job.

Billy had enjoyed several years with John Clark as his central defensive partner and their understanding was bordering on telepathic. However, John moved to Morton in 1971 and Jock Stein was changing things in his line-up with Jim Brogan often brought in. Billy just kept on playing and his consistency was awesome as he led by example. You don't get to play around 800 games for Celtic without being something special. So, was it really any wonder I took the skipper for granted?

When Billy took the training sessions, I often wondered if he had been a frustrated outside-left. He played his entire career in defence. The record books show he also had a few early appearances in my position at right-back before he settled into his centre-half role. But, during our work-outs, Billy McNeill would wander over to the left wing to ping in crosses with his left foot. I thought he was too tall to be a winger! How would he have fared as an outside-left? Let's just say that as an attacking wide player he was a good central defender. We'll leave it there.

It didn't take long for Billy McNeill to bring success to Celtic as a manager. The league championship was the big one and that was our priority. Rangers had won the domestic treble the previous season, but they, too, had a change of manager when John Greig took over from Leicester City-bound Jock Wallace. Greig moved straight from being a player at Ibrox to becoming their manager. At least Billy McNeill had three years away from Parkhead. So, back then, the Old Firm had two of their most famous and influential captains in the respective dugouts. It really was a time of change for football's ancient rivals.

The first Glasgow derby was going to be a massive affair for two club legends and Celtic Park was a sell-out on 9 September 1978 when Greig took his side across Glasgow. I was still coming back to fitness after an ankle injury and I was with the reserves at Ibrox. However, our main thoughts were in the east end of Glasgow and I'm delighted to say Billy drew first blood in a 3–1 success with two early goals from Tom McAdam and George McCluskey. Derek Parlane pulled one back shortly after the interval, but McAdam scored a third for us about fifteen minutes from time. Peter Latchford also saved an Alex Miller penalty-kick.

I made my first top-team appearance since October 1977 when I played against Burnley in the old Anglo-Scottish Cup later that month. We lost 2–1 at Parkhead to go out on a 3–1 aggregate. But, at least, it was great to get through the full ninety minutes without a reaction and, although I was hardly ready for a consistent run of games, I hoped I would be able to play my part at some stage in Billy McNeill's first season back.

Little did I realise how the next visit of Rangers would be such a memorable one for yours truly. It was an absolute belter as we claimed the title with our last game of the season. A goal down at half-time, Johnny Doyle was sent off shortly into the second period, goals from Roy Aitken and George McCluskey turned it around and then they equalised. It was a game we had to win, a draw was no use to us. Then Colin Jackson deflected the ball into his own net with the clock ticking down before Murdo MacLeod netted the fourth with virtually the last kick of the ball. People who know me will tell you I am not a dreamer, but that really was a special night. It was what Billy McNeill had wanted on the first day he walked back through those doors at Celtic Park.

Everyone was delighted for The Boss.

JIMMY LUMSDEN

Here's an interesting quiz question, 'Who was Billy McNeill's first signing for Celtic?' Davie Provan from Kilmarnock? Murdo MacLeod from Dumbarton? If you answered Jimmy Lumsden from Clydebank, go to the top of the class!

Big Billy splashed out all of £10,000 to entice me from quaint Kilbowie to the big-time of Parkhead in the summer of 1978 to place me in that privileged pole position. Davie, who was a fabulous winger with all the skills, cost a little more when he arrived in a Scottish record £125,000 deal from the Rugby Park side in September and Murdo, a completely unselfish team man who could run all day and night, was the third purchase, at £100,000 from the Boghead outfit in November.

But yours truly beat them to the punch and I can only say Billy McNeill could spot a player. He knew talent when he witnessed it, that's for sure. I have to admit, though, Davie and Murdo might have had slightly more memorable Celtic careers than me. In fact, I only played once for the first team, a 2–1 Anglo-Scottish Cup win over Clyde on 3 August 1978. And that was that, I had had my ninety minutes of fame in that iconic green and white hooped jersey. And 10,000 were in Celtic Park on a Thursday night to be enthralled by the performance.

It wasn't the most auspicious of starts to anyone's career at the club. It was Billy's first competitive game in charge after returning from Aberdeen in the close season and, ironically, it was against the team who had offered him his first opportunity as a manager. Clyde, like the Bankies, were a friendly wee outfit no one ever took too seriously; we were never going to win any of the major silverware. On this particular evening, the part-timers of the Shawfield side were out to make it a debut to forget for Billy as Celtic manager and me as a Celtic player. They were a goal ahead in only four minutes when Joe Ward beat Peter Latchford with a fine effort. It stayed that way until half-time.

I can exclusively reveal that Billy was not amused at what he was witnessing and he let us know during the interval. I couldn't blame him. I looked around the dressing room and saw players of the calibre of Tommy Burns, Roy Aitken, Big Shuggy Edvaldsson, Alfie Conn, Ronnie Glavin and George McCluskey and we were struggling against a team that, with the greatest of respect, we should have been decimating. Things picked up a wee bit in the second period and Alfie Conn levelled after a well-worked free-kick and the late, great Tommy Burns hit the winner with a sweet shot with only three minutes to play. I recall what Billy told the newspaper guys afterwards, 'I didn't promise a magic wand. I was happy with some of the players, but we still have a lot of work to do.' Slight understatement from Billy.

We played the second leg of the competition the following Saturday and I sat on the substitutes' bench for the entire ninety minutes. Billy had got his message across to the players after the first game and on this occasion we won 6–1 with doubles from Alfie Conn, Tom McAdam and Ronnie Glavin. I got a few guest appearances on the sidelines, but I never kicked another ball for Celtic's top side. I wasn't one bit surprised. At the age of thirty, and with only Clydebank and Morton on my CV, I didn't think for a moment I would be relaunching my career and reinventing myself as a player at Celtic.

I was brought in mainly to work with the youngsters at the club. That had been my remit from day one. Billy registered me as a player and I knew I would only be used in an emergency or in the reserves to get a good close-up look at some of the emerging talent. That suited me fine. I enjoyed coaching the youths and trying to spot talent and then nurturing and enhancing it.

People have often asked what the connection between me and

Billy was before he took me to Celtic. I can honestly say that there was none. Our paths never crossed. For a start, whisper it, I had been a Rangers fan when I was brought up in Kinning Park and then the Glasgow housing scheme of Castlemilk. If I had dreams of playing for one of the great Glasgow clubs it was for the one who played their football at Ibrox. But that notion evaporated the day I walked into Celtic Park to sign for Billy.

Only three weeks beforehand, I thought I was heading for Aberdeen. Billy was in charge at Pittodrie and John Clark was his right-hand man. John and I had been at Morton together and I can only think it was he who put a good word in for me with Big Billy. I worked with the kids at Cappielow and John must have seen something he liked. I received a cryptic phone call one night from my former Morton teammate. 'I can't tell you too much,' he said. 'Don't do anything until I get in touch.' It was a timely message because I was attempting to sell my house in Kirkintilloch in preparation for heading north to join up with such excellent and ambitious professionals as Billy McNeill and John Clark. The switch certainly appealed.

Then I was left wondering about the call from John. I pondered about the possibility of the move falling through for some reason. All became clear when he got in touch again. 'We're going to Celtic,' he said. 'We want you to come, too.' I was dumbfounded. Me? At Celtic? It was unfathomable. They didn't have to sell the club to me, despite my Rangers leaning early in life.

Stevie Chalmers, Celtic's European Cup Final goal-scoring hero, had also moved to Morton at the same time as John in the summer of 1971. Stevie very kindly used to pick me up at Bishopbriggs Cross to take me to Greenock for training each day. All the way there and back, he would tell me tales of Celtic. He may have been a Morton player, but it was fairly obvious he was still a Celtic fan.

I will always remember the day I signed those forms at Celtic Park. Let's face it, Parkhead was a different world from what I had been used to and, once again, I mean no disrespect to Morton or Clydebank. I went over the details with Billy, everything was in order and I was delighted to get my moniker on that slip of foolscap that proved I was now registered to play for the club. I had a cup of tea with Billy and John and they talked about how they saw me fitting into their plans to take the club forward. It was quite informal, but I knew we would go into more detail later on. I left the manager's office and walked through the exit and out into the sunshine. Back then, there were massive green gates at the front of the stadium. I just stood there for a moment, shook my head and said to myself, 'Good grief! I've just signed for Celtic!'

I had a fantastic time at the club. I found myself working with some fabulous youngsters who were coming through the system; the likes of Paul McStay and his brother Willie, Charlie Nicholas, Pat Bonner, Mike Conroy, Mark Reid, Danny Crainie, Jim Duffy and Davie Moyes. A standard had already been set for these youngsters and I was going to make sure they were ready for the first team when Big Billy gave them the call. It was an absolute joy to work with these kids and I took a lot of personal pride as they emerged and consolidated their first team places.

There were some who did not quite make the grade, but I made sure a few of them didn't disappear without a trace. I had started my career at Leeds United in the mid-sixties without ever becoming an established first-teamer. I was very friendly with Eddie Gray, who also grew up in Castlemilk. We met each other playing for Glasgow schools and kept in touch.

Billy Bremner had been their inspirational captain and I got on well with him, too. Like Eddie, Wee Billy was a huge Celtic fan. Somehow I seemed fated to end up at Parkhead! When his playing days were over, Billy became manager of Doncaster Rovers, then in the old English Fourth Division, in November 1978, a few months after I arrived at Celtic. He saved them from relegation and started to rebuild the following summer.

'Any young players Celtic don't want, Lummy?' he asked. 'Remember to let me know if a good one becomes available.' Through our connection, I could send youngsters such as Colin Douglas and Billy Russell to Billy. Later on, he paid something like £35,000 for midfielder Jim Dobbin. It was an arrangement that suited everyone and Billy, of the tall variety, was always happy to help out Billy, of the small variety, as they remained firm friends after first meeting up with the Scotland international squad.

Big Billy was always good company. We used to have sauna sessions most afternoons after training and chief scout John Kelman would often join in. Billy always had that little bit of mischief in him and he would attempt to wind up John. He would lean back and say casually, 'I see Wolves are looking at that young right-back at Forfar. Do you know anything about him? Should we be interested?' Ten times out of ten, Kelman could answer with chapter and verse on the player. Honestly, his knowledge was encyclopaedic. Billy would simply smile. The following day, it could be the same scenario. 'I hear Ipswich are taking an interest in that wee midfield player at Arbroath. Do you know anything about him? Should we be interested?' It was a game Billy played with his chief scout practically every day.

I was on the receiving end of Billy's rapscallion ways following a prestigious Under-16 tournament in Paris which Celtic won. It was a huge deal and we celebrated big-style that evening. I was with Billy and John Kelman and we might just have over-done it. In the wee small hours, we crept up the hotel stairs to our bedrooms for some much-needed shut-eye. The following morning, my bedroom door flew open and Billy had to awaken me from my slumber. He stood there, as immaculate as ever. 'Come on, Lummy,' he barked, 'time to pack the hamper. We're leaving for the airport in an hour or so.'

I squinted at him and realised he wasn't joking. Only a few hours earlier I was holding aloft a glittering trophy after a great win by Celtic's kids and the next I was being told to get out of my scratcher and help to collect all the grubby gear. Billy really had a wicked side!

I thoroughly enjoyed my time at Celtic. Billy promoted me to a first team coaching position before I left in 1982 to become assistant manager to my old buddy Eddie Gray at Leeds. From Elland Road, I moved on to become a boss in my own right at Bristol City and Rochdale. I hooked up again with Davie Moyes, one of my bright youngsters at Celtic, when he was manager at Preston in 1998 and we both went to Everton and then Manchester United together. Wonderful memories and I can look back and say a gigantic thanks to the man who opened that door to a thirty-year-old jobbing midfielder with Clydebank in the summer of 1978.

Cheers, Billy McNeill!

DAVIE PROVAN

I don't mind admitting I was shaking like a leaf in a storm when I first met Billy McNeill. It was a Monday morning, 18 September 1978, and I will never forget the experience. That was the day I signed for Celtic and putting my scrawl on those transfer forms changed my life forever.

I had been playing for Kilmarnock as a part-timer, working in a Paisley distillery and training twice a week in the evenings. It wasn't ideal, but, at the age of twenty-two, I reckoned – and hoped – the situation would change. I had received favourable press coverage the previous season when I played against Celtic, then managed by the great Jock Stein, in a Scottish Cup-tie and we managed a 1–1 draw at Parkhead. That was against the odds, but people pointed out you rarely got a second chance against Celtic. Remarkably, we won 1–0 at Rugby Park and it was the first time in decades the Glasgow club had been knocked out of the national competition by a team from a lower division. I had played in my usual position of outside-right in both games, up against the legendary Tommy Burns in the first and John Dowie in the second.

I thought nothing more about it, but Billy McNeill, then manager of Aberdeen, must have taken notice of it. I was still staying with my mum and dad in Gourock when I received a telephone call one evening. The voice on the other end of the line identified himself as a reporter from the *Weekly News*, a news-paper from the DC Thomson stable that was usually published on a Friday. I presumed he was on for an interview. I was more than happy to get a little bit of publicity.

Not long into the chat, I was asked about the speculation that had been linking me with Rangers. It was fairly well-known my dad was a Rangers supporter and he had taken me to Ibrox most matchdays when I was a youngster. From that point of view, I was then perceived as a fan of the Light Blues. I was asked a straightforward question, 'Would you be interested in joining Celtic?' I didn't hesitate. 'I'd go to Celtic in a minute,' I informed the caller.

'So, you wouldn't have a problem?'

'None whatsoever.'

There was a pause before the 'journalist' identified himself. It was John Clark, Billy McNeill's assistant manager. 'Just checking, Davie, to make 100 per cent sure.'

And that was that. Everything went quiet until one Sunday when I was out with my pals in Gourock. I received a message instructing me to get home as swiftly as possible. Intrigued? You bet. When I got home I was told to phone Davie Sneddon, the Kilmarnock manager.

'Celtic have made an offer for you,' I was informed.

I took a sharp intake of breath.

'And we have accepted.'

Four words that signalled the end of my part-time football career.

'What happens next?' My mind was in a whirl.

'Get down to Rugby Park tomorrow morning and we'll drive through to Glasgow. You can meet Billy McNeill and take it from there.'

I didn't sleep too well that evening. I was so excited at the prospect of joining Celtic, I hadn't asked the Killie boss how much they had bid for me. How highly did Billy McNeill rate me?

The following day, I discovered he had put in an offer of £125,000 for me. Amazingly, it was a Scottish record transfer fee at the time. One minute, I was a part-timer and the next I was the most expensive player in the country. It was quite a lot to take in during a whirlwind twenty-four hours or so. My life had just performed a 360 degree turn.

So, I walked into the manager's office at Celtic Park to be greeted with a warm smile and a good, strong handshake from the man who had orchestrated the fairly sensational transformation. Billy McNeill might have detected my nervousness. Could anyone blame me? He put me at ease immediately.

'We've paid good money for you, Davie,' he said, 'and I think you will be well worth it.'

What did the Celtic manager expect of his costly purchase?

'Just keep doing what you were doing at Killie,' he added. 'Take on your man, get the ball to the touchline and get your crosses in. I don't want you to change your style. Play as you have been playing and everything will be fine.'

Immediately, I felt reassured. Billy McNeill could have that effect on any individual. He was the embodiment of Celtic; a dignified aura, a genuine presence and, for me, he ticked all the boxes. I was made to feel at home straight away. That was the first time I actually met Billy, but I had the privilege of sharing a pitch with him before he retired. It was 28 December 1974 and I was eighteen years old and looking forward to playing against Celtic at Rugby Park. They were the reigning champions and I wondered how I would fare against such quality opposition. In goal for the visitors that afternoon was former Kilmarnock team-mate Ally Hunter which made the game even more interesting.

Our two main strikers were Eddie Morrison and Ian Fleming and they had scored almost thirty goals between them before the turn of the year. I would like to think a few of them might have come from cross balls from yours truly. I thought I would be up against Jim Brogan, a no-nonsense defender who was also a Scotland international, but I remember Jock Stein brought him in to play alongside Billy and George Connelly in the middle of the rearguard, which must have been some sort of compliment to our front two. Instead, Tommy Callaghan was moved back from his left-sided midfield berth to slot in at the back. Tommy was one of those players blessed with an engine and a long stride that could see him eat up the pitch as he galloped up and down the flank.

It ended 1–0 with Kenny Dalglish hitting the solitary strike not long before the interval. However, I couldn't help but notice Big Billy. The referee was an Edinburgh match official by the name of Douglas Ramsey, but I thought the Celtic captain made a reasonable fist of taking care of business in Ayrshire. There were no tantrums or arm-waving, but if he thought someone had been offside, there would be a little glance towards the whistler or his linesman. Six seconds later, as if by magic, the flag would shoot up!

It had been an education just being on the same park as Big Billy. Of course, he was an imposing, even majestic figure as he controlled the Celtic back-line. He was very much in charge and you couldn't help but be in awe of the man. Look at what he had achieved and continued to accomplish. You got the impression he was every bit as hungry to attain success in his mid-thirties as he had been when he had started out as a teenager.

The man was a winner. Ironically, that would prove to be his last season for his only club before he announced his retirement following the Scottish Cup triumph over Airdrie just over four months later. As an opposition player, I found it difficult to envisage a Celtic team without Billy McNeill at centre-half.

It's a funny old game. I could never have guessed how momentous things would develop for me when I heard the news Billy had quit playing. Some three years and four months later, I was sitting chatting to him in the manager's office at Celtic Park and he was outlining what he expected from me as Scotland's highest-priced footballer. Naturally, I never regretted that move for one second. Playing for Celtic and Billy McNeill was an experience, honour and privilege.

Look at how Billy carried himself, that poise, straight back and the chest thrust forward. It was never more puffed up than when we were playing Rangers at Ibrox. He led by example and that composure and reassurance got through to the players. We would get off the coach at the front door of our greatest rivals and we all felt ten feet tall. That was all Billy's doing. There was never the merest hint of nerves on these days. That sort of confidence, self-assurance, belief, assertiveness, call it what you will, does rub off on players. And Billy McNeill was well aware of that, you better believe it.

Don't get the notion all was sweetness and light between me and the manager. There were a few occasions when I was on the sharp end of his tongue. Aye, we had our moments, Billy and me. But there was never a massive fall-out. If he had something to say, he delivered it how he saw fit and that was the end of it. I recall I was struggling with a knee injury, but Billy was not convinced. 'It's all in your head,' he would say. 'Just you get on that pitch.' I wish! The only way to convince the manager was to get booked in for an operation and then something would show that it was not 'in my head'.

The surgeon opened the knee that was giving me persistent problems. Sure enough, something had become detached. It had been floating around in there, creating all sorts of misery. I asked the surgeon to place the offending piece of tissue in a jar. He must have wondered why I would want such a keepsake. The following day, I hobbled into Celtic Park on crutches. I went to the manager's office, knocked on the door and was told to come in. I placed the jar on Billy's desk and said, 'There's the injury that was stuck in my head.'

172

Billy, like Big Jock Stein before him, had spies everywhere. You could come in for training on Monday morning and he would ask, 'Did you enjoy yourself in Panama Jax on Saturday night, Davie?' Another Monday, it could be, 'Had an enjoyable evening in Henry Afrikas', then?' Or it could be, 'I hear the Warehouse was jumping at the weekend.'

There was no hiding place. The club held your passports back then. They were locked in a safe in Billy's office and not even Raffles could have cracked that code. They were kept under lock and key to make sure a player wouldn't forget the item if we were heading off to play a European tie. Obviously, the club didn't trust us with our own passports.

However, I can now reveal I did manage to flummox Big Billy one day. I was hurt in a game against St Mirren at Love Street and limped off. Normally, in those circumstances, the player was expected to turn up at the ground on Sunday morning for an early assessment of the damage. Unfortunately for me, I had arranged to fly out that day to view an apartment in Spain. And I was going to manage the feat without a passport. Amazingly, you could pull off such a thing back then. I was due to fly from Manchester to Alicante without the necessary legal requirements and get back in time for training on Monday. Outrageous as it may seem in these days of ultra-cautious airport control, I did fly in and out without too many problems.

As I turned up at Celtic Park on Monday morning, Billy was waiting for me. 'Davie, a word in the office now,' he said. I knew I had been rumbled. I had no doubt one of Billy's look-outs had spotted me somewhere along the line. I decided to feign innocence.

'Why did you miss Sunday?' he asked, looking me straight in the eye.

'I was feeling a bit better, boss,' I lied. 'I didn't see the point in putting anyone to any bother.'

I could see he was not convinced.

'Really?' he shook his head. 'So you were in the country all weekend?'

'Of course, boss,' I answered. I pointed to the safe in the corner. 'You know my passport is in there. How could I possibly get out of the UK without it?'

A little game of cat-and-mouse ensued. He would thrust and I would parry. He knew that I knew and I knew that he knew! I was only too aware, though, that I held all the aces, my passport was in beside all the other players' essential travel documents well and truly shut away. It ended in a truce and I went off to training.

Much later, once Billy had finished with management and I had long since hung up my boots, we met at a function one evening. He came over to me, shook my hand and gave me that knowing smile. 'Remember that time when I asked you if you had left the country, Davie?'

'I remember it well,' I replied. 'I'm hardly likely to forget it. It was a fairly unusual conversation.'

'You were spotted at Manchester Airport,' he grinned. 'You were queuing for the flight to Alicante.'

I decided to come clean. 'Yeah, quite correct, boss. I admit it.'

'And you did it without a passport?' he sounded incredulous.

'Yeah, that's right. My passport never left the safe in your office.'

'Incredible,' he laughed. 'You put one over on your old gaffer. You deserve a drink.'

We had a couple at the bar and reminisced about our time together at Celtic.

It was a good time to be at the club. It was a special place, maybe a little idiosyncratic in how it was run, but the manager put together an unbeatable dressing room. Everyone gelled, Danny McGrain, Shuggy Edvaldasson, Andy Lynch, och, I could go through the squad. We all felt part of something exceptional.

That was all down to one man and one man alone – Billy McNeill.

MURDO MacLEOD

Billy McNeill had a wonderfully wicked sense of humour and he demonstrated it one afternoon at Ibrox. It was 19 September 1981 and we had just beaten Rangers 2–0 in a league game. Tom McAdam had given us an early lead with a trademark header and I netted the second with a low shot following a free-kick with four minutes to go. In truth, we should have won a lot more comfortably as we had control of the encounter straight from the kick-off.

As we celebrated in the dressing room, Big Billy said to me, 'Right, Murdo, hurry up and get changed. Let's go upstairs and see Deedle Dawdle – the nickname for Rangers director Willie Waddell – and tell him he's got a lovely new stand.'

Rangers had just spent £4 million, a lot of money back then, on refurbishing the stadium and a lot of the credit went to Waddell, who had been a player, manager, general manager, vice-chairman and director at the club. The Rangers hierarchy had deliberately held back the unveiling of the stadium for the visit of their greatest foes. They had already played a few league and League Cup-ties on their home turf, but they wanted a gala occasion in front of a sell-out Old Firm crowd.

The sun was shining in Govan that day, the brand spanking new stadium gleamed, the fans turned up in their thousands and all they needed was the right result. Celtic, though, were in no mood to be bit-part players in the Ibrox theatre. Billy McNeill made sure of that. We won by two goals, but we could have claimed four or five. So, the Celtic manager was in fine fettle afterwards, but he couldn't help himself when it came to rattling Deedle's cage. Maybe there was history between the pair, I don't know. What I was aware of, though, was that the Rangers man was an acquired taste for many of his contemporaries. He would have been fizzing, having just watched his team be completely outplayed and beaten by Celtic. Billy just had to rub it in.

To me, Big Billy was a god among the footballing fraternity. I held him in the highest regard and will never forget the first day I met him when I signed for Celtic on Thursday, 2 November 1978. For whatever reason back then, it was assumed I would be heading for Rangers when I left Dumbarton. I've no idea where those stories originated, but they were news to me. I just kept working away with the Boghead outfit, did my best and hoped someone would take an interest. I was with the Scottish League Select for a game against our Irish counterparts the evening before I joined up at Parkhead. The match was at Fir Park and ended 1–1. Coincidentally, I had been spending time with Roy Aitken and George McCluskey, but I had no idea I would be lining up alongside them the following weekend.

Dumbarton manager Alex Wright contacted me after the game and told me about the Celtic interest and said we had to be at Parkhead on Thursday to have talks with Billy McNeill. I was in a bit of a whirl, as you might expect. I will always recall that first meting, it was a moment in my life when everything stood still. There I was in the manager's office at Celtic Football Club and I was actually talking to this absolute legend, a footballing giant. I was in awe of the man. I looked at this icon who had held aloft the European Cup some eleven years earlier, the captain of the world famous Lisbon Lions, the winner of a landslide of medals and honours, respected and admired by everyone in the game – and he wanted to sign *me*!

I was aware Billy had taken in a couple of Dumbarton games, but I had no idea he was looking at me. We had Graeme Sharp leading our attack at the time and he was getting some good reviews. Or it could have been any of my teammates who had caught Billy's eye. Fortunately for me, I was the focus of the

Celtic manager's attention. I believe he made a bid of £100,000 for me and that was a fair amount of money in 1978. Billy had paid £125,000 for Davie Provan from Kilmarnock a couple of months earlier and that was a record fee between Scottish clubs, so that might put his offer for me into context. There was no way Dumbarton could afford to turn down that sort of cash. It was just a question of 'where do you want me to sign, Mr McNeill?' and that was the transfer done and dusted. Everyone was happy. I trained with my new teammates on the Friday and went straight into the first team twenty-four hours later for a league game against Motherwell at Parkhead.

Alas, that was when my personal fairy tale came to an abrupt end. Our opponents had sacked their manager, Roger Hynd, only a few days beforehand and John Hagart was put in temporary charge of the team that was toiling at the foot of the table. There was a nice touch before the kick-off when Paul Wilson, who had just left Celtic for the Fir Park side in September, came over to shake my hand and wish me all the best in my new career. I appreciated the gesture. Everything was going according to plan when Tom McAdam scored in twelve minutes and I was delighted to have played my part. I picked up the ball on the left, switched it to Davie Provan on the right and his pinpoint cross was headed into the net by McAdam. So far so good.

Paul Wilson, though, was eager to mark his quickfire return to the east end of Glasgow and he set up the equaliser for Gregor Stevens before the interval. We pummelled their defence throughout the second-half, but with about eight minutes left to play, they broke swiftly and Willie Pettigrew set up Stewart McLaren to roll in the winner. That wasn't in the script. The fans, as you could imagine, were not too happy, but, at least, I received some good notices the following day in the press. Not that they mattered much, I was more interested in the team's performance and the result. I was also aware that our next league match the following Saturday was against Rangers at Hampden, the game being played at the national stadium to accommodate the aforementioned work being done on Ibrox.

Had Billy McNeill seen enough from me, an inexperienced twenty year old, to play me in such an important game? I didn't think it would help my cause that I would be forced to sit out a midweek League Cup-tie against Montrose at Links Park because I was ineligible after playing in the tournament with Dumbarton earlier in the campaign. Ronnie Glavin came back into the side, but Celtic had to be content with a 1–1 draw, Andy Lynch scoring the goal with a penalty-kick. I waited and wondered until the day before the game when Billy named his line-up – I was in. My second game for Celtic against Rangers at Hampden. Wow! I was certainly excited. Two weeks earlier, I had played for Dumbarton against Stirling Albion and the attendance could be counted in hundreds and not thousands.

The official attendance at the national stadium was given as 52,330 and goodness only knows how many years I would have to have played with Dumbarton to reach that total. I enjoyed my first Old Firm confrontation. There was a lot of good football played that afternoon and it wasn't all about bone-jarring tackles, frantic challenges and the ball ending up black and blue. It ended in a 1–1 stalemate which was probably just about right. I was involved when Andy Lynch gave us the lead in the fifty-second minute and well-known sportswriter Hugh Taylor, in his *Evening Times* match report, said, 'Celtic's goal, scored by Andy Lynch, who played a fine captain's part, was a splendid effort. A deft one-two with new boy Murdo MacLeod, who didn't do a thing wrong on his Old Firm debut, split the Rangers defence and Lynch gave Peter McCloy no chance.'

Alas, our lead lasted only three minutes when Rangers levelled with an Alex Forsyth penalty-kick. I had survived my Glasgow derby baptism and I had the taste for more.

One of the many things Billy excelled at was making you feel like a world-beater. On matchday, he would have a quiet word and after that confab you were ready for anything; you were ten feet tall and the opposition were beaten before a shot had been fired in anger. 'Get on the ball, Murdo, he'll not get near you. Run with it, he'll never catch you.' After five minutes of this, you began to feel sorry for your opponents.

A week after the Rangers game, we drew 2–2 with Hibs at Easter Road and I scored my first goal for the club. I blasted in a shot from about twenty-five yards that zipped into the net. I caught it perfectly and the ball simply took off. As we prepared for our next match, Billy told my teammates. 'If you see Murdo in that position, roll in a pass and he'll take care of the rest. Thirty yards, forty yards, it doesn't matter, just tee up Murdo and we'll have the chance of a goal.' I believe I managed to blush every now and again as the accolades flowed. But that was Billy, masterful at man-management. There was no one better for raising your self-belief and confidence. He knew the right buttons to push and he was instinctively aware when one of his players needed a wee gee up. And it worked every time, too.

His chats became legendary, as I'm sure every other Celtic player who was lucky enough to work alongside Billy would testify. 'I fancy you for a goal today. Murdo,' he would say. 'Yes, I'm certain you'll pop one in, no problem.' And then he would move about the dressing room to other players, spreading his psychology around his players. 'Danny, that guy'll be having a laugh if he tries to run past you.' 'Davie, I've seen pipe bands turn quicker than their left-back.' 'Roy, your authority will be all over this game.' And so on until we were all pumped and raring to go. And, outwith matchday preparations, he was thoughtful enough to ask about the players' families, he knew the names of the mums, dads, wives, girlfriends and children.

He was never better than before the remarkable last game of the season, the famous 'ten-man Celtic win the league' crescendo. It was a simple enough scenario. We knew the title was ours if we were triumphant. However, a win or a draw would suit our opponents, who still had two more games to play. Our season had now been contained within a ninety-minute nutshell. Billy didn't go around us individually. Instead, he stood in the middle of the dressing room and told us, 'Listen to that crowd, that's your fans out there. They'll be behind you all the way, they'll be absolutely relentless. Those guys are worth a goal of a start to us.'

I have no idea how many times I have relived that game in my mind. Our supporters still want to talk about it like it just happened yesterday. I can only tell you it was the most amazing, crazy, incredible, pulverising, momentous, topsy-turvy, controversial and enjoyable encounter I ever played in. You'll have to take my word for it and that of the other combatants that dramatic evening. And the supporters in the 52,000 crowd. There was a television strike at the time and, unbelievably, the spectacle was never shown. I've seen snippets of grainy footage shot by a fan from the terracing, but that's all. The Celtic supporters who were fortunate enough to be there have the memory to treasure.

What a game, though! It stormed along from the first shrill of the referee's whistle right to the moment when I gave the ball an almighty dunt and it just ripped into the net behind Peter McCloy. That was our fourth goal and cemented our 4–2 success. I was the last Celtic player to touch the ball. The match official blew for full-time as soon as Rangers kicked off. The title was ours and Parkhead was in bedlam.

Players were cavorting around like kids and when you step back and analyse it, that was an extremely young Celtic team. I was twenty, so too was Roy Aitken, while George McCluskey and Mike Conroy were twenty-one, Davie Provan had just turned twenty-three while Tom McAdam was twenty-five. Goalkeeper Peter Latchford was twenty-six, Johnny Doyle had also just turned twenty-eight that month, Andy Lynch and Shuggy Edvaldsson were also twenty-eight and Danny McGrain was positively ancient at twenty-nine. The only thirty-something in a green and white shirt on the pitch was Bobby Lennox who, at the age of thirty-five, came on as a second-half substitute for Conroy.

Billy McNeill, too, was hardly a veteran of the dugout at only thirty-nine. After an unforgettable evening, he had won his first honour as Celtic manager.

Well, he was always going to mark the occasion with a bit of drama, wasn't he?

FRANK McGARVEY

Billy McNeill paid me one of the most remarkable compliments of my life when he said, 'Frank McGarvey was so good he could have played in any Celtic team at any time.' Long after my career had been over, my former manager made those glowing comments in a book and I had to read them twice to make sure I wasn't imagining things. That wonderful man always had the ability to make me feel ten feet tall.

If it hadn't been for Billy there is every likelihood I would not have signed for the club that had always been dearest to my heart as I grew up in the Glasgow housing scheme of Easterhouse, about five miles from Celtic Park. As a kid, I played a lot of football in the vicinity, but there was never the whiff of interest from Celtic. However, back in March 1980, Billy McNeill was prepared to shell out the biggest transfer fee in Scottish football history to sign me from Liverpool. There was only one snag, Alex Ferguson, my former manager at St Mirren, was eager to get me to join him at Aberdeen. I loved and admired Billy and Alex. What was I supposed to do? I knew I had to get the decision absolutely spot on; there would be no turning back.

Liverpool had bought me from the Paisley side for £300,000 less than a year beforehand and then ignored me and stuck me in the reserves. It didn't seem to matter what I did in the second team; the top side were so successful that I just couldn't get a chance to get in and show what I could do. I was frustrated and, I have to confess, lonely. I was living in Formby, but I was growing increasingly homesick. I wanted back up the road and I had a meeting with the Anfield gaffer Bob Paisley. He explained I would have to be patient, but I had made up my mind I was going home. Celtic and Aberdeen had monitored the situation and both were willing to pay the £250,000 fee Liverpool were looking for. It was down to me to choose. Billy McNeill and Celtic? Or Alex Ferguson and Aberdeen?

I met my old Saints boss in an Italian restaurant on Glasgow's Great Western Road and we had a fairly detailed discussion. He laid it on the line, his plans for me at Pittodrie, where I would fit into his first team, how the side would play, his ambitions for the Dons, everything. Alex Ferguson can be a determined character, just in case you hadn't already heard! And very persuasive. I listened to him and I have to admit I was very impressed. After being a forgotten man at Anfield, suddenly I was very much a wanted man at Aberdeen. And Celtic.

I explained to Alex Ferguson about my situation with Billy McNeill and I couldn't make any promises until I had spoken to him. Alex still tried to persuade me Aberdeen were the better choice. He made the point there was more of a chance of me being successful and winning honours at Pittodrie. He emphasised the strength of the team with international players such as goalkeeper Jim Leighton and central defenders Alex McLeish and Willie Miller. They were the very cornerstone of the formation of the line-up and it seemed more than obvious the club were on a firm footing. And I knew all about the manager's strengths after our years together at Love Street. He had a relentless drive to succeed and it would have been all too easy to follow his thread of thinking. I told him, though, I had given my word to Billy McNeill that I would discuss the matter with him and I hoped he understood. I'm not sure he did.

I met Billy McNeill in his manager's office at Celtic Park. Sitting beside him that day was John Clark, his defensive partner in the team that had won the European Cup in Lisbon in 1967. I was aware I was in the presence of not one, but two very special people. Sitting in the restaurant with Alex Ferguson, my mind said Aberdeen were the wise choice. Sitting in front of Billy McNeill and John Clark, two absolute legends of the club that had always been closest to my heart, I was veering in their direction. I admit I was in a quandary. Both clubs and their managers had strong appeal, but I knew I had to make a decision and stick by it. Once I had committed, my new club could be certain I would give them everything. It didn't seem fair to Celtic or Aberdeen to keep them waiting, I had far too much respect for Billy McNeill and Alex Ferguson.

I chose Celtic; that was down to Billy and my heart.

I admit I was more than a tad relieved once the decision had been made and I could get back to concentrating on playing football. I realised Alex Ferguson would have been upset, but he would also have known it would have been a very difficult decision for me to make. Clearly, I would not have dismissed the possibility of linking up with him at Aberdeen lightly. Now, with all that taken care of, I was just eager to get into that green and white jersey and get out on the park and play for Celtic.

I had performed at Parkhead for St Mirren, but it's an entirely different place when the fans are behind you and roaring you on. There were 35,000 supporters in the ground on a freezing winter's evening and they gave me a fabulous reception when I ran out for my first appearance against St Mirren, of all clubs. My Paisley teammates of not that long ago were in town and they were determined to spoil my homecoming. And they did, too. I didn't score on my first appearance and they took a point in a 2–2 draw.

It was all a bit of a whirlwind at the time. I had just completed the formality of signing twenty-four hours earlier and the club had to rush through my registration with the SFA. Once everything at that level had been okayed, I was given the nod to get out there and show I was worth the money. Did the huge transfer outlay weigh heavily on me? Well, a quarter-of-a-million pounds was a helluva lot of money for any club to part with, but, as you could anticipate, Billy took the pressure off me early on by telling me, 'Frank, as far as I'm concerned, you have already repaid the cash. Just concentrate on your game, it's been money well spent.' He always knew the right buttons to push, which was another of his great strengths.

The stalemate that night was a fairly strange encounter. We were winning 1–0 through a first-half goal from George McCluskey when I managed to slip in Johnny Doyle for the second shortly after the interval. 'So far, so good,' I told myself. And then it all went wrong in five horrible minutes. The referee awarded them a penalty-kick when he indicated Danny McGrain had handled the ball on the line and Doug Somner belted it past Peter Latchford. And in double-quick time he struck again with a header. I was disappointed because I had wanted so much to make an immediate impact, but such tales only belong in *Boys' Own* comic books and not real life.

Billy noticed I was a bit dejected and put his arm around me, 'Don't worry, Frank,' he said, 'it'll be okay next time.' That was the first occasion he ever cuddled me. Do you know he was still doing it years later? He would see me at a function and come up and embrace me. It was like he was still my manager and I was his player. Time had stood still. That was the charm of Billy McNeill, though. There was always a genuine warmth about his character and he wasn't afraid of showing his emotions. 'How's it going, Frank?' would be followed by those big arms engulfing you and you knew you were in the company of a true friend.

In all our years together, he never gave me a row. Not once. He had a lot to say to other players, but I think he knew I had given him everything I had in every game. I might not have played particularly well, but I could never be faulted for my effort. I realised Billy liked having me around the dressing room and I had to laugh when I also noticed in one of his books that he thought I was 'gallus'. In Glasgow parlance, that could be seen as someone who was a bit cocky, an individual who walked with a swagger. I'm not too sure about that. He also believed I could be an infectious character and a good presence about the place. I would certainly hope so.

As for the actual football, he practically gave me free reign to play alongside the likes of Charlie Nicholas and George McCluskey, two exceptionally talented guys to have as colleagues in attack. Billy reasoned he never knew what to expect from me because I never had a clue what I was going to do next myself. Not sure if that's a compliment or a complaint. Let's put it this way, I liked to keep my opponents guessing!

I did play in an off-the-cuff manner on occasion and Billy realised no cause was ever lost when I was on that football pitch. I would chase anything and everything and no defender was going to get any peace when I was around. That was just my natural style. I couldn't give anything less than 100 per cent and Billy could always rely on that. But I was overwhelmed when I read his tribute. I was knocked out to know he rated me so highly. It meant so much to me. If you got praise from this guy, you knew you had earned it.

I had to wait until my third game before I scored my first goal for the club. I drew a blank in a 1–1 draw with Kilmarnock at Rugby Park where the amazing Bobby Lennox, on as a second-half substitute, scored a late equaliser. I could hardly believe I was playing alongside a Lisbon Lion. Bobby was the last of the European Cup-winning side to hang up his boots, but he was so fit I reckon he could have played on for another couple of seasons after he retired at the age of thirty-seven. In fact, it was Bobby who gave us the lead in my goal scoring breakthrough game against Hibs at Parkhead.

The great George Best was in the Edinburgh side's line-up that afternoon. The man known as 'The Buzzbomb' walloped in a penalty-kick shortly after the interval and then we scored three in an incredible seven-minute burst and I'm delighted to inform you I got the effort that kicked off the crazy spell. I recall Danny McGrain and Davie Provan combining on the right before Davie slung over a perfect cross. I just needed to get my head to it and the ball was planted behind keeper Jim McArthur. That was the first of many goals Davie laid on the plate for me. Johnny Doyle and Roddie MacDonald scored the others and I was so overjoyed – and a little relieved – to have notched my first goal.

'There, Frank, what were you worrying about?' smiled Billy McNeill in the dressing room, followed by a customary bear-like hug. Unfortunately, we didn't win the league that season. Our last chance of retaining the championship ended at Love Street and it seemed as though my old club was coming back to haunt me. We were held to a goalless draw and that gave the trophy to Alex Ferguson and Aberdeen by a solitary point. This isn't sour grapes, but how we didn't win that game in Paisley on a May afternoon in 1980 I'll never know. There were only twelve minutes remaining when referee Alan Ferguson – he couldn't have been a relative, could he? – awarded us a penalty-kick after I had put Tommy Burns clear and he was sent flying in the box by an illegal challenge from John Young.

Penalty-kick? The match official had no doubt as he pointed to the spot. The Saints players protested and the ref decided to check with his linesman. Unbelievably, Ferguson came back and gave us a free-kick outside the box. One national newspaper reporter wrote the incident was three feet inside the area. At least! We were robbed!

As we sat in a fairly disconsolate state in the dressing room afterwards, Billy McNeill adopted a positive view. 'Right, lads, we'll just have to win the Scottish Cup next week,' he said. We were due to play Rangers at Hampden and, thankfully, we delivered the trophy in extra-time when George McCluskey cleverly flicked a low drive from Danny McGrain beyond Peter McCloy. The spectacle was ruined when the fans invaded the pitch at the end and police on horseback were called on to try to restore some semblance of order. All the reports the following day and for weeks afterwards were all about the riot. That was a shame because we played very well that day, deservedly won the trophy and I was delighted to get my hands on my first piece of silverware as a Celtic player. What a glorious feeling.

Three years after I joined Celtic, Billy McNeill left for Manchester City and it would be another four years before he returned to his spiritual home. I was on my way back to St Mirren in 1985 after scoring the winning goal in the Scottish Cup Final against Dundee United. I suppose it was the perfect way to sign off, although I didn't see it like that at the time. What a lot of Celtic fans will not be aware of, though, is the fact I almost rejoined Big Billy at Parkhead.

Front players such as Brian McClair, Mo Johnston and Alan McInally all left Celtic in the summer Billy was appointed manager for the second time. His first signing was Andy Walker, who had scored a lot of goals for Motherwell, but he knew he had to get another couple of strikers in to the club, especially after Mark McGhee sustained an injury fairly early on.

Billy made an enquiry to St Mirren about my availability. I was thirty-one years old at the time and felt as fit as I ever did. I would have gone back like a shot, but the Paisley boss at the time was Jimmy Bone and he wasn't interested in selling me. Billy turned to Frank McAvennie and he was in the Celtic team that won the league and Cup double in the club's centenary year. So, it worked out well for Billy McNeill and everyone connected with Celtic.

I could always dream.

PAUL McSTAY

I was only three weeks into my Celtic first-team career when I witnessed at first hand the sheer professionalism and sportsmanship of Billy McNeill. There was the utter delight from the manager at handing a seventeen-year-old rookie his first appearance in the Premier Division against a strong Aberdeen side. It was a bold decision by the manager to demonstrate a lot of faith in my ability and he worked on my confidence on the lead-up to the crucial encounter at Pittodrie. He managed to take the pressure off and said all the right things to make sure I was well prepared for the game.

I went out to face the Dons on 30 January 1982, my first-team league debut and a moment I had been striving to achieve since I had come through the ranks at Celtic Boys' Club. This was my moment of truth, but Billy had stressed I had been selected on merit. He had appreciated what he had seen and, in his judgement, I had a role to play in his plans this particular afternoon against Alex Ferguson's team that was laced with international players such as goalkeeper Jim Leighton, defenders Willie Miller and Alex McLeish and midfielder Gordon Strachan. Billy McNeill could have chosen a less exacting baptism for yours truly!

The pressure was on from the opening sixty seconds when our opponents took the lead before a few of the Celtic players had the opportunity to get a kick at the ball. John McMaster scored with a drive beyond Pat Bonner and I had the feeling we were in for a long afternoon. We knew we had a massive job on our hands even before their early opener and, as positive-thinkers will always insist, it is better to lose a goal in the first minute than the last. At least we knew we had eighty-nine minutes to make a response. With Billy McNeill in the dugout, there was no need to panic. He had set up his team that afternoon with four men in midfield with Dom Sullivan, Tommy Burns and Murdo MacLeod as my partners. I couldn't have asked for better company.

As you would expect from any Billy McNeill side, the players rolled up their sleeves and immediately restarted the encounter with a gritty determination to get right back into the game. And we did that when George McCluskey netted a penalty-kick just before the half-hour mark. Frank McGarvey was an incredible player to have in your line-up and a real menace to the opposition. They hadn't a clue what to expect next when he was on the ball and that day Doug Rougvie was the Dons defender who had been driven to distraction before giving away the spot-kick with a desperate lunge at our all-action frontman. It remained a stalemate until we hit a real purple patch midway through the second-half. We could feel we were in the ascendancy and, naturally enough, it is imperative in these situations to make your dominance count.

I recall Murdo MacLeod accepting a short free-kick from Dom Sullivan and firing in a shot that took a deflection off a defender, wrong-footed Jim Leighton and dropped into the net to give us the advantage. My best moment was something like five minutes away when I scored on my first appearance. I'll never forget that sensation of total elation. I received a ball in their box, made some space for myself and slotted a left-foot effort wide of the keeper. It sounds like a cliché, but it really was a dream come true. As I ran towards the cheering Celtic fans in the crowd, all celebrating like crazy, my eye fell on the front row of the stand and I recognised a friend of mine. And then I noticed a whole row of his pals and relatives. What a feeling!

We won 3–1 and Billy McNeill, as you would expect, was beaming afterwards. I saw him go around the team, pat them on the back, make an observation or two. That was a happy coach journey back from the north-east, I can tell you that. That game is one I will never forget. Billy McNeill had entrusted me with a place in his starting line-up. I had heard the tales Jock Stein would carefully select games in which to bring in a young player for his debut appearance. It was usual for Big Jock to pick a game at Parkhead, too.

That was precisely what Billy had done the previous week when I took my bow in the top side in a Scottish Cup-tie against Queen of the South in the east end of Glasgow. We won 4–0 and, apart from the obvious recollections, there was another memorable moment when Danny McGrain scored his first goal in three years! Playing against Aberdeen at Pittodrie, though, was a whole new ball game. What a massive boost to my self-esteem to understand Billy McNeill thought I was good enough against top-class opposition on their own turf. Remember, please, this was an Aberdeen team that beat Real Madrid to win the European Cup-Winners' Cup the following year.

We were in action again three days later when Hibs came to Parkhead for another league encounter. Celtic were playing catch-up at the time and I believe this was our first game on our own pitch since early December because of the dreadful weather conditions. That didn't mean much to me at the time as I hoped I had done enough at Aberdeen to keep my place in the team. I was delighted when the line-up was announced and I was in again. Unfortunately, there wasn't too much memorable about the game.

Bertie Auld, Billy McNeill's fellow-Lisbon Lion, was manager of the Easter Road side at the time. I knew all about Bertie's reputation as a genius in the Celtic midfield alongside Bobby Murdoch in the historic team that had won the European Cup in 1967. Bertie and Bobby were the main architects of how Celtic played back then. However, he didn't take that adventurous spirit into the dugout. Bertie knew how to suffocate a game and his tactics that evening were for the Edinburgh men to play for a point. They got it in a goalless draw and for the first time I had encountered something like defence in depth from the opposition.

There was little time or room in which to manoeuvre, you didn't get the chance to take too many touches before someone was snapping at your heels and I learned a lesson that evening. I realised I would have to grow up very quickly to play at this level and also if I hoped to remain in the first team. I couldn't help but wonder if the manager would make a change for our next game, which was four days later against Dundee in Tayside. Once again, he showed conviction in a teenager and I was in again. We won fairly comfortably 3–1 and I was fortunate enough to set up Murdo MacLeod for the first goal. Murdo scored a second and Frank McGarvey chipped in with the other. I was delighted when I read a report in one newspaper the following day where the sportswriter, Don Morrison of the *Sunday Mail*, stated, 'Along with Murdo MacLeod, Paul McStay impressed the most. The kid showed a lot of class and style and seems set for a great future.'

Things had been going fairly smoothly, but, as luck would have it, I would be destined to play my fourth game for the club back where my league outings had started only fourteen days earlier. Celtic were drawn against Aberdeen in the early round of the Scottish Cup and we knew Alex Ferguson would be looking to exact revenge for our earlier win.

Celtic had a great tradition in the national competition, but had won it only once in the past five years – the 1–0 extra-time victory over Rangers in 1980 – and Billy McNeill and everyone else at Parkhead was determined to get back on track. The draw had been unkind, but the manager reasoned if you were going to win the trophy you would have to overcome some top-class opposition along the way. He set the team up in much the same way as had been successful in the league match a couple of weeks earlier.

On this occasion, though, Alex Ferguson put Alex McLeish into his midfield to combat our four of yours truly, Dom Sullivan, Murdo MacLeod and Tommy Burns, the quartet who had enjoyed success last time out. Big Eck was a versatile performer who had played most of his games in the back four alongside Willie Miller and they were two of the best centre-backs in the business. But the Dons boss decided Big Eck's strength in the middle of the park would be more advantageous to the team in this crucial Cup-tie.

In the end, Fergie, who became a future boss of mine with Scotland, got it right. John Hewitt claimed the only goal of the game in the nineteenth minute and we just could not get that precious equaliser. Near the end, Tom McAdam smacked an effort off the woodwork and we realised it wasn't going to be our day.

To say I was disappointed would be a massive understatement. I was gutted. A fortnight earlier, I had been celebrating in the same away dressing room in the same ground and now we were out of the Scottish Cup. It was a lot for a young player to take in. Very suddenly, you are aware of the highs and lows of the beautiful game and how quickly fortunes can change. I had witnessed Billy McNeill in triumph and this would be the first time I saw him in defeat. How would he react to an adverse result? I thought he displayed the dignity befitting of such a Celtic legend. He would have been hurting, along with the rest of us.

Billy McNeill had always stressed that Celtic players should think of themselves as winners. Second best was nowhere, as far as he was concerned. So, at Pittodrie, where he had been manager for a season before returning to Parkhead in the summer of 1978, he had seen his team beaten and knocked out of a trophy.

Davie Hay was my Celtic boss when I first got my hands on a Scottish Cup medal three years later as we overwhelmed Dundee United 2–1 in an enthralling and dramatic encounter at the national stadium. We were trailing 1–0 before Davie Provan curled one of his free-kick specials high into the net and Frank McGarvey thumped in a last-minute header. Billy McNeill was back as Celtic manager when we won the silverware again in our centenary year, ironically duplicating our result over the Tannadice men. This time Frank McAvennie was our two-goal matchwinner. We retained the trophy a year later when Joe Miller got the only strike of the game against Rangers and the great Tommy Burns was in charge in 1995 when a header from giant Dutchman Pierre van Hooijdonk beat Airdrie.

There were three league titles, as well; two with Billy McNeill in seasons 1981/82 and 1987/88 and one with Davie Hay in our amazing last-day 5–0 win over St Mirren that pipped Hearts on goal difference. There was also a League Cup with Billy in season 1982/83 when goals from Charlie Nicholas and Murdo MacLeod gave Celtic a 2–1 win over Rangers.

And it all began back at Pittodrie on a freezing Saturday afternoon on 30 January 1982 when the Celtic manager made a colossal commitment to a teenage hopeful. Thank you, Billy McNeill.

PAT BONNER

Billy McNeill was deadly serious. 'Get your act together or you're on the next boat home,' he told me. I was nineteen years old, a boy among men, really. I could have folded. Let's face it, those were extremely hurtful words from the Celtic manager.

So, what was I to do? I didn't really have an option. I determined there and then to show my gaffer I had a future at the club. I had always been a good trainer, but I upped my efforts, working hard and flat-out every single day. I'll admit my form had dipped when Billy McNeill fired his verbal volley. I had been feeling a little homesick, too. My family were a close-knit unit – as the Irish tend to be – and my grandmother had passed away. Unfortunately, I couldn't get time off to attend her funeral and, naturally enough, that had an effect on me. I'm not using this as any sort of excuse for not performing consistently at the required level for a club such as Celtic. Even seasoned campaigners can hit a sticky patch, it happens to everyone in football at some stage in their career.

If Billy was trying to provoke a reaction from a rookie keeper, then he had more of an impact than any psychologist. I was determined to prove the manager wrong. Quite literally, my future was in my own hands. I always arrived early for training, but I can tell you, I never got in before Billy. I think he switched on the lights in the morning when he arrived and switched them off at night when he went home.

I had had something of a meteoric rise after becoming Jock Stein's last signing for the club on 14 May 1978, just ten days before my eighteenth birthday. I often wondered about that. Big Jock must have known he would be leaving the position yet he still took time to travel over to Ireland to sit down with a teen-ager and explain all that entailed in becoming a Celtic player.

He went through everything in fine detail. And then I turned up for pre-season training in July and there was no sign of Jock. Billy McNeill and his assistant John Clark had just taken over after leaving Aberdeen, so we were all starting at the same time. Naturally, they didn't know me, a raw teenager from Donegal Junior football who had been spotted by Sean Fallon playing for Keadue Rovers. That actually worked for me. Billy and John really put me through my paces during the pulverising training routines before they made up their minds. They had to find out fast if they believed I had what it took to be a goalie at the club.

At that time, Celtic had Peter Latchford and Roy Baines as the two main goalkeepers. I was put in the reserve side, but I trained with the first team. Peter had been brought up to Glasgow by Big Jock in what was initially a loan deal from West Brom in February 1975 which became permanent five months later while Roy, who had started his career at Derby County before a switch to Hibs, arrived in an exchange move that saw Andy Ritchie leave for Morton in October 1976. So, I was an Irishman battling with two Englishmen for a place with Scotland's best-loved football team. Having said that, a place in the starting eleven looked a long way off when I first joined the club.

It didn't work out for Roy, a very capable No.1, for whatever reason and he returned to the Greenock outfit after playing fewer than twenty first-team games. When he was transferred in March 1979, that meant an automatic step-up for me as Latch-ford's deputy. Billy realised he would have to toughen me up just in case an injury ruled out Peter and I had to be called in. You could say things got a bit rigorous during training. The manager was determined to work on my ability with cross balls.

As a special treat, he arranged for the likes of Big Shuggy Edvaldsson, Roy Aitken, Tom McAdam and Roddie MacDonald, all six-foot plus and built to match, to make sure I knew they were around when I came for a high ball. I should add Billy joined in, too. He was still fit enough to get into that tracksuit, as he did every single day. There are some managers who spend about fifteen minutes with the players when they go through daily routines and then go off to take care of business elsewhere. Not Billy McNeill. He was eager to get involved in everything we did and, at the same time, he made certain there were no slackers. We would go through the usual loosening-up sessions and then Billy decided it was time for me to face the barrage of balls into the box.

I used to play Gaelic football back home in Ireland, so I was used to going up early to catch the ball. However, with a football, that could prove to be dodgy. One slip and the ball would be behind you and, as luck would have it, there would normally be an opponent lurking around to stab it into the net. So, there was a slight change in timing and rising to meet a ball dropped into a packed penalty area when friend and foe went for it at the same time.

All sorts of crosses were flighted into the penalty area in an aerial bombardment and I had to attempt to clear a path to take the ball at the most advantageous point. Billy, Big Shuggy and the others made it as difficult as possible for me to make a clean catch. I was buffeted around, blocked off, challenged with elbows flying around and you had to maintain complete and utter concentration. If I mishandled a cross, Billy would simply say, 'Right, let's spend another half-hour on this. Take your positions, boys.' And we would go through it all again.

It could be brutal. These guys were my colleagues and they were giving me more of a bashing than our opponents on matchday. After weeks of being clattered by my so-called mates, I decided to do something about it. During another exhausting training session, a ball arrived in the box and, as luck would have it, it was about to land between Billy and me. I saw my chance. I went for it with everything I had. We were two big lads and, remember, Billy had been playing for Celtic just three or four years beforehand. We were on a collision course and I decided to punch the ball clear.

There was a dreadful thud and maybe I got more of Billy's head than the spherical object. The manager was just a wee bit dazed as I said, 'Sorry, boss, I think I might have caught you there.' Those merciless and gruelling training routines came to a halt that day. Of course, it could have been a coincidence.

As a matter of fact, Big Billy actually went into goal one day to demonstrate what he expected of me. 'Step aside,' he said, 'I'll show you what I want.' That was an incredibly brave thing to do because goalkeeping is a specialised position and a lot of outfield players haven't a clue about working on angles, when to come for the ball and when to stick. As Billy had often insisted, goalkeeper and centre-half were the two most vulnerable positions in the team. No argument from me on that assertion. One slip is normally fatal and that will be all the supporters will remember about your performance.

However, I was quite surprised by his display between the sticks. As a central defender, he would have known about the timing, but he also had a good pair of hands. He would come and clutch the ball, turn and smile and say, 'I want to see you doing that.' I couldn't argue with that, either.

Billy could be just as tough with his own backroom staff during training. There was one day he decided to work on crosses to the near post. I recall John Clark was out on the right and someone else was on the left. It was a simple enough routine – or, at least, it should have been. Billy's assistant could be a bit of a wind-up merchant with an extremely dry sense of humour. Billy would get us all in order and then wave for John to send in the first ball to my near post.

The first delivery was so far off target it overshot the far post.

Then in would come one from the bloke on the left and that fell into the designated area. Next up, it was John again. Wallop! The ball flew over the crowd at the near post and went out of play again. Billy didn't look too pleased with his No.2.

'Okay, let's try again,' he ordered. 'Near post, remember.' John might not have been a Bobby Murdoch or a Bertie Auld with the ball at his feet in that unforgettable Lisbon Lions line-up, but he must have been able to guide a ball towards my near post. We all took our positions, I awaited getting knocked around as usual and once more we were all left standing around as the ball was launched into orbit.

'Right, get down the road,' shouted Billy to John, pointing to the exit gate. The Celtic manager was actually sending off his assistant! John, disguising a smile, shrugged his shoulders and walked in the general direction of Celtic Park. Once again, Billy hadn't been joking. I had seen that look before. If nothing else, the exercise proved he had no favourites on the training ground and he would treat his backroom staff exactly as he would his players. There was no discrimination. John Clark found that to his cost that particular afternoon.

I admit I could come home fairly annoyed after a brush with Billy. We had a sort of love/hate relationship, but I hasten to point out we never once fell out. Some things may have been said in the heat of the moment and you had to accept that was part and parcel of the game. I never disliked Billy, no matter what had been uttered in an unguarded moment. There may have been things that had been said between us, but they ended there. There were no grudges. In any case, as far as I am concerned, it is impossible not to have affection for someone for whom you have complete and utter respect. I really can't stress that enough. Billy McNeill may have been my manager, but he was also a person I admired as a human being.

I can reflect on our time together at Celtic and can see how much I owe him. He must have had confidence in my ability to give me my chance so early. It was a big thing for him to hand me my debut against Motherwell on 17 March 1979 – St Patrick's Day! What a date for an Irishman to make his first Celtic appearance. I hasten to add it was not a sentimental choice from the manager. Aberdeen had knocked us out of the Scottish Cup in a replay by winning 2–1 at Parkhead in the previous midweek. Unfortunately, Peter Latchford shouldered most of the blame for two early Dons goals – one in the first minute – and Billy decided to bring me in. Football can be a harsh game and you had to grasp your opportunity when it came along. While I prepared to take my bow in front of those wonderful fans at Parkhead, Peter was with the reserves at Fir Park.

It would have been a perfect day for me if I had managed to keep a clean sheet, but, alas, it was not to be. I would just have to settle for a 2–1 victory, but I was happy to accept that. The newspapers were quite kind to me the following day and one made the point that Bobby Lennox, who scored both our goals that afternoon, was thirty-five years of age – almost double that of the eighteen-year-old debutant. Bobby, still lightning fast at even that advanced stage of his career, had us two goals ahead five minutes after the interval. My aim after that was to keep out our opponents, but a bloke by the name of John Donnelly pulled one back and we were walking on eggshells for the remainder of the confrontation. Happily, we got through without further mishap.

I had to wait a couple of weeks for my next first-team appearance and, coincidentally, that came against Motherwell again, this time at Fir Park. On this occasion, it was a midweek encounter and once again I was in after Peter Latchford had been blamed by some critics for Hibs' winner in the Edinburgh team's 2–1 victory at Easter Road the previous Saturday. And what a game it turned out to be, too. We were a goal down in nineteen minutes, but stormed back to lead 3–1 at half-time before it went to 3–2 and then 4–2. Five minutes from the end, they made it 4–3 and, thank goodness, that was the end of the scoring. Making it even more remarkable, Danny McGrain scored a rare goal. It had been that sort of night in Lanarkshire.

That was my second and last top-team outing of the campaign and I had no complaints. Billy McNeill went with the experience of Peter Latchford for the remainder of the season and was totally vindicated when Celtic won the title on that famous evening when they triumphed 4–2 over Rangers with ten men following Johnny Doyle's dismissal. I was as overjoyed as any Celtic player who was stripped that night. However, I would be lying if I said I didn't want some of that. The scenes at Parkhead that night were simply phenomenal, it was such an outburst of happiness from every corner.

It was Monday, 4 August 1980 when things turned for me big-style. Peter Latchford broke a bone in his hand and Billy put me in against Manchester United for Danny McGrain's testimonial game. There were 45,000 fans in Celtic Park that evening and it rocked from start to finish in honour of a fabulous club servant.

I was up against former Celt Lou Macari, who was the Old Trafford team's captain for the night, Scotland striker Joe Jordan plus other international stars such as Sammy McIlroy, Steve Coppell and Jimmy Greenhoff. It was a glitzy occasion, but the main thing on my mind was to try to get a shut-out at the third attempt. Happily, I managed that as the ninety minutes ended in a goalless stalemate. A trophy was up for grabs, so penalty-kicks had to be taken and United scored three to our one. No one seemed to care and, as far as I was concerned, it was a clean sheet.

Billy McNeill was never a strict disciplinarian, but he was always very protective of Celtic's traditions and the club's image. I think he called it sensible discipline. I can recall one of my first days at the club when trainer Frank Connor, who had been a goalkeeper at the club in the early sixties, told me to get a haircut. I was never a hippy, but I got the message. We were expected to wear a shirt and tie and dress in the manner you would expect of a professional at one of the world's foremost football clubs.

As a youngster, you took on duties such as cleaning the boots of the first-teamers and sweeping out dressing rooms. That order transmitted into your everyday life and outlook. They weren't bad habits to pick up. I can also recall a day when I hung up my jacket on a peg as I got ready for a training session. 'Hang your jacket up properly,' said Billy as he removed the item from the peg, found the little loop on the inside collar and then placed it back on the wall. 'There, that's better,' he said with satisfaction. That little gesture remained with me for life.

Billy left for Manchester City in the summer of 1983 and had a stint at Aston Villa before returning to the club in our centenary year. It was unfortunate Davie Hay had to make way as manager, but Billy came in and created his own environment. We had no silverware to show for our efforts the previous season and it is to Billy's credit he managed to re-energise the club. He brought a positivity with him, he had returned to do a job and, as ever, he would be leading from the front.

Billy bought wisely, too, bringing in Andy Walker, a lively striker from Motherwell, Chris Morris, a right-back from Sheffield Wednesday and Republic of Ireland colleague, and Billy Stark, an experienced midfielder from Aberdeen. Over the next few months he brought in Frank McAvennie, from West Ham, and Joe Miller, another rapier-swift raider, from the Dons. Frank and Joe had never hidden their affection for Celtic and Billy also saw that as important.

It's in the history books now what the team so memorably and so wonderfully achieved as they celebrated one hundred years of existence. The League Championship trophy and the Scottish Cup, both bedecked in green and white ribbons, returned to the Celtic trophy room in majestic triumph.

It was no less than Billy McNeill deserved.

DAVIE HAY

I had two footballing idols when I was a kid – Denis Law and Billy McNeill. There's an eight-year difference between me and these two genuine legends – and I use the word advisably – and they were experienced Scotland international players while I was still at school in Paisley. I could never in my wildest dreams have believed I would one day be a teammate of both.

Denis, for me, was the complete soccer showman; the first football superstar. He was stylish, elegant, flamboyant and could score goals for fun for his country and his clubs, most notably, in my experience, Manchester United. Billy, on the other hand, was mainly in the team to prevent goals, although he could nick a couple of vital ones when he went up for set-plays. His prowess in the air, as everyone in the game has long acknowledged and admired, was superb. His timing, his take-off and the moment of impact were all essentials for a dominant centre-half.

But I can't recall Billy ever bringing the ball out of defence like a Franz Beckenbauer. He rarely, if ever, attempted to dribble past an opponent. Billy's best work was done in the air and John Clark, his fellow-Lisbon Lion, did all the tidying-up on the deck. John was known as 'Luggy' or 'The Brush' to his teammates. Not too sure about the first nickname, but the latter certainly fitted him perfectly. As a pair, they dovetailed exceptionally well, a match made in Paradise, indeed.

I was in awe of Billy when we first met. Initially, I was a part-timer when I joined Celtic in January 1965 while I continued my accountancy studies. I was seventeen years old and didn't really come into contact with the likes of Billy or the other first-team players who would become colleagues. I probably got to know them a lot better when we did pre-season training. There was never anything big-time about Billy McNeill. In fact, you could say that about all the players of that era. They must have known at some stage there was the distinct possibility you would be challenging for their place in the first team, but that never prevented any of them going out of their way to give you advice and hints and make you feel welcome and part of the football club.

I was disappointed to miss out on the trip to Lisbon when Celtic won the European Cup on that unforgettable day on 25 May 1967. I was nineteen years old and a full-timer by that time and I was aware Jock Stein had plans to take some of the younger players to Portugal to give them experience of football at that level. I wasn't among them. Unfortunately, I had left it too late to make travel arrangements or even get a ticket for the match, so I had little option but to watch the game on television. I sat down with my future wife Catherine to view the game, which kicked off at 5.30 p.m. That was an awesome performance from the guys I looked up to every day.

That summer, with Celtic the European champions, Big Jock encouraged the youngsters to take on the established players. It was his way of keeping the first-teamers on their toes. He would organise bounce games between the Lions and the teenagers who became known as the Quality Street Gang; youngsters such as Kenny Dalglish, Danny McGrain, George Connelly, Lou Macari, Vic Davidson, Paul Wilson and yours truly.

I think Billy enjoyed mingling with us and passing on some invaluable tips. That was the thing about Billy; he was always so approachable and genuinely friendly. He had a word for everyone and it made you feel ten feet tall when he remembered your name. He was the same with everyone. He may have been the captain of the team that had just become the first British club to conquer Europe, but he was still so down to earth. Nothing was too much trouble for him.

One vivid recollection I have of that European Cup adventure was going to the quarter-final tie against Yugoslavia's Vojvodina Novi Sad on a frosty, cold March evening at Parkhead. There was a hint of fog, as well, and I could only get tickets for the old Rangers end at the ground. Catherine accompanied me. The official crowd was given as 69,374, but, as a trained accountant, I would have questioned that figure. We could hardly move as everyone crushed together. Remember, there was no such comfort zone as a sitting area at that part of the ground back then. Celtic were 1–0 down from the first leg and I knew from talking to Billy and other players, such as Bobby Murdoch, Tommy Gemmell and Jimmy Johnstone, that the Slavs were no mugs.

It was goalless at half-time and, as you might expect, the supporters were getting just a little anxious. It was a bit of a rarity to stand in among the fans and I was amazed at how quickly they could react to a player missing a chance and then, just as swiftly, change their mind when the same player did something good. One minute someone was 'woeful' and the next they were 'wonderful'. It was a real eye-opener standing in the midst of the spectators that evening. The one thing I did realise, above all, was their devotion to the team. It was quite an experience.

The place erupted when Stevie Chalmers equalised after Tommy Gemmell had fired over a cross from the left that wasn't dealt with by the Vojvodina defence. The ball hit the net right in front of me, Catherine and a few delighted supporters, and it was just bedlam. I had never witnessed anything like it. You could just sense how much it meant to the team's followers. There was a bloke beside me simply screaming with delight. I thought he was going to shatter my left eardrum.

There were no fancy electric scoreboards or clocks at the ground. Many of the fans continually asked, 'How long to go, mate?' The yelling gent to my left quizzed me every minute on the minute. I tried to concentrate on what was happening out on the pitch, which was becoming increasingly difficult as a heavy mist rolled in around the east end of Glasgow. Identifying the players wasn't made any easier by the fact Celtic were playing in their dark all-green strip that night.

Celtic won a corner-kick on the right wing with time running out. I can remember Billy McNeill looming into focus. Our centre-half didn't score a lot of goals, but he did score important goals. He made them all count. The Slav defenders had done their homework and tried to pick up the captain as he came forward. He was clearly the centre of attention. I had a quick glance to see Charlie Gallagher shaping to take a short corner-kick, but a Vojvodina player raced out to take up a covering position. That made up Charlie's mind and he swung a right-footer into the penalty area. Big Billy, as he did umpteen times in training every day, rose and majestically powered the ball high into the roof of the net. Catherine and I were getting swung all over the place by delirious fans. Celtic were in the semi-finals and the rest, as they say, is history.

Is it any wonder the Celtic fans adored their skipper? Could anyone be surprised Big Jock's first pick on his team sheet every week was Billy McNeill? That evening, as a fan, I realised just how much Billy and Celtic really meant to the man on the terracing.

When you talk about Billy McNeill you remember the Celtic captain standing in Lisbon holding aloft the European Cup that glorious sunny evening. You recall his special goals in Cup Finals and crucial league games. But a lot goes on behind the headlines and I witnessed a moment that crystallised how important Celtic were to Billy McNeill. It was a league game against Ayr United at Somerset Park in November 1973 and I was in the stand that afternoon. I had a thigh strain, so I didn't bother to strip and, once again, I took my place among the fans.

Billy teamed up in central defence alongside George Connelly, who had become a close personal friend of mine. Ayr were never easy on the eye and the ball would spend a lot of time in the clouds as they hammered it down the length of the field on their tight, little park. A guy called Alex Ferguson was playing for Ayr United that day and he was always eager to let the opposition defenders know he was around. Fergie liked to unsettle the centre-backs and he could be a bit of a handful.

During the game, for no good reason, I turned my gaze to Billy and George while the ball was at the other end of the pitch. There were 16,000 supporters squeezed into the confines of the ground and I think everyone else was watching the action around the Ayr goal. Billy was having a right go at my mate and, at one stage, I thought it might come to blows. Billy was gesticulating furiously and was obviously unhappy with something his defensive partner had – or hadn't – done. George, clearly, wasn't just going to stand there and accept an ear-bashing. Thankfully, nothing came of it. The game roared on and Celtic won 1–0 with a goal from Kenny Dalglish.

The manager missed the incident, as did the media. If there were TV cameras there that afternoon, they missed it, too. I've never mentioned it until now. It was just a little cameo of Billy McNeill taking his duties as Celtic captain very seriously. It wasn't all about glory games and performing in the spotlight. Here was a match Celtic would be expected to win against opposition who were still part-time. It didn't matter to Billy. It could have been the San Siro Stadium and not Somerset Park, this was a game in which Celtic were involved and he demanded the absolute best from everyone around him. Now that's what you call a thorough professional.

In Billy's line of work out on the pitch, no one ever remembered the last-ditch tackles, the keen anticipation or the clearing headers. But, of course, our wonderful captain did have the exceptional knack of rising to the occasion.

I signed forms with Celtic in January 1965 and at that time Celtic hadn't won anything in ages. Three months later, we were due to play Dunfermline in the Scottish Cup Final. Somehow it seemed fitting Billy McNeill was the man to alter that sad trophyless state of affairs. I don't think I'll be the only person in this book to mention that towering header from Billy that flew into the net to ensure that the silverware polish was being looked out again in the Parkhead trophy room.

My personal favourite Scottish Cup Final memory as a spectator, however, came four years later when Celtic walloped Rangers 4–0. I was excited for my big mate George Connelly who had become the first player from our group to achieve regular first team football. Wee Jinky Johnstone was suspended for the showdown with our age-old foes and Big Yogi, John Hughes, was injured and he, too, was forced to miss out. That left Big Jock with a bit of a dilemma with both wingers ruled out of the Hampden game. Well, it might have been a problem for most managers, but Big Jock wasn't any other manager. He simply changed the formation of the team and played without wide men with Big George and Bertie Auld told to get inside the opposition's full-backs, Kai Johansen and Willie Mathieson. As the scoreline would indicate, it worked a treat.

Billy got the show on the road in the second minute when he rose imperiously to a left-wing corner-kick from Bobby Lennox and the best was yet to come. As half-time approached, Wee Lennox raced through to lash a second beyond the exposed Rangers goalie. And, only moments later, came my pal George's memorable moment. Martin took a short goal-kick to his skipper John Greig on the edge of the box. He tried to knock the ball wide, but George read the play and intercepted the pass. He took it round Greig, enticed Norrie Martin from his line, nonchalantly drifted wide of his frantic efforts to retrieve the situation and rolled the ball into the net – right in front of the Celtic supporters. I was so happy for my chum. I was quite chuffed for myself, too, of course. Stevie Chalmers notched a fourth to round off a great day at the national stadium.

I could never have believed it, but the roles were reversed six months later. I was picking up a Cup medal and Big George was cheering me on from the Hampden stand. I was chosen to play left-back against St Johnstone in the League Cup Final after Big Jock had surprisingly left out Tommy Gemmell. We won 1–0 with an early goal from Bertie Auld and once more our skipper, Big Billy, was being invited to go up to receive the silverware.

Billy McNeill waving trophies at celebrating Celtic supporters at Hampden is quite an endearing and enduring image.

11

Hampden Hails the Centurians

On the tranquil, breezeless afternoon of 14 May 1988, the lingering sun over Hampden Park bestowed its radiance through the cloudless pale blue skies. Every blade of grass on the lush green pitch appeared to be caressed in the brightness of a perfect day.

Celtic, with one encounter left to overcome, were a momentous ninety minutes away from completing a glorious League and Cup double in their centenary year. The national stadium, with the elements in flawless harmony, was the ideal setting for such a glorious achievement. Hollywood at its most extravagant could not have staged a more salubrious production.

Billy McNeill, a year after returning to his first love, was yet again on the brink of making Celtic history. But, following Dundee United snatching the advantage shortly after the interval with a slick run and finish by Kevin Gallacher, the manager realised he would have to gamble to bring success.

He said, 'Big decisions had to be made when we went a goal down. I was prepared to leave Celtic short at the back. I said to Tommy Craig, "Right now we've lost the Cup … we've got to go and win it." That's why I brought on Billy Stark for Derek Whyte to give Joe Miller freedom on the other side. Andy Walker had probably been asked for too much during the season, so I changed him for Mark McGhee's strength and determination. We stretched United while stretching ourselves.

'While the players were out on the pitch celebrating at the end, I went to the dressing room. I was alone there with my thoughts. The players deserved their moment of triumph because they had won the Cup, not me.

'It is unlike me to want to be by myself, but for once I did. Eventually, Jack McGinn came in and said, "I think they want you out there, Billy." Later, I reflected on the past twelve months. I had gone from one extreme to another as a manager – booted by Aston Villa and now lauded by Celtic.'

With fifteen minutes to go, Celtic were pushing forward frantically when Anton Rogan surged down the left and slung in a magnificent cross. Frank McAvennie, as courageous as ever, threw himself at the ball and pulverised a header beyond goalkeeper Billy Thomson.

With one minute to go, Joe Miller didn't connect with his right-wing corner-kick properly. It swept low across the surface where Billy Stark fed it back to McAvennie and he swivelled to hit an effort sweetly into the net.

The charismatic frontman laughed afterwards, 'We had to finish the game in ninety minutes because we couldn't handle extra-time. It had been a really hard season and we felt the effects of the tiredness in the last couple of weeks as we wrapped up the league title.'

There was one slight hitch before the champagne flowed – there wasn't any! Billy McNeill added, 'I believed we had thought of everything, covered every eventuality. The only mistake we made in our preparation was forgetting to bring champagne. So, we had to borrow some bottles from Queen's Park. Thank goodness the amateurs had a few in stock.'

No bubbly on the big day? It could have ruined Frank McAvennie's afternoon.

ROY AITKEN

Billy McNeill is the Greatest Ever Celt. Without hesitation, I would place my former manager right at the pinnacle of all those who have been associated with this famous club since it came to life in 1888. There will be those who may query my choice when you consider the names of so many other legendary individuals sprinkled throughout Celtic's remarkable history. For me, though, Big Billy is the best of the lot.

Jock Stein? What he achieved at the club was simply breath-taking. He took over a team that had won nothing for eight dismal years and, two seasons later, had become the first UK side to conquer Europe. What an incredible feat and you have to also take into consideration the nine-in-a-row title triumphs and umpteen Cup victories. Even getting Celtic to a second European Cup Final three years after Lisbon was extraordinary. Big Jock has deserved every bit of praise and acclaim that has come his way.

Jimmy Johnstone? The Celtic supporters voted him their Greatest Ever Player and the Wee Man merited that award for entertainment value alone. He could turn a game on its head with a shake of his hips, a mazy run through a forest of legs and set up a goal or claim one for himself. He was an exciting individual as well as being a colourful character. The Celtic fans, quite rightly, loved their wee winger with the ability to illuminate dull, grey afternoons in the dead of a Scottish winter.

Kenny Dalglish? A special talent, no argument. The Lisbon Lions, including my pal Bobby Lennox who was so helpful to me in the early years? Each and every one of them, including Billy, a genuine legend. Henrik Larsson? Another fabulous showman the supporters took to their hearts. Danny McGrain? Danny was the best I ever played alongside. If he had a bad game, I must have missed it. Danny's consistency was such I have no recollection of any winger giving him a hard time. I could go all the way through history and mention names such as Willie Maley, Jimmy McGrory, Charlie Tully, Bobby Evans and so on. Everywhere you look there is an iconic figure at this great club.

That is why I believe it is even more of an achievement for Billy McNeill to get my vote. Why Billy? What has he got that places him ahead of the other worthy and outstanding candidates? Billy McNeill, in my eyes, was the complete package. As a player, he made almost 800 appearances, more than any other performer in the club's history. Take a look at his medal haul, twenty-three as the club's on-field leader. As a manager, he appeared to be the logical choice to take over from Jock Stein in 1978. There are a few who would have shirked that responsibility of stepping into those shoes. Billy embraced the awesome challenge and won a league title in his first season.

It also seemed only right and proper that he was in charge when Celtic claimed the league and Cup double in our centenary year. In his seasons in the dugout, he picked up five titles, three Scottish Cups and a League Cup. As an ambassador, he was first class, a proud character who knew the true worth of Celtic Football Club and a gentleman who possessed the charm, warmth, wit and intelligence to spread the word about the traditions of the club.

And those are just some of the reasons I rate Billy McNeill as the Greatest Ever Celt.

I remember the first time I saw the great Billy McNeill. I travelled up from Ardrossan regularly to play for the Celtic Boys' Club when it was run by Frank Cairney. Billy would often take in one of our games when he had a free day and what a lift you got when someone informed you, 'Billy McNeill's here today!' You would search for him on the touchline and then you would spot this unmistakeable figure, standing straight-backed, almost to attention. Then he quit playing after winning his last medal in the 3–1 Scottish Cup Final triumph over Airdrie at Hampden in May 1975. Coincidentally, I signed for Celtic the following month at the age of sixteen.

About six weeks later, Jock Stein was involved in the car crash on the A74 motorway at Lockerbie that almost killed him and left him hospitalised for a few months. Sean Fallon, his long-time assistant, took over team matters for the season while Big Jock recuperated. I made my debut on 10 September in a League Cup-tie against Stenhousemuir at Ochilview when I came on as a second-half substitute for Shuggy Edvaldsson, the Icelandic defender who had been brought in as an obvious successor in the middle of the rearguard for Billy. We won 2–0 with goals from Bobby Lennox and Kenny Dalglish.

A fortnight later, I made my first start against the Larbert side when I stepped in at right-back for the injured Danny McGrain. Pat McCluskey slammed a penalty-kick past the post before my full-back partner Andy Lynch scored the only goal about ten minutes into the second-half.

I then dropped out until I returned for my first appearance in the Premier League against Aberdeen at Pittodrie on 2 February 1976. On this occasion, I was pitched in at centre-half and a goal from my Saltcoats buddy Bobby Lennox gave us a 1–0 victory. Clearly, Sean Fallon was happy enough with my performance because he played me in that position for the remaining eleven league games of the campaign. I was mainly partnered by Shuggy or, on a couple of occasions, Roddie MacDonald. As you might expect, Celtic clearly missed the presence of Jock Stein that season and I mean absolutely no disrespect to Sean Fallon when I say that. It was a massive period of transition and we failed to pick up any silverware.

Jock Stein returned and, as if by magic, we won the league and Cup double in his comeback campaign. At the start of September, he signed Hibs' experienced defender Pat Stanton in a swap deal with Jackie McNamara and played him alongside Roddie MacDonald as twin centre-halves. The manager took me aside and explained he didn't think I was strong enough to sustain playing in the middle of the defence for an entire season. Instead, he switched my position to a central midfield defensive area to operate just behind Kenny Dalglish and in front of the back four.

It was a different role for me, but I was just happy to get a game. I was played in that position in a League Cup-tie against Arbroath at Parkhead near the end of August and we won 2–1. It wasn't a particularly memorable game and even Big Jock told the press afterwards, 'It wasn't the most interesting, was it?' I think that's what is known as a rhetorical question.

The league didn't start until September that season with the six games in the League Cup qualifying sections taking up all of August. After we had drawn 2–2 with Rangers at Parkhead and lost 1–0 to Dundee United at Tannadice, I got the go-ahead to start in our home game against Hearts. Jock played me at centre-half alongside Pat Stanton while Roddie MacDonald was on the substitutes' bench. There was no place for Shuggy Edvaldsson and I recall Joe Craig, a striker bought for £60,000 from Partick Thistle the previous evening, played up front alongside Kenny Dalglish.

We drew 2–2 and Jock was obviously still putting his jigsaw together. However, he must have seen something in me because he kept me in the side for the rest of the league season, apart from one game. I even had the enjoyment of slamming in two goals against Rangers in a 2–2 draw at Ibrox in March 1977.

I played in the League Cup Final against Aberdeen which

we unluckily lost 2–1 in extra-time. A newspaper reporter wrote the following day that 'Celtic had enough chances to win half-a-dozen games, but ended up winning nothing but sympathy'. I wouldn't disagree with that.

I was selected for all five Scottish Cup games and I was delighted to sample a Final triumph at Hampden when we overcame our old Ibrox rivals 1–0 with a penalty-kick from Andy Lynch. We had earlier clinched the league title in mid-April with four games still to play. A goal just after the hour mark from Joe Craig against Hibs at Easter Road did the trick. At only eighteen years of age, I had won the double, something so many players do not achieve in their entire careers. Throughout the summer, there was so much to look forward to in the upcoming campaign. However, everything unravelled in an awful season – and that opened the door for the return of Billy McNeill.

Even before a ball was kicked in anger, there was a massive blow when skipper Kenny Dalglish joined Liverpool for £440,000 before the opening league match against Dundee United. The game ended in a goalless draw, Pat Stanton sustained a knee injury and never played again. Another six leagues into the term, Danny McGrain was ruled out for the remainder of the term with a foot injury following a tackle with Hibs' John Blackley, a personal friend of our world-class defender. It was a triple setback from which the team never recovered.

Kenny, Pat and Danny had been three of our most consistent and influential players the previous season. Other players were signed to replace them, but it proved to be an impossible task. Celtic dropped out of the league race far too early and finished fifth, nineteen points adrift of Rangers. We also lost 2–1 in the League Cup Final when Gordon Smith headed in an extra-time winner for the Ibrox team and First Division Kilmarnock dismissed us, the holders, from the Scottish Cup 1–0 in a replay at Rugby Park. We didn't get beyond the second round of the European Cup, losing 4–2 on aggregate to the Austrians of SWW Innsbruck.

Changes had to be made and Billy McNeill, after a season at Aberdeen, decided to return to his spiritual home. Immediately, he won the support of the players – he made sure we all got a pay rise. The basic weekly wage was seventy quid, but we could earn virtually the same again in bonuses and appearance money. Billy checked the figures and had a chat with the board. He informed them the basic at Aberdeen was £120 per week plus they received lucrative add-ons, too. At a stroke, all the players at Celtic got a hike of £200 on their monthly wages. We would have given the new manager every ounce of effort in any case, but that act emphasised he cared about his players. That mattered to all of us.

Danny McGrain took over as captain following the departure of Kenny Dalglish and I accepted that role when Danny left the club in May 1987. Davie Hay moved out that summer, too, and Billy returned to take over the team as we prepared for our centenary season. I won a league and a Scottish Cup with Davie in charge and I enjoyed working with him for four years.

One of the things Davie and Billy shared was their love for Celtic. Many players at the time could connect with that because we were Celtic fans, too. I'm thinking about the likes of myself, Tommy Burns, George McCluskey, Andy Lynch and Johnny Doyle. Others who joined the club may not have had an affiliation for the team, but they soon realised what this club stood for and how special it was.

In Billy McNeill's first season as Big Jock's successor, I believe he proved himself as being a first-rate manager. Two requirements for a team boss must be results and success in the transfer market. Billy ticked both boxes in his first year. He wasn't afraid to back his judgement of a player's ability with cash and he paid

£125,000 to Kilmarnock for their outside-right Davie Provan. Sounds peanuts today with all the multi-million pound deals that are commonplace, but it was a Scottish record back in 1978. He also parted with £100,000 for midfielder Murdo MacLeod from Dumbarton. Without argument, that was money well spent and these two players repaid those fees over and over in their initial campaign.

Who could forget the evening when ten men won the league? I was only twenty – still the youngest in the team – when we beat Rangers 4–2 to lift the Premier Division championship in Billy's first season. We had to win in our last league game of the campaign or the title was going to Rangers. And we managed the feat on a night of electrifying tension.

When Billy came back in 1987, we had a special relationship as manager and captain. I realised I had extra responsibility on and off the pitch as skipper and if anyone knew what it meant to be in that position at Celtic it was Billy. We had a great deal of communication and we had a lot of trust in each other. He would take me aside some days and ask, 'How are the boys? What's the mood in the camp?'

On occasion, I would tell him they are feeling a bit leggy, maybe the training could be scaled down a little. Sometimes I could get a subliminal message to the boss. He would nod and, later on, present it as his own idea. 'Right, lads,' he would say, clapping his hands together, 'let's take a break. How about some golf tomorrow?' or something along those lines.

I really admired Billy for so many reasons. He was honest, for a start. He could be a hard man in the dressing room when he was getting his messages across, but he could also be the life and soul of the party when we were allowed to let our hair down. But we all knew who was the boss; that fact was never in doubt. Everything Billy McNeill did was for the betterment of Celtic

Football Club. He made sacrifices, as we all did, to bring success to the team and the supporters.

I mentioned Billy proving his ability in the transfer market with the purchases of Davie Provan and Murdo MacLeod in his first season, but I could also point to Frank McGarvey and the boys he brought in during the centenary year, performers such as Andy Walker, Billy Stark, Joe Miller, Frank McAvennie and Chris Morris. He got the right blend, mixing new signings with the likes of myself, Pat Bonner, Tommy Burns, Peter Grant, Paul McStay and Mark McGhee, all of us out-and-out Celtic fans.

Celtic's one hundredth birthday celebrations had to be extraordinary. Billy McNeill and his players delivered in style with the league and Cup double. Billy, quite rightly, won the Manager of the Year award and Paul McStay deservedly took the top player honour. I was humbled, though, when the boss went on record as saying, 'I don't think Roy Aitken has had a better season'. Forget the money, the fame and the many other rewards, words such as those from an authentic legend make everything so worthwhile.

It was my pleasure and privilege to play for and get to know the real Billy McNeill. Greatest Ever Celt? For me, that will always be the case.

ANDY WALKER

I owe a former Rangers player big-time for making it possible for me to join Billy McNeill in Celtic's centenary celebrations in 1988, that never-to-be-forgotten year when the club took its place in glorious history by winning the league and Cup double.

If it hadn't been for Tommy McLean, there is every likelihood I would have been playing for Motherwell that memorable Saturday afternoon of 23 April 1988 when Celtic won the Premier Division title with a 3–0 triumph over Dundee. My dad, Frank, would have been in the Parkhead stand to witness the success. As it was, I was out there in the thick of the action and I managed to knock in a couple of goals.

I had just signed for Celtic the previous summer from the Fir Park side for £350,000 as Billy McNeill, who had just returned after four years in England, reshaped his squad. I arrived at roughly the same time as Billy Stark, from Aberdeen, and Sheffield Wednesday's Chris Morris. Frank McAvennie joined us from West Ham in October and Joe Miller, from the Dons, the following month. In under a year, my move to Celtic had turned my career upside down. The previous season with Motherwell, we had settled for eighth position in the twelve-team league and had been beaten twenty-one times in the forty-four game campaign. It was a fair old contrast in fortunes, I must say.

I netted twelve goals during my last term with the Lanarkshire outfit, but, by the completion of my debut year at Celtic, I had thirty-two strikes to my name. And league and Scottish Cup winners' medals. The remarkable transformation was all down to the day Tommy McLean told me I would never be good enough to perform as a winger. I had played schools, amateur and Junior football, but no one came in for me until Tommy made his move. I was with Baillieston Juniors at the time and we were due to play Bo'ness in the Junior Cup Final. However, before that game, Tommy came along to watch me in another match. I don't know what impression he got because I only played something like fifteen minutes as a substitute.

Back then, the Junior Cup showdown at Hampden was televised live and, although we lost 1–0 , the Motherwell manager watched the ninety minutes on a video at some point and then signed me. It was a six-month contract worth sixty quid a week and I thought I was on my way. It didn't quite work out as I had anticipated.

Tommy, who had played for Scotland and picked up a European Cup Winners' medal in 1972 during his eleven years at Ibrox, had been an excellent outside-right in his playing days. Or so he told me. He had an idea what a player on the touchline should be providing for his side and his teammates. I think it would be fair to say he wasn't overly-impressed by the performances from yours truly. He had a word with me about my abilities as a wide player and was fairly frank and straight to the point.

'You're not going to make it as a winger,' he informed me, adding for good effect, 'You've no pace, you've no flicks or tricks and you can't cross the ball.'

Well, at least I wasn't getting any mixed messages. However, for reasons known only to Tommy, he thought I could hack it as a leader of the attack. To be honest, I didn't fancy it. I had never envisaged myself as a centre-forward. I debated the point that it would be better for me to stick to the one position I knew and that was on the wing.

'You've got a good touch,' he insisted, 'and can go right or left. I think you can do it if you persevere. I see you as a back-to-goal striker.'

Now that left me just a shade perplexed. What on earth was a 'back-to-goal striker'? I had never heard the expression before.

Tommy attempted to explain it to me. Basically, he would tell the team's best passer of the ball and future Scotland international captain Gary McAllister to get the ball up to me quickly, I would take it under control and bring other players up the pitch and into the game. One thing I would say in my favour is that I always felt comfortable in front of goal and in and around the penalty box.

Tommy wanted me to give it a try and I gave it my best shot. I eventually settled in, picked up a few hints, kept at it and made steady progress. In fact, I began to play quite well and enjoy it.

In my first season, I made the odd first-team appearance. My debut was in a goalless encounter against Kilmarnock. We were in the First Division at the time and I got a run in the side near the end of the term. I played for about six minutes in the Scottish Cup semi-final against Celtic in 1985. I was put on as a substitute for an injured teammate not long before half-time and I thought, 'This is wonderful. Playing against Celtic, with all my pals at the Celtic End and my wee brother there with his Celtic scarf'. The adrenalin was pumping so much that when I went into a tackle I felt nothing. It was only after a few minutes when there was a stoppage that I looked down and saw my sock covered in blood. The trainer had to haul me off. I didn't want to go as I had hardly been on the pitch in the biggest game of my life. Despite my protests, the decision was made and John Gahagan came on for me.

We actually led in the first-half for about ten minutes with a Gary McAllister goal, but Tommy Burns, who would become a very good friend, equalised and we ended up getting a 1–1 draw. Unfortunately, the injury made sure I wouldn't get the opportunity to figure in the replay in which Motherwell gave a reasonable account of themselves until about fifteen minutes or so to go when Roy Aitken scored and then Mo Johnston added two more for a 3–0 scoreline. On the plus side, we were promoted at the end of that campaign.

I received some favourable reports in my last year at Mother-well. I was only twenty-three years of age and had adapted and changed my entire style of football and my thinking. Okay, I only scored a dozen goals in that campaign, but I would say in my defence, we didn't make many chances. Most of the time we were fighting a rearguard action and the front players had to scrap and battle for everything when the ball dropped into the opponents' half which, unfortunately, wasn't often enough. It was at some stage that year I was tapped by Davie Hay, who was then the Celtic manager.

All very hush-hush and against the laws of the game because I was under contract, but if you don't believe it went on in football then presumably you think the Planet Earth is flat. My dad was a massive Celtic supporter, as I was too, and, in his role as a chartered accountant, had been involved in some business deal-ings with folk at Parkhead, Billy McNeill included. In fact, he acted as a financial advisor when Kenny Dalglish left Celtic for Liverpool in 1977. My father, who was in Lisbon in 1967 and Milan in 1970 to cheer the team on in the European Cup Finals, wasn't an agent and he did most of his work on a friendship basis. He did make some interesting contacts, though.

I still had a year of my Motherwell deal to run when they offered me an extension at the end of the 1986/87 season. By this stage my heart was set on a move to Celtic. Dundee United, managed by Tommy McLean's brother Jim, showed an interest, but there was only one club for me. I wondered if the move would be scuppered when Davie Hay left, but I was then made aware Billy McNeill had me in his plans when he made his Celtic comeback. Thank goodness!

However, things didn't go too smoothly in the first few

matches of our pre-season tour of Sweden and I couldn't help but think if it had been too big a step up from Motherwell to Celtic. You begin to imagine all sorts of things. Then, in the last game of the tour against a First Division side, IK Oddevold, we were awarded a penalty-kick and I grabbed the ball to get a chance of scoring. I potted the spot-kick and got another couple before half-time as we won 4–1.

It had been our fifth game, so I thought it was time I contributed a goal or two. That was my thinking, too, before my Premier Division debut for Celtic against Morton at Cappielow. I realised it was important to deliver for the fans and I thought if I could just get a goal I could take it from there.

I scored twice as we won 4–0 – Billy Stark and Mark McGhee chipped in with the others – and those goals were crucial to me. Billy McNeill had told the players it was vital we got off to a good start to show we meant business and to give everyone a signal to that effect. I was fortunate as I scored a lot of goals in that early spell. It got the fans on my side and it wasn't long before I had scored more than I had throughout the previous season with Motherwell. I was grateful the Boss and his assistant Tommy Craig never put me under any pressure about scoring. I was just told to play well and everything would come right. Their vote of confidence was well appreciated.

Right at the start, Tommy stressed the first line of our defence was our front three and we started working on that in Sweden. I recall an early game against my old club Motherwell where Mark McGhee put a lot of pressure on Fraser Wishart and he pushed his clearance to Tommy Burns, who immediately crossed for me to score with a diving header. I got two that afternoon as we won 4–1. The front players challenged for everything in our opponents' half, making sure they weren't given any time or space to pick their passes out of defence. Frank McAvennie and Joe Miller arrived within six weeks of each other and they bought into the idea.

I really enjoyed playing up front alongside Frank. There was a chemistry between us, we didn't have to work too hard to develop an understanding. Instinctively, I knew when to go short when he went long and vice versa. Frank was quicker than me, better in the air and more aggressive. My role was as the second striker to link up play and Frank was just brilliant to have as a teammate. He was just so unselfish and would run all day. I think he thrives on this image of Jack The Lad, but, trust me, all those stories insisting he missed training every Monday are a lot of baloney. He was a great trainer and wanted to win at all costs.

We could be having a wee knockabout, but he wanted to make sure he scored goals and his side emerged victorious. He was just that type of guy. He simply had to win. Frank was great for me and I thought we dovetailed really well.

In the centenary season, Billy McNeill had to make some hard choices in his frontline. He had to perm three from four most of the time with myself, Frank, Wee Joe and Mark McGhee. He told me he had a similar problem first time around at Celtic when he played a system with two strikers and he had Charlie Nicholas, Frank McGarvey and George McCluskey to choose from. He admitted it was made even more difficult because he was loathe to leave out Charlie because he was so skilful and could virtually win a game on his own with a flash of his undoubted quality.

And Billy knew he could rely on Frank and George, two big Celtic fans, to always produce their best in all circumstances. It was the same with us in 1987/88. There was a strong camaraderie within the team. In fact, it's still there. We had a thirtieth anniversary ball to celebrate the centenary team in a top Glasgow hotel in May 2018 and the friendship among the guys was evident. Mind you, our memories of events from three decades ago weren't in complete synchronisation.

It was superb to work alongside Frank and I was annoyed when he left to go back to West Ham. He wasn't even at Celtic two years, but he wanted to return to live in London. It had something to do with a model girlfriend and Billy McNeill reluctantly allowed him to leave. The Boss figured the dressing room would be a more comfortable place without the presence of an unhappy player.

Frank and I simply had fitted each other's styles and our intuition brought fifty goals between us in our debut campaign, with his eighteen added to my thirty-two. Remember, I had a twelve-game head-start on Frank before he arrived.

He will always be remembered for his two goals that gave us a 2–1 victory over Dundee United in the Scottish Cup Final that brought the curtain down on an exhilarating season. On the build-up to the game, Billy reminded everyone that the Tannadice team had been in five recent Cup Finals and had lost the lot. He reckoned the players might not get over the line for their boss Jim McLean when they were up against it. The United manager had a hard taskmaster reputation and a few of his players, well away from the dressing room, would tell tales about how they were treated. I think you could say man-management was not one of Jim's strengths. Billy had no fears on that front.

I had scored a few goals leading up to the Scottish Cup Final and I thought I might be good enough to get one against United. However, with half-an-hour to go at Hampden, with us trailing to Kevin Gallacher's early strike after the turnaround, I was struggling to make any sort of impression. Billy then made a double substitution to take me and Derek Whyte off and put on Mark McGhee and Billy Stark.

Afterwards, the boss admitted he was taking a risk by leaving the team a bit short at the back, but reasoned the introduction of Stark would give Joe Miller a bit more freedom to express himself and Mark would provide a fresh pair of legs in attack. I was disappointed to be taken off, but I didn't dwell on it – things were too exciting on the field. Frank equalised with about fifteen minutes to go and then scored the winner in the fading moments. When that final whistle went, I was the first on the park to jump on Frank's back. I was so pleased for him.

Four years after that wonderful centenary year, I left for Bolton Wanderers. Billy had gone before me and had been replaced by Liam Brady. I caught up briefly with Billy McNeill at Hibs in 1998. Jim Duffy was manager at Easter Road at the time and he took me on loan from Sheffield United. He also brought Billy on board to lean on his experience. Let's face it, who wouldn't want a man of the quality of Big Billy in their corner?

My old gaffer had been out of mainstream football for about seven years and was quite happy to take on the role which carried the title 'Director of Development'. I recall at the time he stressed he did not want the manager's job. Jim Duffy would never have had to look over his shoulder with Billy around. Unfortunately, though, Jim did get the bullet only a few weeks after working with Billy. Hibs were struggling at the foot of the Premier Division – they would be relegated at the end of the season – and the end came for Jim after a 6–2 defeat from a Motherwell team managed by Alex McLeish. And who got the Hibs job? The same Alex McLeish.

Billy was in charge of team selection for one game only and I recall it was against Aberdeen at Pittodrie where the home side won 3–0. Billy moved out shortly afterwards and one of Big Eck's first tasks was to tell me I would be following him. It didn't surprise me at all because, believe it or not, there were *fifty-five* signed players at Hibs at the time. For any club in the world, that is a phenomenal amount. The new boss was tasked with the job of slimming down the staff and, as a guy on a temporary deal, I was clearly among those who were expendable. It had been good to work again with Billy McNeill, even in those slightly unusual circumstances.

Who would ever turn down the opportunity of being associated with Billy McNeill?

BILLY STARK

I thought I was heading for Hearts in the summer of 1987. However, that was before Billy McNeill intervened and my career took an altogether different route, one I couldn't have envisaged possible for a midfielder aged thirty coming to the end of his contract at Aberdeen.

Alex Ferguson – then just a plain 'Mr' – had already left Pittodrie for Manchester United in November the previous year and his assistant boss, Archie Knox, later caught up with him at Old Trafford. There had been talk of Sandy Jardine, Fergie's former Rangers teammate who had been working in managerial tandem with Alex MacDonald at Tynecastle, taking over. That never materialised and Ian Porterfield, who had left Sheffield United in March 1986, arrived to become our new gaffer eight months later.

Fergie was always going to be a tough act to follow and around that time I made up my mind I would not be extending my deal.

I had four great years at the Dons after Fergie, who had originally signed me for St Mirren, paid the Paisley club £80,000 for me in 1983. I won a European Super Cup medal in my first season, followed that up with a league and Cup double the following year, a league title in 1985 and then enjoyed victories in the Scottish Cup and League Cup the term after that. So, it had been a fairly successful period in my life, but I realised it was time to look to pastures new. The kids had started school and, as a Glaswegian, I thought about a switch back to the West of Scotland. I just didn't know where, though. I had to be realistic and think I had enjoyed my best days in the game as a player, but I still believed I had at least a good couple of years in my legs.

I did receive a few offers, but the best one at that stage was from Hearts – it looked as though I was going to work with

Fergie's pal Sandy Jardine, after all. Contact was made, everything seemed reasonable enough and I thought Edinburgh would be my next port of call. John Kelman was the Celtic chief scout who made the phone call that somewhat changed my career path. I was given a number, dialled it and got straight through to Billy McNeill. It was all very pleasant and he intimated he would like me to join him at Celtic. He had just returned in May that year and was putting his plans together. Fortunately, I figured in them, much to my amazement.

Clearly, Billy had to begin rebuilding. I realised he thought the easiest thing would have been to go out and buy a string of players, but he insisted in buying sensibly. However, time did not appear to be his ally. There were a number of players who would be leaving around that time, including Mo Johnston, Brian McClair, Murdo MacLeod and Alan McInally. Billy knew he needed replacements in position for the start of the campaign, which was an enormous one for the club, Celtic's centenary season. Billy wondered if I was interested in coming to Celtic. I was in like a shot. Any thoughts of going anywhere else were dispelled in the span of that fairly brief telephone conversation.

I was Billy's first signing, but he held the news back from the media. He wanted his debut acquisition to be a headline-making, big-money transfer and I perfectly understood the situation. I have never been one to seek the spotlight and, in any case, I had penned my signature on that contract, I was a Celtic player and I was fit and raring to go. That was all that was important to me. I knew Billy liked the look of Motherwell striker Andy Walker who had been making a bit of a name for himself with the Fir Park outfit.

Therefore, Billy made his move for Andy while admitting there would be massive pressure on the player to deliver. The reported transfer fee was £350,000 and once the newspapers were informed and had their story, Billy took the opportunity to introduce me, his slightly more modest £70,000 purchase from Aberdeen.

Mick McCarthy had already arrived in the summer as Davie Hay's last signing. The Republic of Ireland centre-half cost £500,000 from Manchester City and, rather oddly, never got the chance to play for Davie. Billy inherited him and, suddenly, he had three new signings and he was searching for more, but, of course, they had to be quality recruits. Right-back Chris Morris, a future international teammate of McCarthy, arrived in a £125,000 switch from Sheffield Wednesday. In time, Frank McAvennie came in from West Ham and then Joe Miller, my old Aberdeen colleague. Miller, McAvennie and Walker became a fairly potent force, gelled well together, defended from the front and got their fair share of goals.

I was a nervous wreck before the opening Old Firm encounter against Rangers at Parkhead in late August. Even after all my years in the game, this occasion got to me. I had never felt so on edge as the minutes ticked down to kick-off. Billy McNeill pulled off a bit of a masterstroke by introducing his fellow-Lisbon Lion Tommy Gemmell to the dressing room as we got prepared. Tommy was a naturally larger-than-life character who possessed a real happy-go-lucky nature. He moved around the players with a word here and there as he helped put us all at ease. Tommy, like Billy, had done it all and had big-game savvy. His presence helped ease the pressure. He spent some time with Andy Walker, in particular, because this would undoubtedly have been the front player's biggest match. Allen McKnight, the Irish keeper who was making his debut, got a special message from Big Tam who had signed him on loan the previous season when he was manager at Albion Rovers.

So, we were well primed by the time referee Davie Syme blew

his whistle to get the action underway. There were 60,800 spectators in the ground that beautiful afternoon and the sun was certainly shining on me when I scored the only goal of the game in the fourth minute. It's a moment I will never forget.

It started when Tommy Burns intercepted a pass and rolled the ball out to Mark McGhee on the left. He controlled it nicely before sending over a deft cross. Peter Grant stepped over it as the ball swept in my direction at the angle of the eighteen-yard box. I resisted trying to put my laces through it. Instead, I steered the ball low across Chris Woods at his right hand side and my effort nestled in the back of his net. Suddenly, there was this crescendo of noise and I was mobbed by my teammates as I headed for the supporters in the Jungle.

I may have been a midfielder, but I like to think I chipped in with a reasonable quota of goals. That might even have been in Billy's thinking when he first moved for me in the realisation the team would miss the strikes from Murdo MacLeod since his move to Borussia Dortmund. I had played as an old-fashioned centre-forward with my school team and, as I developed, I wanted to continue scoring goals, although I was no longer in the frontline. Seemed perfectly logical to me.

But my memorable debut in this fixture still had another twist. Nine minutes into the second-half, my left boot came off as I made a tackle – there are those who will insist that was my one and only challenge in my entire career – and I was still holding it when Peter Grant thought it was a good idea to knock the ball to me.

I caught sight of Graeme Souness charging in from behind me in an effort to intercept the pass. There was a collision and down I went. The Rangers player/manager had already been booked and he must have had a fair idea what was coming next. The match official waved the red card at him and off he went. My goal was good enough to separate the teams at the end of ninety hectic minutes and Billy McNeill was very complimentary to all the players. It had been a big performance from his team and, possibly, an even bigger result for the returning manager. In a huge season for everyone at the club, we had put down an early and important marker.

As our title challenge gained momentum – and that was undoubtedly boosted by the October arrival of Frank McAvennie and the purchase of Joe Miller a month later – there was serious talk of making it a league and Cup double to mark the club's one hundredth birthday. Unfortunately, it would not be a clean sweep of domestic silverware because, only three days after our win over Rangers, we were knocked out of the League Cup by my old Dons team at Pittodrie when Jim Bett got the only goal of the game on the hour mark. However, in this season of seasons, we were not going to dwell on that setback, frustrating though it may have been.

It wasn't classic Celtic when the Scottish Cup kicked off and we beat Stranraer with an early goal from Frank McAvennie at Parkhead. In truth, we toiled and we had Pat Bonner to thank for a great penalty save. We had to settle for a goalless draw against Hibs in Glasgow at the next stage and we realised we were on dangerous territory in the replay. There were only eleven minutes to play when Peter Grant fired in a ferocious effort that walloped against the woodwork. I followed it in, got my head on the ball when the shot bounced out and we were through.

Before the quarter-final against Partick Thistle at Firhill, Billy warned us of a potential upset on a heavy pitch. We were told to dampen our opponents' enthusiasm and exuberance right from the off. I think we managed that when Andy Walker gave us an early lead, Tommy Burns added a second and, following an effort from Frank McAvennie that rebounded from the crossbar, I was lucky enough to pop a header into the net for the third goal in a 3–0 victory. Billy very kindly praised me in the press when he said, 'Billy Stark again showed that when there is even a sniff of a chance, he'll always be there at the kill.' Thanks, boss, I do my best!

We were a couple of minutes from extinction in the trophy when Hearts led 1–0 in the semi-final with a bit of a freak goal. A long, high punt forward by Brian Whittaker was contested by Pat Bonner and Dave McPherson almost on the goal-line. The Hearts player certainly looked to have impeded our keeper as the ball dropped into the net. Referee Kenny Hope turned a deaf ear to our pleas, so we just had to get the sleeves rolled up that extra inch and go for it. This Celtic team was not afraid of hard work and that fact could be emphasised by the amount of late goals we collected. That was down more to fortitude than fortune.

With time disappearing far too swiftly, Tommy Burns, with that lovely left foot, caressed over a right-wing corner-kick. Henry Smith, in the Hearts goal, had come for most crosses on the afternoon and taken them cleanly, but this one eluded his grasp. It fell nicely for substitute Mark McGhee to squeeze over the line. Our fans were still in raptures when we decided to go for a winner. As long as we hadn't heard that shrill from the referee's whistle, we still had a chance of a goal. And so it proved.

I took a quick throw-in on the right touchline, Frank McAvennie clipped it towards the far post and once again Smith mishandled. The ball dropped in front of Andy Walker and he fairly blasted it in from practically under the crossbar.

Now it was the grand finale at Hampden on 14 May with the Premiership trophy already won. Dundee United were our opponents and they were always well organised, competitive and dangerous on the counter-attack. All week Billy McNeill had insisted it would be a thirteen-man job to win the Scottish

Cup. He laid his plans accordingly and they worked as the 2–1 scoreline in our favour tells you.

What didn't quite come off was our defensive formation of three at the back, which was designed to combat the pace of Kevin Gallacher. It was goalless shortly after the turnaround when he raced through to crash a shot past Allen McKnight, who had taken over from the injured Pat Bonner. I was on the substitutes' bench at the start along with Mark McGhee, but I had taken our manager at his word that this would indeed be a game when all thirteen players would be utilised.

With twenty minutes to go and the team still trailing, Mark and I got the nod from Billy to get ready to go on. I replaced Derek Whyte as the defence got another reshuffle while Mark was a straight swap for Andy Walker. A manager has to be extremely brave to make these calls and Billy never shirked a tough decision. With fourteen minutes to go, Anton Rogan raided on the left before sending in a dangerous cross. Billy Thomson, the United keeper, missed it and Frank McAvennie read it perfectly to get in before centre-half Paul Hegarty to head into the net. We knew we would win it now, but I can't say the winner came straight from the training ground.

The contest was into its fading moments when Joe Miller miskicked a right-wing corner-kick in my direction on the edge of the box. I sclaffed an effort into the box, it hit off a defender and Macca pounced to knock the ball into the net off his shin. Cups are won and lost in these moments.

Billy McNeill, in the space of ten months or so, had instilled that winning mentality in a set of players, several of whom had been with other clubs at the completion of the previous season. That's a special talent. No one should have been surprised the manager had pulled it off. All things considered, it was a phenomenal feat. His personality and presence gave everyone a lift. He possessed a wonderful ambassadorial persona and projected himself well at all times.

There was always an endearing down-to-earth quality about him, someone who could enjoy a laugh and a joke and when you talk about greatest-ever Celts, it's difficult to see beyond Billy McNeill.

FRANK McAVENNIE

Billy McNeill fined me enough cash to wipe out the national debt back in the late eighties. Well, that's if you believe all you hear and read.

Yes, I'll hold my hands up and admit I was late for training most Mondays following 'difficulties' getting home after a weekend in London. This happened only about four times a month. Honest!

It was never quite as bad as that. Big Billy would pull me aside and say something along the lines of, 'Okay, what's the excuse this time, Macca?'

I didn't even attempt to lie to him. It was fairly well documented I liked a party. 'Ach, you know how it is, Boss,' I would shrug and say lamely.

'Do I?' he would look quizzically at me. Then it would be followed with the inevitable remark, 'Okay, that's a grand out of your wages.'

People on the outside must have thought I was playing for my boyhood idols Celtic for virtually nothing as the fines mounted up. Not quite. I loved the club and the wonderful support, but I couldn't quite afford to go about my business with zilch coming into my bank account. Have you any idea how much they were charging for a bottle of champers in Stringfellows back then?

Actually, Billy and I had a wee arrangement that saved me a few bob. As that week's game approached, the Boss would have a quiet word in my ear. 'Hey, Macca,' he would whisper, 'play well and I'll forget about docking your wages. Okay?'

How could I say no? It was an unusual incentive, that's for sure, but anyone who knows me – or who has played alongside or against me – will tell you that once I got on that pitch I always gave 100 per cent. That's just the way I was. In any case, I knew my dad Bernard would be somewhere in the Celtic crowd and if he thought I wasn't pulling my weight he would give me pelters. So, money wasn't my sole concern when I pulled on that green and white shirt.

Billy McNeill was great with me from day one, let's get that absolutely straight. I idolised him when I was a kid growing up and going to the games with my dad and taking our place in the old Jungle. Growing up, I heard all sorts of wonderful stories about this genuine Celtic legend. When he came down to the Holiday Inn in London to sign me from West Ham in October 1987, he must have realised he wouldn't have to work too hard for me to agree to the move.

I took a drop in wages, but Billy made the point that living in Scotland was a lot less expensive than in London. Also, we had an agreement that I would receive a signing-on fee of something in the region of £140,000. The Celtic board would take care of the tax liabilities and I would be left with the agreed amount. In effect, as far as I was concerned, it would be tax free and everything would be completely legal. These were the days before EBTs, I hasten to add. I knew Billy McNeill would honour the agreement, but I discovered to my cost the directors at the club weren't singing from the same hymn sheet as the manager.

The money was due to be paid in quarterly instalments, which was perfectly acceptable and understandable. Handing over that sort of cash to an individual on the first day would never be a good idea. A lot of footballers, including me, come from working-class backgrounds and that sort of cash can go straight to your head. It's the sort of money you thought you would never see in your lifetime. I didn't have a problem with the arrangement.

Unfortunately, though, my first payment was included in my salary and, as you would expect, it was fully taxed. I thought there must be some sort of mistake in administration. I mentioned it to Billy and he told me he would sort it out. I left it with him.

However, the other three payments also came through as my wages and were hammered by our friends at HMRC. I reckoned I stood to lose around £50,000.

I didn't want to be continually in Billy McNeill's face as he tried to put a Celtic team on the park that could combat a Rangers side managed by Graeme Souness who reversed the trend and brought England international players such as Terry Butcher, Chris Woods, Graham Roberts, Trevor Francis, Butch Wilkins, Trevor Steven and Gary Stevens to Scotland. Souness would probably have signed Uncle Tom Cobley, too, if he had been English! It seemed money was no object as our old foes signed massive cheques and chucked dough around like confetti.

The last thing Billy needed was me knocking on his door every second day complaining about missing dosh from my salary. I know he took it up with the board on several occasions. It couldn't have been an easy task. The directors had been labelled as having a 'biscuit tin' mentality and certainly worked hard at giving everyone that precise impression. So, Billy was up against it and I respected him for finding the time and making an effort on my behalf.

Don't get the idea my time at Celtic was all about bickering over cash. Nothing could be further from the truth. I loved my seventeen months with Billy McNeill and the boys who were at the club back then, most are still good friends to this day. Winning the league and Cup double in the club's centenary year is something that will live with me forever, no one will be able to take that away from me. Same goes at being given the honour of performing in front of the greatest supporters in the world. I lived that dream.

However, after almost two full seasons and with fifteen months to run on my deal, my situation had not been resolved. And right in the middle was Billy McNeill trying to play the peacemaker and attempting to get everything sorted. However, there comes a time when you realise you are wasting your time. Your working environment isn't right and you begin to resent some people. And for me that was the board, who didn't seem one bit interested in the position within which they had placed their manager and one of their players.

The press soon got wind of things not all being quite right behind the scenes at Parkhead. Stories were finding their way into print that I was demanding a transfer. That was never the case although, at the same time, something had to give. Billy McNeill and I had a couple of heated discussions, I'll admit to that. It was all very frustrating. Believe me when I tell you I thought I would be a Celtic player for life when I signed. I never gave playing elsewhere a second thought. But the attitude of the directors got right up my nose.

Tales somehow leaked into the newspapers – I wonder where they came from? – that I was heading back to West Ham. I had talked to my old Upton Park gaffer John Lyall and, like Billy, he was a real man's man. I rated John and Billy as the two best managers I ever had the privilege of working alongside. You don't want to get me started on international boss Andy Roxburgh!

A Scottish Cup quarter-final encounter against Hearts at Parkhead was due on 18 March 1989. The entire week leading up to such an important game seemed to be dominated by me and my desire to quit the club I had always supported; still do, as a matter of fact. There had been a few misunderstandings along the way and I didn't believe I had a chance of playing. So, imagine my surprise – shock would probably be a more accurate word – when Big Billy told me I would be leading the attack that afternoon. My original reaction was, 'No way!' I understood Celtic fans and their feelings for the club. It's never about individuals, it's all about Celtic. My God, they even booed Henrik

Larsson when he scored for Barcelona in a Champions League game at Parkhead in 2005!

I knew I would be forced to run the gauntlet. The supporters had been force-fed tales I was turning my back on the team they adored, but, of course, they didn't know the facts. It had even escalated into what was being termed as a public row between Billy and me. That was never the case. I didn't think I was in the right frame of mind to line up against Hearts, but Billy wasn't having any of it. Tommy Craig, his assistant manager, pulled me aside and told me to get out there and prove what Celtic meant to me, even if it was to be my last game. Of course, I returned in 1993 when Liam Brady was the boss, but that was well in the future.

On the afternoon of the game, I ran onto the park and was aware of some jeering at the start. You could say I got a mixed reception. Tommy Craig's wise words stayed with me, though. As usual, I was getting in about it as the boots flew in every direction. Two Hearts players, Alan McLaren and Tosh McKinlay, who would later join Celtic, and our centre-half Mick McCarthy were ordered off in a bit of a roughhouse. I got my sleeves rolled up and I'm delighted to say, as the game progressed, I heard chants of 'Macca must stay!'

We won 2–1 – I helped to set up the second which was a penalty-kick from Roy Aitken – and headed for London later that evening. Talks had gone well with John Lyall and I also met Arsenal manager George Graham. I'm an emotional guy and my heart led me back to West Ham. They paid £1.25 million for a twenty-nine-year-old player and that was the end of that chapter.

I think I can safely say that life with Billy McNeill at Celtic wasn't dull, that's for sure. It appears I don't do boring. When I scored the two goals that defeated Dundee United and gave us the Scottish Cup in our centenary year in 1988, the late and much-missed Tommy Burns was crying at the end. He cuddled me and exclaimed, 'Macca, do you know they'll be talking about this team in a hundred years?'

I'm sure they'll be talking about Billy McNeill a lot longer than that.

JOE MILLER

Billy McNeill gave me the opportunity to play for Celtic in front of the best supporters in football. How could I ever thank him enough? I was walking on air the day I signed for my boyhood idols from Aberdeen on 13 November 1987. I was already feeling fairly pleased with myself, but my confidence was given another massive boost when the manager told the press I was 'the final piece in the jigsaw'.

It was the club's centenary year and there can be no doubt Billy had his eyes on the league title. That was his priority and if we threw in the Scottish Cup as well that would be even better. When I joined the club, Celtic had already been knocked out of the League Cup by the Dons 1–0 at Pittodrie early in September. Whisper it, I played that evening when Jim Bett scored the only goal.

However, on the day I fulfilled my ambition and became a Celtic player, I can reveal it almost didn't happen. As ever, these things don't pass without some sort of drama. In my case, I simply couldn't afford to take a drop in wages to make my dream come true. Ian Porterfield had taken over from Manchester United-bound Alex Ferguson as manager of the club and things changed fairly dramatically. We didn't click, put it that way. Chairman Dick Donald accepted Celtic's offer of £650,000 and the rest was down to me agreeing personal terms. And that's where the hitch occurred. One of the last things Alex Ferguson did at the Dons was give me a welcome hike in my pay packet.

It was obvious Billy didn't know what I was earning and, accordingly, put an offer on the table he clearly believed I would snap up. I looked at the figures and I wasn't impressed. Yes, I was desperate to join Celtic, but I was only looking for what I thought I was worth. I was being far from greedy. Billy told me he would have to go back to his board and tell them they would have to come up with more cash. I told him I would sit in my car outside the ground, he could meet with the directors and then let me know if the move was on or off. After about half-an-hour, I was told to go back inside and see Billy. Thankfully, the matter was resolved and everybody was happy.

Apart from my old boss Alex Ferguson! He believed he had first refusal on me and had been interested in taking me to Old Trafford. When he heard about Celtic's move for me, he was desperate to get in touch with United's chairman Martin Edwards, who was on a break in the States. As luck would have it, he couldn't contact him and there was little he could do to stop me joining up with Billy McNeill in the east end of Glasgow, my old stomping ground as a schoolboy. Fergie later admitted he would have paid £1 million for me.

Tommy Burns, my all-time favourite player, was at Celtic Park to greet me the day after I had completed the formalities and I was in the team to play Dundee at Parkhead that afternoon. Tommy took me aside and said, 'You are here for a reason, wee man. You are a good player and when you score today, get yourself over to those guys in the Jungle. They are Celtic Football Club. Share your joy with them.'

Fortunately, I did get a goal against the Dens Park side as we won 5–0 and I took Tommy's advice. I raced over to where the most fanatical supporters dwelled and 'shared my joy'. It wasn't always sweetness and light at Celtic, though. I learned you had to accept the rough with the smooth.

There was one unforgettable occasion when I had a major fall-out with Billy McNeill. I wasn't one bit happy with my Celtic gaffer and I didn't hold back as I let him know my feelings. My timing could have been better, though – there was a crowd of 45,367 at Hampden Park to witness my furious reaction during a League Cup semi-final against Aberdeen on Wednesday, 20 September 1989. Millions of TV viewers also saw the flashpoint incident.

What had my manager, a man who always had my total respect, done to provoke such an explosive response? Billy sent me on at the start of the second-half as a substitute for Stevie Fulton with the tie balanced at 0–0. We were forty-five minutes away from another Cup Final and I had enjoyed scoring the only goal of the game against Rangers at the same venue exactly four months earlier as we lifted the Scottish Cup. Could I be Celtic's match-winner again? I could always hope.

This time my presence at the national stadium was remarkable for all the wrong reasons. Ian Cameron scored for the Dons in the seventy-fifth minute and I couldn't believe it when I was told I was being taken off with Andy Walker coming on in my place. A substitute substituted? I was totally embarrassed and then my reaction quickly turned to anger. I couldn't help myself. That was my first appearance for the team – I had missed the entire pre-season through injury – and there I was getting hauled off after only half-an-hour on the field.

I trudged towards the bench and had to sit there and simmer throughout a miserable evening for everyone connected with Celtic. Putting the tin lid on everything, Roy Aitken was sent off in the dying moments as we tried desperately to grab an equaliser. Our captain went up like a rocket, even eclipsing me. He was convinced Jim Bett had taken a dive as he made a challenge. As the midfielder went down a wee bit too theatrically, referee Brian McGinlay, who had booked our player in the first-half, bought it. Even Bett looked surprised as the red card was flashed and Big Roy had to leave the field.

Three days later, we played Motherwell in the league at Parkhead. No one was unduly surprised when the name Joe Miller was absent from the squad that afternoon. Instead, I found myself playing for the reserves at Fir Park and I even scored in a 3–2 win. The first team were held to a 1–1 draw with the visitors taking the lead in the seventh minute and Paul McStay equalising with a header just before the interval. Billy McNeill, though, proved he was not a man to hold a grudge. Our next game was a home midweek European Cup-Winners' Cup-tie against Partizan Belgrade, who held a 2–1 advantage from the first leg.

There was a crowd of almost 50,000 at Parkhead that evening – just a week after my Hampden flashpoint – and the manager took me aside in training a couple of days earlier to inform me I would be in from the start. He was aware he had hurt me deeply. It had been an unfortunate incident all round and we decided to get on with taking care of business for Celtic. That's all we ever wanted to do.

As I sat in the dressing room before we lined up to take the pitch, I wondered how the supporters might react to my inclusion. Any worries I may have had were dispelled when we raced out of the tunnel. I was given a marvellous reception and I realised they accepted I had only acted in such a manner because I was one of them. Against the Yugoslav team, we not only won, we scored five goals. We also went out of the tournament. Unbelievably, they snatched a fourth goal in the last minute to tie the game 6–6 on aggregate and go through on the goals away rule. Jacki Dziekanowski, signed from Polish outfit Legia Warsaw in the summer, didn't know whether to laugh or cry at the end. He had just scored four goals and had seen his team eliminated.

Yes, there were ups and downs during my time at Parkhead, but I wouldn't have missed performing alongside Tommy Burns, being managed by Billy McNeill and playing in front of the Celtic support for all the world.

CHARLIE NICHOLAS

This may sound a little strange, but I was always a bit nervous when I was in the company of Billy McNeill. When I looked the Celtic manager straight in the eye all I could see was that image of the Celtic legend holding up the European Cup. I just couldn't get past it. Billy and that massive piece of silverware had taken up permanent residence in my mind's eye.

Of course, I shouldn't have been one bit distracted because Billy McNeill, despite his iconic status and for all the things he achieved in the name of Celtic, was one of the humblest guys I ever had the privilege of meeting. There was a humility about Big Billy and the rest of the Lisbon Lions that was really quite astounding. They were always such an approachable bunch of guys, but what they accomplished that evening in the Portuguese capital on 25 May 1967 is well and truly etched in the club's history books. Quite right, too.

There was a lot to like about these guys and what they did for Celtic. Having said that, I knew I would have to leave Big Billy massively disappointed one May afternoon at Hampden; the Scottish Cup Final in 1990 when Billy was in the Celtic dugout and I was playing for Aberdeen. Big Billy and his players went into the game with the realisation they had to win to earn a place in the UEFA Cup or miss out on playing in Europe for the first time since 1978. They were sitting behind Rangers, Aberdeen, Hearts and Dundee United in the league as they prepared for this one. The pressure must have been immense.

Their league form had been fairly awful and, in fact, they had failed to win any of their previous eight games before arriving at the national stadium on 12 May – only ten days after the Dons had beaten them 3–1 at Parkhead. Our manager, Alex Smith, rested many of his first-team players for the visit to Glasgow, including me, Alex McLeish, Jim Bett, Hans Gilhaus and a couple of others. Yet we could even give Celtic a goal of a start – Andy Walker scored early on – and come back and beat them with three goals after the interval, two strikes from Eoin Jess and one from Graham Watson. We were already assured of a place in the UEFA Cup because we had beaten Rangers 2–1 in the League Cup Final in October. Incidentally, we had overcome Celtic 1–0 in the semi-final. So, to a certain extent, there wasn't as much strain on us to deliver.

The actual game was not that memorable. I had a shot kicked off the line by Paul Elliott after only five minutes and, remarkably, that was the nearest either team got to scoring. It ended goalless after the extra half-hour and for the first time in the history of the competition it would be decided on penalty-kicks. Both teams scored with eight of their first nine spot-kicks – two were missed, Brian Grant for us and Dariusz Wdowczyk for Celtic. I scored with mine – the fifth – which took it to sudden death.

It's an understatement to say it was tense as it reached the shoot-out stage and you had to feel for Celtic left-back Anton Rogan when his effort was stopped by our keeper Theo Snelders. Anton looked distraught as he slumped to his knees and I doubt if it is any consolation at this late stage, but it wasn't a bad penalty. It was low to Snelders' left, but our athletic Dutchman managed to dive full length and beat it away. Brian Irvine had the responsibility to win the Cup for the Dons and duly thumped a vicious effort into the net.

Alex McLeish then had the opportunity to lead us up those famous steps to receive the silverware. At that moment, many people would not have noticed Billy McNeill's compassion. It was all too much for Anton Rogan, who lay on the turf, totally crestfallen, the chance of a third successive Scottish Cup win gone, the opportunity of playing in European competition lost.

Billy would have been hurting, too. However, he went over to console the defender, helped him to his feet and had some comforting words in his ear. Typical of the man.

When I stepped up to take my kick, did I know I would be signing for Celtic in the summer? I was out of contract at Pittodrie and they were keen to offer me an extension. I had always fancied playing abroad, especially France. There was the opportunity to go to Nice on a trial basis which would have led to a full-time contract. However, it made a lot more sense to remain in Scotland. I was about to get married and my future in-laws were all Celtic mad. But, as I stepped up to the penalty spot. I couldn't let anything interfere with my professionalism. I realised it would more than likely be my last kick of the ball as an Aberdeen player, but that didn't enter my head. They paid my wages and I had a job to do. Plus I knew they had an open-top bus parade planned for the city the following day. I couldn't miss and let everyone down. I put it in my big pal Packie Bonner's top left-hand corner of the net. I didn't celebrate.

My agent, Jerome Anderson, had already been in touch with Billy McNeill to go through a few details. It looked odds-on I would be going back, but, at that stage, nothing had been finalised. The eventual outcome saw me returning to Parkhead having left seven years earlier for Arsenal. For a Celtic fan, Jock Stein had been the ultimate icon. It was Big Jock who put me on the ground staff at Celtic after I had been down at Ipswich and Wolves on trial. I was fifteen-and-a-half years old at the time. Later on, he selected me a few times for Scotland. However, there was never a relationship with Big Jock. It was totally different with Billy – he was just such an open big chap with time for anyone.

I first came in contact with Billy when I was playing for Celtic Boys' Club and he was helping out with the Under-16s after retiring from playing in 1975. He took notice of me almost immediately and I could see he thought I might have something. He talked to me a few times and I was in awe of the man. Very charitably, Billy admitted in a book he thought I was 'a cut above' the rest of the lads in my age group. It wasn't long before Billy was back in mainstream football when he had a brief stint at Clyde before taking over from Ally MacLeod at Aberdeen in June 1977 when I was fifteen years old. Billy was aware I had not been made a formal signing offer by Celtic and it was fair game to try to take me to Pittodrie. That's when things moved a bit more quickly at Parkhead and I was put on a schoolboy form, but I had yet to be offered a full-time contract. Billy would eventually try to rectify that situation.

I wonder, though, if he ever came up against a more difficult opponent than Christina Nicholas, my mum. She was a wee bit apprehensive about her son not having a trade behind him and attempting to become a full-time footballer. There were no guarantees things would work out in that profession. No one possessed a crystal ball and, as a mother, she cared about her offspring's future and welfare. I was on the ground staff at Celtic and trained on Tuesday and Thursday evenings, but I had yet to take the gigantic step up. My mum would have known about the thousands of young kids with stars in their eyes who never made the grade and had nothing to fall back on. Naturally, she worried about her son's choice of career.

I was serving my apprenticeship as a car mechanic with the local Citroën franchise and my mum believed it was right and sensible that I had a safety net if things didn't work out elsewhere. It was now Billy McNeill's job to persuade my mother that Celtic were the right club for her son and football should be my profession. We were a working-class family from the Maryhill district in Glasgow and were fairly well grounded. You didn't get something for nothing, you earned your living. So, quite rightly, my mum wasn't being distracted by thoughts of her son's name up in lights and all over the sports pages' headlines. Now it was over to Billy to attempt to persuade her that I had a chance to make it as a footballer. He would have to turn on the charm.

My dad, also called Charlie, was a huge Celtic fan and used to take me to Parkhead as a kid, so he was sold on the idea of his son playing in the green and white hoops. Naturally, he was all for taking a chance and seeing how far I could progress. My mum, though, still had to be convinced, so Billy paid us a visit. He drove a huge grey Audi and parked it at Maryhill Barracks. My mum would get excited. 'Oh, there's Mr McNeill coming to talk to you, Charlie!', but even the presence of Big Billy didn't immediately dissuade my mother of the notion her son should hang up his working overalls.

One day, Billy phoned my mum at home, going into overdrive on the smooth talking. He realised she was worried about her boy and that was perfectly normal. He reassured my mum I had a better than average opportunity of becoming a footballer. He insisted I had all the qualities to be a top-class professional and that he would personally keep an eye on me at Celtic. He would look after her son and she need have no worries on that score.

Billy then provided her with his home telephone number. 'If you have any issues, Mrs Nicholas, just call me immediately and I'll take care of it,' he promised. And Big Billy always delivered on his promises, I can tell you that. Obviously, I don't know the entire conversation between Billy and my mum, but it certainly did the trick. I believe it lasted ten minutes or so, but it changed my entire life.

I came home later that day in my working gear and was told by my mum, 'Billy McNeill has just phoned me,' she said, adding the words I yearned to hear, 'it's okay for you to go to Celtic.' Just like that. Whatever was said in that informal chat calmed my mother down, suddenly she was aware her son just might have a chance of making a living out of kicking a ball.

I signed in June 1979, just a month after ten-man Celtic had famously beaten Rangers 4– 2 to win the league title. Billy McNeill, needless to say, was as good as his word. He did take me under his wing. Actually, there was a bit of a father/son relationship between Billy and me and I'll always be grateful for that. His interest in an individual's well-being went way beyond ninety minutes of action on match day. There are some footballers who can tell you stories that if you are not in the first team then you are largely ignored. Unless you are playing, you're the invisible man. That was never the case with Billy McNeill.

I recall the concern that was displayed by the Celtic manager when I suffered a broken leg at the age of twenty. I was playing against Morton reserves at Cappielow when I sustained the injury. It was a simple accident, but such incidents can end careers. The day after the game, Billy paid me a visit. Celtic were due to go to Hong Kong for a ten-day toning-up session and the manager reassured me he would see me as soon as he got back. Once again, he didn't disappoint. I made up my mind I would work as hard as I could to put the strength back into my leg. Billy took a personal interest in my progress and I'm glad to say I came through the recuperation, but it was fairly frustrating spending most of the remainder of the campaign on the treatment table.

Billy has admitted he might have been slow in giving me my first-team chance, but I don't necessarily see it that way. I think he got his timing right and if he had pushed me in earlier it might have set me back. Billy did with me what Jock Stein had done with my all-time hero, 'King' Kenny Dalglish.

My debut was a Glasgow Cup-tie against Queen's Park on 14 August 1979 when I was seventeen years old. I recall a snippet in a Glasgow evening newspaper where Billy was quoted as saying, 'It's a good opportunity to give him experience at a higher level. He has shown he has the necessary ability.'

I scored on my first appearance as the team won 3–1 at Hampden. How about that? I took my bow at the national stadium. Mind you, I didn't let it all go to my head – the attendance that evening was given as 1,673. There would be bigger crowds when I revisited the ground throughout my career.

So, I have a lot to thank Billy McNeill for; not least his ability to persuade my mum that I should give football a try as my chosen profession.

JOHN COLLINS

Graeme Souness offered me more money to join Rangers than Billy McNeill could match to take me to Celtic. So, naturally, I accepted Billy's offer when I became his first £1 million purchase from Hibs in July 1990. Well, who could say no to Billy McNeill?

Actually, it was an easy choice and that's no disrespect to Graeme Souness. Coming from a Celtic background, the mantle John Collins of Rangers would not have sat comfortably with me. Money is important, of course, and we all know it is a short career and you have a family to look after, but cash is not the be all and end all. Back then, the Ibrox manager could scour Europe for talent, so I could take it as a compliment that, with so many players from which to choose, he wanted me

In the season I made my move to Celtic, Souness brought in England international striker Mark Hateley from AS Monaco, a club I would get to know well six years later, and USSR international defender Oleg Kuznetsov from Kiev Dynamo. He wouldn't have got much change out of £2.5 million for those two players; a massive amount of cash at the time. Later on, they could afford to pay over £4 million to take Paul Gascoigne from Serie A outfit Lazio.

In the battle of the cheque books, it didn't look like a fair fight, did it? Rangers won the league every season in my six years at Celtic. Did I ever regret my decision? Not for a moment. As a team, we did our best and, as an individual, I did my utmost to help turn things around. And these were exciting times at Celtic. Every day was a challenge and Billy McNeill was the right man for an extremely difficult task.

I'll always remember the first day I met him. In the family home in the border town of Galashiels, there had always been talk of Celtic's greatest captain and the likes of immortal manager Jock Stein and players such as Jimmy Johnstone, Bobby Murdoch, Bertie Auld and Tommy Gemmell. I was born eight months after the European Cup triumph in Lisbon, but I was brought up steeped in the knowledge and folklore of this historic victory. Relatives would talk about the game against Inter Milan like it had been played that weekend!

Photographs of me as a kid kicking a ball around had me wearing an assortment of Celtic tops. So, although I had never actually met the great Billy McNeill in person, I certainly knew of him and his sporting exploits at my favourite team. I had just returned from the World Cup Finals in Italy that summer when I received a phone call to inform me Celtic were interested in signing me. There had been a few rumours flying around when it became obvious I would be leaving Hibs. I had informal talks with Bordeaux, but any thoughts of moving to France were ditched in my initial phone call from Billy.

We agreed to meet at Peebles Hydro and I was excited at the prospect of sitting down with this legendary figure. It was also gratifying to feel rated by this man. His knowledge of football was second to none. Money wasn't to the forefront of my thinking that day as we sat and chatted. He told me Celtic had made an offer of £1 million for me and Hibs had accepted. It was the biggest transfer deal in the club's history and it was remarkable to believe it was for a little lad from Gala.

Rangers had made their pitch, the Celtic manager would now talk to his board and, hopefully, we could get the deal done and I could get my dream transfer. I'm well aware that's a cliché, but it just happens to be true. Once everything had been put in place, I couldn't wait to get started. I was embarking on a new adventure. My dad and my family were ecstatic, too!

People commented on the seven-figure fee for my services, but the amount never bothered me. It didn't weigh me down one bit and I can honestly say I wasn't put under any extra pressure to perform. As a footballer, you concentrate on training every day as you prepare for the game. That's your entire focus. Billy McNeill and Celtic reckoned I was worth £1 million, so it was up to me to prove their evaluation was correct and the best place for that was out on the football pitch on match day. I am not exaggerating when I say I gave Celtic every ounce of energy I possessed on each occasion I wore that shirt. Take it from me, Billy McNeill wouldn't have settled for anything less – nor would I for that matter.

There was something very special, even unique, about playing for Celtic. I got a thrill every time I raced down that tunnel and out onto the pitch. That's something that will stay with me forever. My dad would be at the game and I knew where he sat. I could look up and see him and give him a little wave before kick-off. I was one of the lucky ones. The Celtic support in full throttle bring about an atmosphere you won't find anywhere else. I felt at home at Celtic right from day one and Billy McNeill played his part in welcoming me to the club.

I was the new boy in the dressing room, but I knew the likes of Paul McStay from teaming up with him in the Scotland midfield. I was looking forward to playing alongside him on a consistent basis because he was such a skilful player with a fabulous range of passing and the ability to shoot powerfully and accurately from any distance. Like myself, he was passionate about Celtic, as were so many of the other players, such as Pat Bonner, Peter Grant and Joe Miller. So, there was no settling-in period at Parkhead; it was the place I wanted to be and I was prepared to make my family proud of me.

I looked forward to my first game against Graeme Souness and Rangers and that took place at Ibrox on 15 September, only a couple of months following my arrival. The family had talked about Old Firm encounters in almost mystical terms and now I would get the opportunity to sample it first-hand. The game zipped by, but the atmosphere was electric. Wherever you went before the Saturday, you would bump into fans who reminded you that Celtic *must* win this game, defeat was not an option. So, no pressure there then.

The match ended honours even at 1–1. I was delighted to play my part in our goal which opened the scoring a few minutes after the turnaround. We received a free-kick on the left and I curled it into the area around the penalty spot. Derek Whyte timed his leap to perfection and sent a superb header low past Chris Woods to the keeper's left. The Celtic fans behind the goal went crazy. Unfortunately, a long-range shot from Terry Hurlock took a deflection and left Pat Bonner helpless for the leveller after the hour mark. That was my first experience of an encounter between the great Glasgow rivals and I could see why Henrik Larsson said years later that it was the biggest derby in the world.

We beat Rangers twice in successive Saturdays in March the following year. We had slipped in the league, had lost 2–1 in extra-time to the Ibrox side in the League Cup Final and our best bet for a piece of silverware was the Scottish Cup. The first game against Graeme Souness's men was a quarter-final in the national trophy at our place and we won 2–0 with first-half goals from Gerry Creaney and Dariusz Wdowczyk. It turned into a controversial encounter when they had three players – Terry Hurlock, Mark Walters and Mark Hateley – ordered off in a towsy second period while we had Peter Grant dismissed for two quickfire yellow cards. There's nothing like an Old Firm game to get the adrenalin flowing.

It was a little more sedate a week later when we won 3–0 in a Premier League confrontation in the east end of Glasgow.

Thankfully, there was only one red card in this one – Rangers' Scott Nisbett being invited to leave the action after a foul on Paul McStay – and Anton Rogan, Joe Miller and Tommy Coyne claimed the goals. However, one glance at the league table showed Celtic in fourth place on thirty-three points, eleven adrift of the Ibrox team with only seven games left to play. You only got two points for a win back then, so the title was gone, despite our good work in that game. Aberdeen were three points behind Rangers and Dundee United were three better off than us. So, it was all eyes on the Scottish Cup if I was going to pick up an honour in my first season as a Celt.

Four clubs went into the semi-final ballot: ourselves, Motherwell, Dundee United and St Johnstone. We were drawn against the Fir Park side and the first game on 3 April ended in a goalless draw. In fact, we had reached the last-four without conceding against Forfar, St Mirren and Rangers. Now Pat Bonner had kept another clean sheet and it would be back to Hampden six days later for the replay. We led twice in the second game before losing 4–2. It was a real sickener for everyone. Billy McNeill looked fairly distraught in the dressing room afterwards. The following day he admitted, 'I can't remember ever feeling so flat after a semi-final defeat either as a manager or a player.'

I did get my hands on a Scottish Cup medal when we beat Airdrie 1–0 in the Final on 27 May 1995, my only trophy at Celtic. Billy McNeill had left the club in the summer of 1991 to be replaced by Liam Brady who moved out in October 1993 with Lou Macari getting a brief stint. Tommy Burns took over in the summer of 1994. Then came the Cup win over the Broomfield side, astonishingly the club's only piece of silverware during a tough six-year stint.

Although Billy wasn't around the team at Hampden that sunny afternoon, you knew he would be celebrating our success.

It was a privilege to play for him and I thank him for giving me the opportunity to wear the green and white hoops as a grown-up. Billy McNeill was such an impressive individual. He simply commanded respect and when he talked, you listened. A gentleman, a true legend, well-mannered, bright, astute and polite, he was all of these things.

Billy McNeill also exuded charm and warmth. To a wee boy from Gala, he was one classy guy.

CHIC CHARNLEY

I cornered Billy McNeill one night at a sporting function; it was too good an opportunity to pass up.

'Why have you never signed me for Celtic?' I asked, cutting to the chase. Big Billy didn't even blink an eye.

'There's a very good reason for that Chic, son,' he answered. 'I like to sleep at night.' Then he paused and added, 'In any case, there's no way I could have you and Frank McAvennie around the place at the same time.'

Point taken, Billy. I didn't pursue the debate. There was another chance meeting at a dinner when I was chatting to Celtic's Greatest Ever Captain. He was in a philosophical mood. He told me, 'You know, Chic, my right hand tells me to sign you and the left hand says no.' Unfortunately, for me, the left hand won that particular argument.

I've always liked Big Billy. Remember when he had that quadruple heart bypass operation in the mid-nineties? It was still the days of good old telegrams. I sent him a message while he was recovering in hospital. 'You could have had that op years ago if you had signed me.' I hope he saw the funny side.

I've never hidden my admiration for Celtic and I pride myself that I have a 100 per cent success rate when playing in the green and white hoops. Not too many players can boast that fact. I might even be unique in the club's history.

My one – and, sadly, only – game for the team came at the end of the 1993/94 season. Lou Macari was the Celtic manager when I was invited to play in a testimonial match against Manchester United at Old Trafford. I received the telephone call from Partick Thistle boss John Lambie and thought he was pulling my leg. I knew him well enough over the years to realise he was prone to the odd prank or two. I loved that guy.

When I realised he wasn't joking, I couldn't wait to get involved. I thought it was a marvellous gesture by Celtic because I had never hidden my passion for the club. It was well-known where my affections lay – just ask any Rangers fan! No matter who I was playing for, they always gave me stick. To be fair, I wound them up at every opportunity, too. All good fun!

I boarded the coach with the rest of my new teammates and am not afraid to admit that my eyes filled up as we made our way through the thousands of Celtic supporters on our way to Old Trafford. Me? Crying like a baby? Given my so-called reputation that may be difficult to imagine, maybe, but it's the truth nevertheless. Eventually the players were escorted to the away dressing room and the moment I had waited for all my life was only minutes away – I was about to pull that coveted hooped shirt over my head. My chest was pumping and my heart was beating like never before. I was going to play for Celtic and I was going to enjoy every minute of it. And I did.

As we kicked the ball about in the warm-up I looked up at the vast stands of Manchester United's superb stadium and all I could see were green and white scarves everywhere. This was a testimonial match for United's Mark Hughes, but there seemed to be more Celtic fans in the ground than their United counterparts. It was a truly amazing experience. Awesome and unforgettable. Suddenly I was aware the Celtic support were chanting, *'There's only one Chic Charnley ... there's only one Chic Charnley.'* To be honest, I was so overcome I started to cry. I couldn't prevent the tears from streaming down my face.

Those wonderful fans had just taken me to a place I could only dream about. Lou Macari was so concerned about my welfare and ability to carry on that he sent on Frank Connor, one of his assistants, to see if I was okay. 'Chic, can you play?' asked Frank. 'Just try and stop me,' I answered. This was the biggest moment in my entire career and I wasn't going to miss out. I reassured him I would be fine. I have a tape of the supporters chanting my name and I still feel as emotional today as I did all those years ago.

What a night it became as Celtic won 3–1. I set up one of the goals for Simon Donnelly with a through pass into his tracks and he stuck it away with a fair amount of style.

There's a photograph of me running away from Eric Cantona with a broad smile on my face that evening. I've been asked countless times what I was laughing at. Eric, a genuine world famous superstar, had tried to play the ball through my legs, a nutmeg as it's known in football. I wasn't having any of that. I snapped my legs shut, got the ball under control and swerved past the Frenchman. I looked at the Celtic dugout and caught the eye of Brian Scott, the club's physiotherapist. 'Who does he think he is?' I said and the Celtic bench dissolved into laughter.

Ironically, Lou Macari was sacked during the summer after a fall-out with the club's owner Fergus McCann. Tommy Burns took over and I might just have been his sort of player. Tommy, a true Celtic legend, had been an elegant left-sided midfielder during his glorious playing days. I knew he appreciated my style of play.

Tommy actually once tried to sign me for Kilmarnock when I came back from my stint in Sweden with Djurgaardens in 1993. I had already had talks with John Lambie and chairman Jim Oliver at Partick Thistle just before Tommy came in. I was in a sweat. I really fancied playing for such a wonderful gentleman as Tommy, but I had given my word to John and Jim I would accept their offer. I couldn't go back on that and, unfortunately, I had to tell Tommy. He fully understood and wished me the best of luck.

I must end with another wee tale about Big Billy. He had a spell as Director of Football at Hibs in 1998 when I was a player there. I was haggling with the club's chairman Rod Petrie about a payment. I think it was for £500 and I was determined to get my cash. 'Why don't we flip a coin for it?' I said, reasonably. 'Heads, I win. Tails, I lose.'

The Easter Road chief thought for a moment before he agreed. Naturally, he didn't trust a born-and-bred Glaswegian. Billy just happened to be walking past at the time and Petrie stopped him and asked if he would mind doing the honours. I handed the coin to one of my great Celtic heroes. He studied both sides, grinned and asked me to call. I shouted 'Heads' and he flipped it into the air and then caught it. He looked at it and then said, 'It's heads.' I smiled at the Hibs supremo and pointed out, 'I think you owe me £500, Mr Chairman.' I got my money.

Shortly afterwards, I was at another sporting function and I spotted Billy. A friend had asked me to get his autograph, if it wasn't too much trouble. I wondered if he would sign one for me at the same time. Of course, it was no bother to this wonderful gent. He signed both and handed the scraps of paper back to me.

Later on, I looked at my prized possession. Billy had written, 'To Chic. Are you still using that two-headed coin to win the toss?'

Hail Caesar! Celtic Fans' View

PAUL BRENNAN, 51, Celtic Quick News blogger

To live among your heroes, for them to be accessible, normal even, but still imperious heroes, is a remarkable thing. This was Billy McNeill to several generations of Celtic fans.

I have memories of meeting him as a child, when he was Celtic captain and a footballer of enormous reputation across Britain and Europe. He had stature, patience for all of us and a confidence that can only be gained from genuine achievement.

My dad was a year below Billy at Our Lady's High School in Motherwell. They were both in their twenties when Celtic scaled the ultimate height, so I grew up hearing about the great man, as a schoolboy, as well as on the field. We had a family tradition when I would go with my dad to Billy's Halfway House Bar in Bellshill to deliver butcher meat to his mother. You can imagine the excitement this ritual brought.

I knew Billy better as a manager than a player. Twice he took over a Celtic team on the ropes and inspired a remarkable turnaround, even if the latter occasion was not enduring. His first five years as manager saw some of the most attacking football imaginable. During this era, the coaching staff and players would often use the phrase 'playing the Celtic way', which meant attacking at every opportunity. Having won the game's greatest honour by overcoming its most defensive formation, attacking football was Billy's gift to the world. Although he and his assistant John Clark were defenders, to play attacking football was an act of faith.

When he returned as manager in 1987, Celtic had been out-thought by a revolution at Rangers, which saw their rivals use enormous financial resources, as well as huge personalities, to claim their first title in nine years. Celtic did not have the imagination or financial wherewithal to reciprocate by signing English internationals. Instead, they had Billy McNeill, who not only had the personality to fill every inch of Celtic Park, he dominated the moneyed reputations at Ibrox. The result was a glorious double in our centenary season, which remains one of the greatest in our history.

That will to win can only be spread so thinly, however, and Celtic's time at the top was over. Billy returned to a role he was equally passionate about – engaging with Celtic fans wherever he found them. During these years, the Celtic media team caught him lost in the moment, in the tunnel at the Estádio Nacional, Lisbon, when he recounted the team's walk from the dressing room to the pitch on 25 May 1967. He explained how ordinary men raised themselves to become extraordinary champions. Of all the times I have seen or heard Billy, this clip is my most cherished.

News of Billy's dementia spread before the family made the announcement and I met him a few times during that period. On one occasion, he stopped my son with a question, 'When did Celtic win the European Cup?' On hearing the right answer, Billy joked, 'You've got a better memory than me.' And with a smile, added, 'I suppose I should stop making jokes like that.' The inner strength the man had was astonishing.

The last time I spoke to Billy he was in the company of John Clark and I was with my dad. After a few moments' chat, Billy said, 'I remember you, you delivered butcher meat to my mother.' Forty years had passed since that was true, and Billy was well on the road to dementia, but he remembered the ordinary Celtic fans who returned the joy he gave them for so many years. We were gifted a true hero.

KEVIN McKENNA, 55, journalist

Some of the most thrilling memories of a Celtic childhood occurred when I was admitted into the company of older men in our family when they talked about football. In these tribal gatherings, wreathed in cigarette smoke and fortified by Johnnie Walker, you were expected not to say anything but simply to listen. Occasionally, a kindly uncle would seek to include me in the conversation with the same question, 'So who's your favourite player, Kevin?' And my answer was always the same, 'Jimmy Johnstone.' This always seemed to please them.

These were men who had recently emerged from a decade-long famine when Celtic had lifted only two League Cups between 1955 and 1965. Now under Jock Stein it seemed as if they would not rest until each of those barren years was redeemed with corresponding Cups in the next decade. Even after a few trophy-laden years under Jock it seemed they still could not quite believe what they were seeing and their faces became like children's as they discussed the individual attributes of their favourite players. I remember that Bertie Auld, Jimmy Johnstone and John Hughes figured most in their conversation. Years later I concluded that in these three players they perhaps saw character traits that they recognised in themselves: hard, cheeky, skilful and flawed.

But when they talked of Billy McNeill there was only pride. It was as if, having been blessed with this team of outrageous talent, they had been further anointed with a special captain. Their pride stemmed not merely from his ability as a footballer but from something much more profound. These men and women and the families that bore them had been accustomed to rejection, discrimination and a thinly-disguised contempt that regarded them as simple and ill-educated.

Here was a young man from a community like theirs who held overseas press conferences in the language of his hosts; who spoke with the quiet authority of a diplomat and who in his good manners and thoughtful demeanour seemed to command respect as soon as he walked into a room. He wasn't just Celtic's ambassador; he was theirs too.

Because of Billy McNeill and what he seemed to represent, my dad and his family and his friends walked a little taller each day and felt a little better about themselves.

LIAM DONNELLY, 55, businessman

I have never known a time in my life when Billy McNeill was not part of it. I was brought up in a 100 per cent Celtic family. My father was a Celtic fan, his father was a Celtic fan. In fact, my grandfather's season ticket was Number Six.

Celtic Football Club was – and still is – an incredibly large part of our lives. And Billy McNeill has been there all the way. Billy was the team's leader – and what a leader. The Lisbon Lions were an extraordinary collection of talents and they all had their part to play in the legend that is our football club, but there was never any doubt who was the leader. His name was Billy McNeill.

He was tall and handsome, intelligent, articulate; a gentleman in every sense of the word. To so many thousands of Celtic supporters, he will be forever Caesar. Yes, we are aware it started as Cesar after an actor by the name of Cesar Romero who drove the car for Frank Sinatra and the Rat Pack in the movie *Ocean's Eleven*. We understand Billy, Bertie Auld, Mike Jackson and a few of the lads took nicknames from the Hollywood stars in the film.

But I can only say Cesar surely morphed into Caesar over the years. Just take one look at that iconic image of Billy McNeill holding aloft that European Cup in the Lisbon sunshine on an unforgettable May day back in 1967. Is that not a sporting individual of noble stature? Of course it is. Billy McNeill is Caesar.

I have been fortunate enough to spend some quality time with the great man. Hard to believe when I was growing up, I must admit, but a real pleasure to be in this man's company. One evening, before he had ever met me, I was wearing a garish green, white and gold shirt at a Celtic function. He came over to me, slung his arm around my shoulders and said, 'I must get a photo taken with you. I love that shirt!'

271

On another occasion, I was fortunate enough to be in Moscow when Celtic played Spartak Moscow in 2007. Billy was with me and a couple of friends during the trip, when we did all the sightseeing stuff and even had lunch in the Kremlin.

On the day of the game, we were in the stadium where Allan Wells won an Olympic gold medal in the 100 metres. As you would expect, there weren't too many away fans in attendance. We were in a small cordoned-off area and weren't keen to attract attention to ourselves. To be frank, the locals didn't look too friendly.

And then Paul Hartley scored with an exquisite header to give Celtic the lead. We couldn't stop ourselves. We rose in unison to cheer the effort. Before we knew it, all eyes were on us. We had been rumbled.

One fan rose from his seat and was quite obviously coming over to have a word. I thought he was a Moscow version of Rab C. Nesbitt or Rab C. Nesbittski, if you prefer. He had a rolled-up programme and was swinging it about menacingly as he edged closer to us.

'Leave this to me, boys,' said Big Billy. He rose to his full height, chest expanded and let the guy come closer. He then said something that stopped Mr Angry in his tracks before beating a hasty retreat back to his seat.

I'm not sure what Billy had said, but I'm fairly sure it wasn't, 'Do you want an autograph?'

Billy McNeill, a giant among men.

SANDY DEVERS, 55, musician

When life's cards were dealt to me and my twin brother, Peter, I suppose there were key things that meant Celtic were going to be a big part of our lives. My mother worked as a nurse for a while at the Bon Secours Hospital in Battlefield. At the time, this was the hospital where Celtic would often send their injured players for surgery and other treatment. Having your mother nursing players back to good health meant that we sometimes had an edge over our pals, when it came to get autograph books signed by the team.

Back then, autograph books were quite the thing and I clearly remember the excitement of getting the books back with signatures of legends like Wee Jinky and Bobby Lennox. There was one signature that stood out, however. 'Boogie'! I was told that this was the autograph of the mighty Billy McNeill.

I remember my mother holding him in high esteem, particularly around the way he presented himself to the world. She was a big fan of Val Doonican's *'Walk tall, walk straight and look the world right in the eye'*. This was something that she tried to instil in her boys.

For a few years, I'd encounter 'Boogie' in different situations. Going to school ten minutes' walk from Celtic Park meant that there were regular trips along the road to haunt the players and look for autographs. My mother's words rang true and every time I saw Billy McNeill when I was a kid, he looked like a colossus. Over the years, I ended up with plenty of 'Boogie' signatures in my autograph books.

Billy McNeill reminds me of good times. One of the best times I've had as a Celtic fan was watching ten men win the league against Rangers in Paradise. Commonly known as 'the 4–2 gemme', it was great to win the league against all odds, after

Johnny Doyle was sent off. It was magical to see Billy McNeill celebrate with the team and, clearly, he had instilled a huge sense of belief in his team, which meant that they were to give me one of my most unforgettable moments as a Celtic fan.

One hazard of being a Celtic fan was coming home after a Cup Final with the left half of your face crimson with sunburn. Cup Finals conjure up memories of sunshine. Often the sunburn was worth it and one unforgettable moment for me was when we won the double in our centenary year. Like 'the 4–2 gemme', an enduring memory for me is the post-match carnage, with all the players celebrating the last-minute winner and in amongst it all was our manager, Billy McNeill, straight as a dye as always, with his suit on and flower in his lapel. Even as a young daftie, I always looked at him as something to aspire to.

Over the coming years, I played in a band called The Peat-diggers, alongside my twin brother. In the early years, we played in Billy's pub in the south side and met him on occasion. We also played regular gigs in supporters' clubs, all over Scotland and abroad. This gave us the opportunity to meet him in person and he always presented himself as a great ambassador for the club and football in general. For the last few years, I've been living pretty far away from Glasgow, but I hardly miss a Celtic game.

It's hard to explain the reasons why there's such an appeal and my wife will sometimes call me a no' righter. I just tell her, '*Don't blame it on the sunshine, don't blame it on the moonlight, don't blame it on the good times . . . blame it on the Boogie!*'

GREGORY MACLACHLAN, 36, Celtic blogger

Growing up on the outskirts of Glasgow and supporting the magnificent Celtic, I endured the highs and lows of following such an illustrious club. Most of my closest friends supported our great rivals Rangers. In fact, my father was a fan of the Ibrox club.

Little was I to know that, during the summer of 1987, my attachment and fondness for Celtic would transcend to a whole new level after meeting a man I consider one of my all-time heroes – the legend himself, Mr Billy McNeill. July 1987 is my most memorable holiday even to this day. My family were going to Butlins, a fun-filled holiday for any child and adult alike. Three days into our holiday, I recall my grandad telling me he had seen Billy McNeill walking around the park.

At the time, being only six years old, my knowledge of Billy McNeill was limited at best. However, it more than piqued my curiosity to quiz my grandad about Billy. After learning about his achievements and exploits for the club I hold so dearly, I knew I had to meet one of Celtic's most iconic players of all time. Later, we went to the evening entertainment and I was informed that a football tournament for children and parents was to be held the following morning. The most enthralling thing for me, though, was that Billy McNeill was to attend the event to greet and meet the participants.

That evening, sleep was close to impossible. I could not wait and my anticipation grew and grew. The following morning, I rummaged furiously through the suitcase for my Celtic strip, grabbed my football and rushed my family along to the event. There was already a large gathering of families around the area.

About twenty minutes later, Billy appeared dressed in a Celtic tracksuit and I could not contain my excitement. Waiting my turn in line, which seemed like an eternity, it was finally my time to meet Billy and get my photograph taken with him. I could feel my heart beat faster and faster, I had no idea what I would say. All my nerves and excitement were displaced as Billy asked me my name and what I wanted to be when I grew up.

Like every wee bhoy's dream I proclaimed, 'A footballer just like you, sir!' Billy serenely replied, 'Well you have to stick in at school also, you know, Gregory.' I then got my photograph taken with Billy and my grandad.

In my elation, I walked off forgetting my ball only to hear, 'Gregory, you forgot something.' Billy passed the ball to me and at that precise moment I felt elated as I controlled the ball with my right foot. Billy stayed to watch the tournament unfold, I was on the losing side of the semi-final. However, after scoring a goal in our 4–2 defeat, I glanced over to Billy and noticed him applauding me.

To this day, it is a moment I recall with glee. Looking back now, as a thirty-six-year-old man, I know in my heart that meeting the great Billy McNeill is precisely what shaped my love and emotion for such a great club as Celtic. Without effort, he had moulded a segment of my heart for both Billy and Celtic Football Club. It is a memory I hope one day to pass onto my grandkids and, hopefully, emulate in them what Billy McNeill did for me. It truly was a wee bhoy's dream!

EDDY GRADY, 50, Celtic memorabilia collector

When we speak of Billy McNeill, it is difficult to identify an adjective that someone else has not already used to describe this man of great stature. In my humble opinion, Billy will always be 'Mr Celtic'.

There are two iconic images of Celtic's greatest captain that will remain in my mind. The first one is Big Billy holding aloft the European Cup in the marble palatial setting at Estádio Nacional in Lisbon in 1967 and the other is of him being carried aloft by Celtic teammates after having just completed nine league championships in a row in 1974.

I have memories of going to my first Celtic home match in 1978 at the age of eleven when Billy and John Clark had not long taken over from Jock Stein. Although my most favourite season with Billy as manager was during the famous 1987/88 campaign.

He managed the squad impeccably and his pre/post-match delivery was always a credit to his professionalism. In his own words, Billy refers to Celtic as a fairy tale club in winning significant trophies during its history.

That indeed was the case when Celtic became the first club to win a double in its centenary year. Since 1998, I have had the great pleasure of getting to know Big Billy as a Lisbon Lion, ex-manager and ambassador for Celtic. This has been achieved through collecting memorabilia.

With my specialisation being the 1967 European Cup Final, special anniversaries and the centenary year, Billy has played a significant role in helping me have numerous items autographed by him and others from the 1966/67 European Campaign squad.

Chatting with Billy in different capacities has always brought great satisfaction, not only on the basis of him being an absolute gentleman, but his knowledge and recollection of memories of his time as a player and manager have been tremendous. He is truly a very inspirational person.

One of my favourite times in his company was at Celtic Park in 2007 at the fortieth anniversary of the winning of the European Cup. Billy was posing for a photo with my daughter, my son and the European Cup when he decided to lift my daughter onto the table to hold onto one of the handles. It made a fantastic photo. The family man and kindness shone through in that moment, to which I was very thankful.

Billy, many thanks for the great achievements you brought to Celtic and for helping me to grow my collection!

PETER MARSHALL, 66, IT manager

I was born in the early 1950s and, growing up at that time, my heroes were gleaned from American DC and Marvel comics, guys such as Batman, Superman, Spider-Man and the like. My one UK hero was Alf Tupper from *The Victor*!

I was introduced to Celtic in late 1958, still only six years old, but I soon picked up on what this was all about. Sadly, not a successful five or six years ensued, but around 1965 I picked up on a player who soon became my sporting hero, not because of him being brilliant like Johnstone, Larsson or even Patsy Gallacher, but because he stood out as a leader. He was always there and seemed to turn up at the right time to score that ever-important goal.

Billy McNeill is his name and, to this day, he is still my all-time sporting hero. Not my all-time favourite footballer, that's Bobby Evans, but my all-time hero. Why hero? Well, Billy fits the definition perfectly: brave, fearless, intelligent and a leader with strong character. And noble.

Being a hero is not just about being the best, or the urge to be the best at all costs, it's more about that urge to serve at all costs and Billy has certainly done that for the Celtic family, as player, captain and manager. Perhaps only Willie Maley and Jimmy McGrory are up there with him.

So, I hold Billy in high esteem. He nurtured the intense feeling I have for Celtic since way back in 1965 and for that I am eternally grateful. Hail, Hail Billy!

Epilogue by Liz McNeill

There is a possibility dementia could be connected to heading the ball, but I think we need more research into it. I wouldn't like to think the possible link would discourage my grandchildren or anyone else's children from enjoying sport. It's great to see the young ones getting exercise in the fresh air. Heading the ball was Billy's forte. I look at photos of him doing it and I think, 'That was his career. That was his life.' The majority of goals he scored were with his head. He wouldn't have stopped playing, even if he had known. A big part of his life was his football. That was very important to him. I don't feel any bitterness or resentment, as he lived doing something he loved.

July 2018

Postscript

The most colourful rainbows often follow the darkest clouds.

In the late evening of Monday 22 April 2019, Billy McNeill, at the age of seventy-nine, finally succumbed to the illness he had battled with such fortitude for far too long. The Celtic legend passed away at home in the company of his family and friends.

The following morning, the world awakened to the sad news of the loss of a fine human being.

Touching and heartfelt tributes were made, treasured memories exchanged, sentiments shared among the many whose lives had been enhanced by the mere presence of a humble man who just happened to be an excellent footballer, a leader of fellow professionals.

Billy McNeill possessed the extraordinary God-given talent to reach out and embrace total strangers, regardless of colour, creed or station in life. First and foremost, Billy McNeill was a good man. Everything else fell into place after that. He was a devoted husband to Liz, a proud father and grandfather.

And a friend to those who needed his gift of comradeship.

A week after Billy McNeill's passing, his Celtic colleague Stevie Chalmers died at the age of eighty-three. Like his captain, the man who scored the European Cup-winning goal against

Inter Milan in the sunshine of Lisbon on the unforgettable day of 25 May 1967 had fought with equal resilience against a terrible affliction.

As time goes by, sunsets will replace darkness, smiles will overshadow sorrow, fondness will succeed grief.

One standard in life will remain steadfast, though.

None shall eclipse the legacy of Billy McNeill.

Alex Gordon, May 2019